Scarlet Fields

MODERN WAR STUDIES

Theodore A. Wilson
General Editor

Raymond Callahan
J. Garry Clifford
Jacob W. Kipp
Allan R. Millett
Carol Reardon
Dennis Showalter
David R. Stone
Series Editors

Scarlet Fields

The Combat Memoir of a World War I
Medal of Honor Hero

———◆———

John Lewis Barkley

Introduction and notes by Steven Trout
Afterword by Joan Barkley Wells

Published by the University Press of Kansas in association with the
National World War I Museum at Liberty Memorial

Published by the University Press of Kansas (Lawrence, Kansas 66045), which was
organized by the Kansas Board of Regents and is operated and funded by Emporia
State University, Fort Hays State University, Kansas State University, Pittsburg
State University, the University of Kansas, and Wichita State University

Library of Congress Cataloging-in-Publication Data

Barkley, John Lewis.   [No hard feelings!]

Scarlet fields : the combat memoir of a World War I Medal of Honor hero /
John Lewis Barkley ;
introduction and notes by Steven Trout ; afterword by Joan Barkley Wells.

p.   cm. — (Modern war studies)

Originally published: New York : Cosmopolitan Book Corp., 1930, with title
No hard feelings!

Includes bibliographical references and index.

ISBN 978-0-7006-1842-2 (cloth : alk. paper)

ISBN 978-0-7006-2019-7 (pbk. : alk. paper)

ISBN 978-0-7006-2060-9 (ebook)

1. Barkley, John Lewis. 2. World War, 1914–1918—Personal narratives, American.
3. Soldiers—United States—Biography. 4. Medal of Honor—Biography. 5. United
States. Army. Division, 3rd—Biography. 6. World War, 1914–1918—Regimental
histories—United States. 7. World War, 1914–1918—Campaigns—France. I. Trout,
Steven, 1963– II. National World War I Museum at Liberty Memorial. III. Title.

D570.9.B28 2012   940.4'1273092—dc23

[B]   2012000697

British Library Cataloguing-in-Publication Data is available.

Printed in the United States of America

10 9 8 7 6 5 4 3 2 1

Contents

Illustrations follow page 142.

Acknowledgments

Published under the title that John Lewis Barkley preferred—*Scarlet Fields*—this new edition of *No Hard Feelings!* would have been impossible without the cooperation and support of Joan Barkley Wells. The editor also wishes to thank Doran Cart and Jonathan Casey, both on staff at the National World War I Museum at Liberty Memorial, for their invaluable assistance with the John Lewis Barkley Papers, and Eli Paul of the Kansas City Public Library for suggesting this project. An expert on both the Meuse-Argonne campaign and World War I memoirs, Edward G. Lengel made suggestions that improved the editorial apparatus immensely. Other World War I historians—Edward M. Coffman, Jennifer Keene, and Michael S. Neiberg—provided beneficial input as well. And, finally, the editor wishes to thank John Bratt for generously sharing his photographs of the spot near Cunel where John Lewis Barkley made his heroic stand in October 1918.

S. T.

Scarlet Fields

John Lewis Barkley (1930) by Howard Chandler Christy. (Courtesy of the National World War I Museum Archives, Kansas City, Missouri)

Introduction

Steven Trout

On the afternoon of October 7, 1918, while serving as a reconnaissance observer far ahead of American lines near Cunel, France, Private John Lewis Barkley climbed into an abandoned French tank and single-handedly held off a German force of perhaps several hundred men as it advanced toward positions held by the American Third Division. Because the tank's crew had removed the vehicle's cannon, Barkley armed himself with a captured German light machine gun, which he pointed through a dangerously wide aperture in the turret. Deafened by the sound of his weapon, which he fired until the gun became super-heated, and surrounded by ricocheting bullets, some of which landed *inside* the tank, Barkley probably killed more than a hundred enemy soldiers and completely disrupted the Germans' advance. Even an enemy 77mm cannon, which targeted the tank from just a few hundred yards away, could not drive Private Barkley from his personal fortress. He held off one wave of attackers, then another. Finally, after enemy bullets and stick grenades stopped striking the tank and a detachment of American troops appeared on the scene, he slipped away to rejoin his unit.

He told no one what he had done. However, several American soldiers witnessed the exploit; one of them even counted (or at least estimated) the number of empty machine-gun cartridges piled up inside the tank—more than 4,000 expended rounds! Weeks later, as Barkley's unit settled into occupation duty in Germany, General John J.

Pershing personally awarded the private the Congressional Medal of Honor. When summoned before the supreme commander of the American Expeditionary Forces (AEF), Barkley, a notorious trouble-maker, was certain that he was about to be court-martialed and sent to Leavenworth. He had, after all, mastered the art of smuggling liquor into camp, going AWOL, illicitly romancing *mademoiselles* as well as *fräuleins*, and engaging in just enough mischief to avoid being promoted to the rank of sergeant. No one was more surprised than this rowdy enlisted man from the Show-Me State when Pershing, a fellow Missourian, pinned the nation's highest medal for valor to his chest.

Among the most decorated American soldiers of World War I—in all, he would receive six medals for bravery, each conferred by a different Allied nation—Barkley was also a talented storyteller. In 1930, with the help of a friend who served as an unacknowledged collaborator, and with the assistance of several professional wordsmiths at a New York publishing house, he recounted his wartime adventures, which reached their climax in the action for which he received the Congressional Medal of Honor, in a vivid memoir titled *No Hard Feelings!* (here reprinted as *Scarlet Fields*). With its matter-of-fact, even self-deprecating description of heroics no less impressive than those of Alvin York, the legendary Tennessean later played on screen by Gary Cooper, or Charles Whittlesey, the leader of the famed Lost Battalion, Barkley's book should have been a hit. However, reviews of *No Hard Feelings!* were small in number and mixed in their appraisal, not because Barkley's memoir was poorly written or insincere, but because its vision of war experience perhaps reached the public too late, at the tail end of a wave of books such as Erich Maria Remarque's *All Quiet on the Western Front* (1929), Ernest Hemingway's *A Farewell to Arms* (1929), and Robert Graves's *Good-Bye to All That* (1929) that for a time set the tone for literature about the Great War. Unlike the authors of these now-familiar narratives, Barkley sometimes relished combat, and he made no apology for having dispatched scores of enemy soldiers.

In short, his perspective did not line up with accepted wisdom (at least among artists and intellectuals) about how soldiers of the Great

War were *supposed* to remember their experience. Like Germany's Ernst Jünger, whose controversial memoir *Storm of Steel* (1921) shares many similarities with *No Hard Feelings!*, Barkley was something of a war lover—or, as the dust jacket for the first edition of his memoir put it, one of those "warriors . . . who fight and like it." Other literary commentators on the Great War—like Richard Aldington, Siegfried Sassoon, William March, and Thomas Boyd—emphasized the powerlessness of soldiers on the modern battlefield, as poison gas, high explosives, and machine guns reduced battle to a senseless lottery. In contrast, while acknowledging the horrors of combat and mourning lost comrades, Barkley celebrated toughness and aggression. And, based on his own experience, he remained convinced that individual effort had made a difference even in this most industrialized and seemingly impersonal of conflicts. His chronicle of battlefield endurance and initiative will come as something of a surprise to readers today—a precursor to Audie Murphy's *To Hell and Back* (1949), set during a war that if we are to believe the canonical literature offered only impersonal carnage.

Born in 1895, John Lewis Barkley grew up on a farm near Holden, in west-central Missouri, and delighted in woodcraft. He would later claim, probably with good reason, that the marksmanship and stealth that he perfected while hunting amid the fields and forests of the region saved his life on the battlefields of France. The son of a local neighbor still remembers hearing childhood stories of Barkley as a crack shot and as a teller of tall tales who was once asked by his mother to carry a bag while hunting—a bag for all the one-that-got-away stories that the future Medal of Honor recipient tended to accumulate.[1] In *No Hard Feelings!*, the reader will encounter this penchant for exaggeration, but far less frequently than one might expect. Though sometimes implausibly cast in the language of hard-boiled fiction (a sign of Barkley's editors at work) and sprinkled with contrivances (the overseas romances that Barkley describes perhaps fall into this category), *most* of the narrative corresponds with information contained in Barkley's wartime letters or matches up with accounts by other soldiers. The violence depicted in *No Hard Feelings!* is brutal. Indeed, when confronted with the gory pages that follow, readers may wonder, did World War I combat, as experienced by the AEF's most seasoned soldiers, really involve so much killing and at such close quarters? The answer is yes—even though, as we will see, Barkley understood his audience's appetite for carnage and was more than willing to highlight the horrors of war.

By the time the United States entered the Great War in April 1917, Barkley had momentarily abandoned his favorite local hunting spot, the woods along a waterway named Scalybark (or Scaly Bark) Creek, and enrolled at Warrensburg Teachers College (today the University of Central Missouri), where he played football and boxed. How he got into the U.S. Army despite a significant speech impediment is a story too amusing to repeat here; the reader will find it in the opening chapter of Barkley's narrative. However, the particular branch of infantry to which he was assigned requires some comment. Among other things, *No Hard Feelings!* provides one of the best accounts we have of service in an American intelligence (what we would today call "reconnaissance") platoon on the Western Front.[2] In much of its historiography, the AEF is, of course, synonymous with poorly trained soldiers—bumbling sad sacks rushed through a few weeks of boot camp before shipping out to France, sometimes without ever having fired a rifle. Such troops existed, and Barkley encountered plenty of them. However, his own training was of a higher order. Wiry, a fast runner, and with sight and hearing quickened by years of hunting, Barkley was a natural choice for intelligence duty. In 1917, shortly after his arrival at Camp Funston, Kansas, he landed a spot in an intelligence training program at nearby Fort Riley and later received additional specialized instruction in France. In both instances, Barkley studied under British and French officers who knew the Western Front and its lethal hazards intimately. He took his studies seriously, mastering Morse code, military map reading, and a host of other technical skills. While other doughboys remained uncertain how to operate their standard-issue rifles, Barkley learned how to disassemble, load, and fire captured enemy long arms, machine guns, and pistols. He learned how to kill up close with a trench knife or shotgun. As explained in *No Hard Feelings!*, every intelligence serviceman had to master three jobs, all dangerous: observer, scout, and sniper. An observer studied the enemy from a static position, such as a shell hole, and relayed information via field telephone; a scout obtained information by going after it, behind enemy lines if necessary; and a sniper, equipped with a rifle scope and appropriate camouflage, hunted for human prey. Barkley would prove exceedingly capable in all three roles—especially the latter.

In France, intelligence platoons operated at the battalion level, but only when needed amid combat conditions.[3] Thus, Barkley's formal home in the U.S. Army was Company K of the 4th Infantry Regiment, part of the "Rock of the Marne" Third Division. American divisions in World War I were massive organizations (twice the size of those deployed during World War II), and they contained artillerymen and engineers, as well as infantry regiments. A division at full strength held 28,000 men and stretched out for miles when en route to a new sector. A realist when it came to the scale of bloodshed that awaited the U.S. Army, General Pershing's chief of staff, James G. Harbord, made these units massive so that they could hemorrhage thousands of casualties while remaining functional on the battlefield.[4] Like other American outfits that arrived in France in the spring of 1918, well ahead of the bulk of the AEF, Barkley's division put Harbord's organizational scheme to the test. Thrown into almost every major American battle— including the defensive action at Château-Thierry (where the Third Division earned its nickname), the Aisne-Marne counteroffensive, the St. Mihiel offensive, and the Meuse-Argonne offensive—the division suffered more than 16,000 total casualties.[5] Nearly 13,000 received wounds; an additional 3,177 qualified as "battle deaths," meaning they expired on the battlefield or subsequently at aid stations or hospitals.[6] Even more revealing, however, is the number of replacements fed into the Third Division—24,033.[7] An eyewitness to all of Third Division's bloodiest campaigns, Barkley does not indulge in hyperbole when describing companies, each starting off with approximately 200 soldiers, winnowed down by one grinding day of combat after another to a mere handful of semifunctioning survivors. Neither does he exaggerate the prevalence of mental illness (so-called shell shock) at the front or the debilitating effects of sleep deprivation and near-constant stress, both of which became too much for some men. At times, Barkley admits, he also came close to total mental and physical collapse.

Spectacularly resourceful (as evidenced by his feat near Cunel), full of endurance (which never *quite* gave out), and able when necessary to suspend empathy (as any capable frontline soldier must), Barkley was perhaps perfectly suited for war; however, his book paints with a complex palette of emotions, not all of which fit the image of a natural-born warrior. At Château-Thierry, where he receives his first taste of combat, he is momentarily unable to process the surreal spectacle before him, unable to understand why a French officer would exclaim "magnificent" while gazing at a bridge over the Marne littered with dead and dying enemy soldiers—"poor devils," Barkley calls them—shot to pieces by American machine-gunners.[8] Later, during the same battle, Barkley takes obvious delight in his cat-and-mouse duties as a sniper—until he recognizes a human being in the crosshairs:

> It was the first time I'd had a target like this. Always before there'd been just a quick movement in the distance, the top of a helmet, or a glint of sun on glass or metal. This wasn't a target. It was a man. It made a lot of difference. And he was a brave man. I could tell by the way he stood there, by the way he held his head. Perhaps he was young, and had a girl at home like mine. Or a mother who wrote to him the kind of letters my mother wrote me.[9]

This image of a soldier suddenly and queasily reminded of the humanity that he shares with his adversary is nearly universal in World War I literature, and its variations appear in the literary records of multiple armies. For example, in *Sardinian Brigade* (1939), perhaps the finest Italian memoir of the Great War, Emilio Lussu describes a nighttime patrol into No-Man's Land that brings him within easy shooting distance of a young Austrian officer. Lussu studies the other individual in detail. Then, after minutes of indecision, he concludes that "to detach one man from the rest" as a specific target would be an act of murder.[10] He hands his rifle to a corporal, who also refuses to fire. The same situation appears in Robert Graves's classic autobiography *Good-Bye to All That*. When sniping from a "concealed loophole" in the British trenches, Graves notices an enemy soldier taking a bath in the German third line, but he cannot bring himself to shoot a naked man.[11] He leaves the job to a sergeant without staying to watch.

The fact that Barkley pulls the trigger, albeit with regret and a sleepless night afterward, makes him a much different creature than the more familiar protagonists of World War I literature. As literary critic Adrian Ceasar has observed, when analyzing the Christ imagery that so often surfaces in the work of Wilfred Owen and other war poets, the British literary mythos inspired by the war of attrition on the Western Front tended to cast soldiers as passive victims, not as proactive killers.[12] And the same applies to many notable works by American writers, including John Dos Passos's *Three Soldiers* (1921), E. E. Cumming's *The Enormous Room* (1922), and even Ernest Hemingway's *A Farewell to Arms* (1929). Hemingway's hero, one recalls, is seriously wounded "while eating cheese," not while engaged in direct combat, and the only fatality to his credit is an *Italian* sergeant shot in the back during the Caporetto retreat.[13]

Thus, part of what makes *No Hard Feelings!* so fascinating is its portrait of a soldier who, after initial hesitation, kills frequently and well, at times with a sportsmanlike spirit more typically identified with World War I aviators. Like many of the most celebrated aces of the air war, Barkley admired his adversaries as brave men, even as he relished their destruction, and he collected trophies from those he slew, especially the distinctive shoulder straps (or boards) that designated a soldier's regiment and branch of service in the Imperial German Army. (Ironically, his behavior in this regard reminds one of a German hero—namely, Manfred von Richthofen, a warrior and huntsman perhaps cut from the same cloth as the young Missourian. Nicknamed the "Red Baron" for the color of his plane, von Richthofen decorated his quarters with pieces of Allied aircraft he had shot down.) When promoting his memoir, Barkley made frequent reference to three very special shoulder straps in his collection: each came from the uniform of an enemy sniper who fell prey to Barkley's superior marksmanship.[14]

However, if Barkley's single-handed attack on the Germans near Cunel marks the pinnacle of his lethality, his greatest coup as a hunter of men, then a later scene marks a climax of a very different sort. Just two days after the adventure that would earn him the Congressional Medal of Honor, and immediately following a moment of ferocious hand-to-hand combat, which leaves the Americans' uniforms "spattered with blood and brains," Barkley takes a young German prisoner.[15] In this case, his quarry bears little resemblance to the bloodthirsty Hun depicted by Allied propaganda. The German is "just a kid, tow-headed and with baby-blue eyes," and he begins "to cry like a baby."[16] But days of unrelenting combat have pushed the Americans too far; someone yells—"Kill the yellow son-of-a-bitch!"—and a crowd of menacing doughboys forms around Barkley and his captive.[17] Halfway out of his mind after weeks without adequate sleep, still recuperating from his adrenaline-draining ordeal in the tank, and tormented by mustard-gas burns to his scalp, Barkley sides with the German and holds his fellow countrymen at bay with his .45-caliber pistol. The situation seems certain to turn ugly—until Barkley's closest comrades, Jesse James (this was the soldier's actual name) and William Floyd, arrive on the scene and help him escort the prisoner to safety. Like similar moments in Eugene Sledge's acclaimed World War II memoir *With the Old Breed at Peleliu and Okinawa* (1981), this remarkable episode takes us deep into war's most mysterious psychological territory—the shadowy region where brutality wrestles with compassion and mercy. Here Barkley points to the survival of a sense of decency that no amount of violent conditioning on the battlefield could quite extinguish. In that derelict tank near Cunel, one man against hundreds, he achieved one kind of victory; when saving a helpless enemy solder, he achieved another.

The two men who come to Barkley's rescue in this scene figure prominently in *No Hard Feelings!*, and both are Native Americans who served in the prewar military. According to the terminology adopted by the War Department in 1917, the Third Division formed part of the Regular (i.e., professional) Army, as opposed to the National Guard or the National Army, a euphemism for the huge portion of the AEF comprised of draftees. In actuality, volunteers and conscripts flooded the Third Division, just as they did every other unit. Indeed, Barkley was plucked from Camp Funston and assigned to the Third Division, along with thousands of other drafted men who would otherwise have served in the 89th ("Middle-Western") Division, because there were not enough professionals on hand to fill regular army units before they left for France. However, the "Rock of the Marne" could still boast that it contained some salty veterans, including regulars who had been posted in China or the Philippines, and Barkley quickly fell in with two of the division's most formidable and experienced professional soldiers.

In his portraiture of Native Americans Jesse James and William Floyd, Barkley invokes more than a few stereotypes. Both men are depicted throughout this story as naturally stealthy, possessed of an innate sense of direction, largely immune to pain, easily inebriated, and utterly merciless in battle. Wild Indians, in short. A typical description of Floyd appears immediately after he rescues Barkley and the German prisoner. For a moment, it appears that the diminutive Hun may still lose his life:

> Floyd had two guns in his belt. His hair hung down to his eyes. All the time I was arguing with him, he kept those eyes on the prisoner's face. I never saw anything whiter than that face. The kid wasn't crying any longer. He was too scared.[18]

Elsewhere, we are told that "the look in Floyd's black eyes would have scared the devil."[19]

However, if Barkley perceived his comrades as inherently warlike and savage in their unwillingness to give quarter to the enemy, it is also possible that they did their best to cultivate this image. As historian Thomas A. Britten has observed, many of the 10,000 Native Americans who served in World War I "felt considerable pressure to 'measure up'" to the expectation (operative both on and off the reservation) that they were naturally strong and fierce soldiers.[20] Through acts of often spectacular courage and endurance, such men sought to perpetuate the martial traditions of their indigenous cultures *and* win approval from white America (perhaps in return for opportunities and resources long denied them). Whatever the case, while Barkley probably exaggerates the aggressiveness of his hard-boiled companions (at least a little), there is no question that James and Floyd were tough men in real life—probably *very* tough men—and accomplished soldiers. Like Barkley, James impressed his superiors enough to qualify for intelligence training (evidence suggests that the AEF's leadership viewed Native Americans as especially attractive candidates for such instruction),[21] and both James and Floyd received the Distinguished Service Cross, the nation's second-highest award for valor. Their names appear below Barkley's on the list of decorated soldiers that concludes the *History of the Third Division* published in 1919.[22] Moreover, if Floyd objected to the treatment that he receives in *No Hard Feelings!* or found the narrative in any way unrealistic, he certainly gave no indication of these feelings when he renewed his friendship with Barkley later in life. After their discharge in 1919, the two men went their separate ways and quickly lost touch. Decades passed. Then, in 1946, Floyd, now national commander of the Regular Veterans Association (RVA), finally tracked down Barkley. The two veterans began a warm and lively correspondence, and ultimately they met in person at an RVA conference. Readers wondering about William "Nigger" Floyd's seemingly pejorative nickname, which was inspired by his exceptionally dark complexion, may be surprised to learn that he referred to himself as "Nig" or "Nigger" Floyd in his letters to Barkley and apparently regarded the title as anything but insulting.[23]

It is also important to recognize that Barkley's clichéd emphasis on Native Americans' ferocity forms just part of the ultimately compelling picture that he draws of his two comrades. A closer reading of *No Hard Feelings!* reveals numerous subtleties that undercut the stereotyping. For instance, when Barkley is first introduced to Floyd, the Native American soldier hardly occupies the subordinate position of noble savage. Barkley must prove himself a "white Indian"—a brave and capable fighter, that is—in order to gain the other man's approval.[24] Barkley's Native American comrades are a far cry from Tonto. They never function as sidekicks. Instead, the two men form an elite clan within the larger tribe of the U.S. Army and pick their initiates carefully. From the start, Barkley struggles to meet *their* standards, not vice versa. At the same time, the narrative acknowledges the vulnerability that James and Floyd keep hidden behind their hyper-masculine personas. One of the most vivid and disturbing episodes in the memoir appears early on, as a French hospital train passes the inexperienced Americans, who are, of course, heading in the opposite direction—toward the battlefield. "That was our first sight," Barkley writes, "of what the war might be going to do to all of us. Of what it would surely do to some of us."[25] Confronted with this scene of ghastly horror—"Everywhere bandages . . . bandages . . . bandages . . . and blood"—Barkley turns to James and Floyd, and finds them just as shaken as he is:

> Those two Indians were standing there in the car door as straight and stiff as bronze statues. And as still. Not a thing about them moved except their eyes. They'd look at each other . . . then at the train . . . then back at each other . . . then at the train again. It was like a machine.[26]

Finally, *No Hard Feelings!* concludes with a tragedy that underscores the sad contrast between the secure social status of Native Americans within the AEF, where their supposedly innate abilities as warriors won them acceptance and even acclaim, and the grim socioeconomic battlefield that awaited them back at home. Soon after his discharge, Jesse James discovers oil on his reservation land in Oklahoma and for a time seems to have achieved the American dream. But like Jay Gatsby, that tragic literary icon from the same era, his success story ends badly: "Not very long afterwards," Barkley writes, "I got word that his body had been found thrown in a creek near the town. It was murder for money, of course."[27]

Barkley's own return to civilian life was less dramatic, though not without turbulence. In the early 1920s, he worked for a time as a detective in a Kansas City agency—a way, perhaps, to retain some contact with the world of violence and raw emotion that he had known on the battlefields of France. He also deepened his association with the U.S. Army, becoming a lieutenant in the Reserves and briefly teaching marksmanship at John Tarleton College in Texas. However, even as the Medal of Honor recipient accumulated credentials as a man of the world, he continued to spend much of his time on the Barkley family farm—and to delight in the woodcraft that had so effectively prepared him for open warfare on the Western Front. He remained a familiar presence on Scalybark Creek. In 1930, Barkley described his feelings for the outdoors in a letter to his friend Mike Mulcahy, a Regular Army captain who oversaw the military cadet ("Vidette") program at Tarleton during Barkley's stay there: "I wouldn't give these Missouri woods up for all the bright lights, army camp theaters, and gay times [in the world]. I like to get out once in a while and tear hell out of things— but I was born in the woods—I love the woods and swamps."[28]

Yet Barkley was a divided man, simultaneously desirous of rustic solitude *and* lucrative renown. The latter eluded him. Other American heroes of the Great War, such as Alvin York and Eddie Rickenbacker, became celebrities, accruing significant material benefit from their wartime bravery. But Barkley's name remained obscure, at least outside Missouri. His relative lack of notoriety did not result from want of trying. Indeed, in the years immediately following the war, Barkley told his story before various audiences on the lecture circuit, but, unlike York, he never became completely comfortable as an orator. And despite his best efforts, neither was he able to secure the kinds of interviews and endorsements that kept the exploits of other war heroes prominent in the popular imagination. Fate, which had allowed him to succeed so spectacularly on the battlefield, now seemed to conspire against him. In 1921, while they were en route to the American Legion Convention in Kansas City, General Pershing and Field Marshal Ferdinand Foch, the former supreme commander of Allied forces on the Western Front, stopped in Holden to honor the young man who had fought so courageously in 1918. But Barkley wasn't at home. It was a typical piece of bad luck—though Barkley would later claim that he contacted Foch at the convention and met with him privately. The former field marshal supposedly greeted the Missourian as one of "the world's greatest heroes."[29]

By the late 1920s, the farm economy in the Midwest was in freefall, and Barkley, increasingly hard pressed for cash (or "jack," as he put it), pinned his hopes for fame and fortune on the publication of a book about his wartime adventures. His ambitions involved much more than mere self-aggrandizement: He was supporting his widowed mother now and struggling to keep the family's property intact as the Great Depression closed in. Tentatively titled *Scarlet Fields*, his story had the makings of a publishing sensation. But there was just one problem: He wasn't a writer, and he knew it. Thus, apparently possessed of at least some talent for narrative, Barkley's friend Captain Mike Mulcahy would play a major role in the prepublication history of *No Hard Feelings!* In 1929, the former Tarleton faculty member agreed to ghostwrite the memoir in exchange for half of the royalties.

To ensure accuracy, Barkley provided his friend with pages of detailed notes, nearly all of which found their way into the finished book. Indeed, a comparison of these notes, which form part of the John Lewis Barkley Papers at the National World War I Museum Archives, with the final version of the text reveals that while the sentence structure in *No Hard Feelings!* may have come from Mulcahy—or, as we will see, from the team of editors who worked for Barkley's publisher in New York—the memories presented are essentially Barkley's. Here, for example, is a section of Barkley's notes, which describes an incident from the 4th Infantry's first rail journey in France, followed by the corresponding passage in the memoir:

Large wine train on side track. Wine is hauled in France in cars
like our oil tankers only the tanks are made of wood. Couldn't get
any wine out of car. Jess James shot thru wine tank with 45. Wine
sperted [*sic*] out in a stream 15 ft long was red wine.[30]

The train didn't pull out right away, so we began to look around
for something to take our minds off our troubles. Someone discovered a wine train standing on a track near by. Several of us
slipped out with our canteens, but we couldn't find any way to get
the wine out of the car. They were the usual kind in which wine
is shipped in France—tank cars made of wood. So Jesse blew a
hole in one of them with his forty-five, and the wine spurted out
in a stream ten feet long. We filled our canteens.[31]

Apart from a few altered details (such as the conversion of the fif-
teen-foot stream of wine into a more believable ten-foot stream), the
published version of this anecdote corresponds almost exactly with
the one originally penned by Barkley, only rendered grammatical and
enlivened by a consistent first-person voice.

While Mulcahy translated notes into narrative, Barkley kept a close
eye on the market for war literature, which in 1929 was booming after
a ten-year lull. In a letter mailed to Mulcahy on September 23, he
enclosed a newspaper clipping that described the runaway success of
All Quiet on the Western Front, the most popular war novel of the twentieth century. Remarque's bestseller would prove inspiring not only to
Barkley but also to better-known authors, such as Richard Aldington
and Robert Graves, who rushed their own literary products onto the
market. "I'll bet that hiney makes plenty of money," Barkley wrote,
speaking for war writers everywhere. "Why can't we?"[32] At the same
time, he scoped out his closest competition—namely, other Medal of
Honor recipients with books in the offing. On October 27, for example,
Barkley warned Mulcahy that Lowell Thomas's biography of Samuel
Woodfill, a famed junior officer who single-handedly captured several
German machine-gun nests, was about to appear. Barkley could see

that the time to publish his own story was at hand, and he pressed Mulcahy to complete as many chapters as possible: "I think it's time we are doing something. . . . This whole war book proposition is going to be a fad . . . and the one that gets his book in first is more apt to get the grapes."[33] Three weeks later, Barkley queried, "Don't you think we should make this story from here on out very bloody?"[34]

Barkley's sense of market timing could not have been better, but months slipped by as one publisher after another rejected the project. Then, in January 1930, Mulcahy showed *Scarlet Fields* to Bradley Kelley, the fiction editor at King Features, a New York newspaper syndicate (part of the Hearst Corporation) best known today for its connection with classic comic strips such as "Blondie" and "Flash Gordon." Pending a successful revision of the manuscript, which needed a major overhaul, the syndicate agreed to arrange book publication through a subsidiary, the Cosmopolitan Book Corporation. Unfortunately, dental problems, which required immediate surgery, prevented Barkley from being on hand when Mulcahy and Kelley drew up the contract, a misfortune that would have serious implications later on.

In March, King Features summoned Barkley to the Big Apple, expenses paid, to work on the memoir with a team of four professional editors—all women, led by a "Mrs. Darioux." For weeks, Barkley spent his days sequestered with the editors, who tore Mulcahy's version of the narrative apart, making it, in Barkley's words, "more pathetic in places—more hard punch in others."[35] At night, he hit the town. For the woodsman from Missouri, it was a heady time, filled, he wrote, with "more liquor and parties than I could stand."[36] At one soiree, he encountered none other than Howard Chandler Christy, a New England illustrator best known today for his "Christy Girl" sketches (these were meant to compete with Charles Dana Gibson's popular "Gibson Girl" series) and his iconic World War I propaganda posters. Christy admired the plainspoken war hero from the Midwest, and over the course of several evenings he painted his portrait, free of charge. The completed likeness, which today hangs in the National World War I Museum, shows the Medal of Honor recipient resplendent in his officer's uniform, his chest covered with decorations, his left hand grasping a sword—just about the only weapon that Barkley had not actually used in combat. In the background stands Barkley's lone tank, dramatically silhouetted against the horizon.

New York nightlife may have offered Barkley a respite from his daily editorial labors, but it did little to calm his financial anxieties. He would later comment that the process of bringing *No Hard Feelings!* into print was a nightmare far worse than the war itself: "This thing is causing me a hell of a lot of worry," he wrote, "more than the best sniper I ever came up against on any dam [*sic*] front I was ever on."[37] Perhaps not surprisingly, now that there was real money involved (or at least the illusion thereof), his partnership with Mulcahy became strained. Looking over the contract, Barkley suspected a double-cross, and after a few days in New York he wrote to his friend in a fury, accusing him of "collecting all the money" that the memoir would earn.[38] In retaliation, Barkley threatened to cut Mulcahy's 50 percent share in the royalties down to 25 percent. Or how about zero? After all, it had taken an entire team of editors to salvage Mulcahy's version of the narrative. If the ghostwriter was incompetent, why should he be paid anything? Mulcahy apparently smoothed things over, because Barkley's subsequent letters to his partner show little sign of anger or distrust. But Barkley remained wary of the entire process; after consulting his lawyer, he repeatedly confronted Kelley, insisting that the contract be rewritten with more profits assigned to the man whose name appeared on the title page.

In the end, the legal wrangling made little difference. No one connected with *Scarlet Fields* (now retitled *No Hard Feelings!*) made a fortune on the project—not King Features, not Mike Mulcahy, and certainly not John Lewis Barkley. Priced at $2 per copy, the book came out on September 5, 1930, just as the international boom in war literature began to peter out and just as disposable income became a thing of the past for most Depression-era Americans. The Cosmopolitan Book Corporation promoted the memoir aggressively enough, producing more pieces of advertising for it, Barkley claimed, than

Little, Brown, and Company had for *All Quiet on the Western Front.* But, as Barkley conceded, "times [were] hard in the publishing business."[39] The first printing of *No Hard Feelings!* (there would not be another) numbered just 3,800 copies. By January 15, 1931, 2,285 copies had sold, earning Barkley $130.97 in royalties, the largest single sum that he would ever receive from his publisher.[40] As the 1930s wore on, his proceeds dropped pitifully. For example, on October 27, 1932, King Features sent him a royalty payment of 37 cents.[41] But perhaps the most depressing news related to *No Hard Feelings!* reached Barkley in March 1938, long after the trickle of royalties payments had stopped altogether. The publishing house Farrar and Rinehart, which had bought out the Cosmopolitan Book Corporation several years earlier, wrote to inquire whether the Medal of Honor recipient would be interested in purchasing the electrotype plates for his memoir. Otherwise, they would be melted down, along with the plates from other books that "hadn't been printed for a long time."[42] Barkley went ahead and bought the plates, but never found a publisher for them. They reside today in the garage of his daughter Joan Barkley Wells's home in Kansas City, Missouri.

Along with unfortunate timing, poor to lukewarm reviews also played a role in killing Barkley's dreams of publishing success. Few of the newspapers and periodicals that received copies of *No Hard Feelings!* chose to review it, and those that did often betrayed a sense of impatience with the narrator's élan in the midst of battle. The most scathing notice, written by Lambert Davis, appeared in *Books* magazine:

> One reads this book with breathless haste to get on to the next thrill, but at the end there is no conviction that Mr. Barkley's version of the war is a representative one or even a real one. Certainly Mr. Barkley's enjoyment of it will appear to most people as somewhat abnormal. Even when we allow him the natural fighting temperament of a descendant of pioneers there is a certain unreality in the extraordinary gusto with which he fought. . . .

Mr. Barkley's facts may be correct, but the emphasis which he continually puts upon them taxes the reader's sense of reality past the breaking point. The general air of bravado with which he tells his story gives it more the atmosphere of a Dumas melodrama than a narrative of the World War. And somehow we are still too close to the reality to enjoy it as a blood and thunder tale.[43]

Other reviewers stressed the memoir's dubious literary merits. "The title 'No Hard Feelings!' is better than the book itself," declared James B. Wharton in *The Nation*. "The best portion of the book is the writer's modest description of the feat which earned him [the Medal of Honor]. But good soldiers do not always make good writers."[44] In his review for *The New Republic*, E. G. Taylor offered a similar appraisal of the writing but was somewhat more generous in his evaluation of the content: "[Barkley's] story, which seems to have been written in collaboration with some very competent journalist, is flavored with cognac and perfumed with French ladies; it proves that life sometimes resembles a blood-and-thunder movie."[45] The most favorable notices appeared in *The Bookman* and *The Saturday Review of Literature*. In the former, an anonymous reviewer praised *No Hard Feelings!* as a "straightforward and unassuming narrative, which more than compensates for its undeniable lack of literary value by the quality and abundance of its material."[46] And in the latter, critic Leon Whipple paid the memoir a backhanded compliment: *No Hard Feelings!* was a "thrilling book," he conceded, but "dangerous" for that very reason. Whipple feared that Barkley's exciting account would serve as "an invitation to war—for fun!—addressed to the Class of 1932 who will learn about war from books."[47]

In 1930, the question of what the Great War meant to America—or, rather, how it would be constructed within collective memory—was still a painful and unsettled one, and the reviews that *No Hard Feelings!* received perhaps say more about the turbulent cultural dynamics of the period than they do about Barkley's book. As evidenced by the definition of "reality" implicitly operative in Davis's biting review, the antiheroic war literature of the late 1920s, perhaps best represented by *All Quiet on the Western Front*, offered a version of the past that made sense to many Americans. Thus, Barkley appeared "abnormal" for celebrating an experience that, as presumably everyone knew, involved nothing but misery and terror. In reality, however, more than one vision of the Great War took hold in America during the interwar period. Speaking for many citizens, the American Legion, which included nearly a quarter of the nation's four million World War I veterans in its ranks, celebrated the war as a time of "Americanization" when citizens of varying ethnicity had shed their differences and come together in a common cause. (Barkley presents this very theme at the close of his narrative, where he describes "two Indians, an Irishman, an Italian, a Jew, a Syrian, and a middle-western farm boy" as "an honest to goodness American gang.")[48] Moreover, through military service, the Legion argued, American males had become *real men*; in the pages of its national magazine, which reached far more readers than any of the antiheroic war books that appeared in 1929 (with the possible exception of Remarque's), the Legion glorified the Great Adventure of 1917–1918 as just that—a great adventure that had toughened its male participants, enlarged their scope of experience, and prepared them for middle-class success. Ironically, this nostalgic vision of war experience would remain intact even as the Legion came to support isolationism on the eve of World War II.[49]

Thus, conflict among eyewitnesses, not consensus, was the dominant theme as the United States struggled throughout the 1920s and 1930s to digest an ambiguous episode in the nation's recent past. Hollywood understood this dynamic from the beginning and, of course, played to all sides. Indeed, as copies of *No Hard Feelings!* arrived in bookstores, contradictory images of the Great War appeared on movie screens. Significantly, 1930 saw the release of Lewis Milestone's screen version of *All Quiet on the Western Front*, the most celebrated pacifist film in American history, *and* Howard Hughes's legendary *Hell's Angels*, an aviation epic whose breathtaking dogfights and steamy romance (a love triangle with Jean Harlow in the center) overshadowed its own antiwar message.[50] By offering action and adventure, incongruously paired with denunciations of armed conflict, *Hell's Angels* resembled earlier cinematic treatments of the Great War such as *Wings* (1927) and *The Big Parade* (1925), both major hits at the box office. "Thrill," "enjoyment," "melodrama," "blood and thunder"—the vocabulary of Davis's blistering notice fits these Hollywood products perfectly. So was Barkley's account really so deviant? Taylor, the critic for *The New Republic*, perhaps said more than he intended when claiming that *No Hard Feelings!* "proves that life sometimes resembles a . . . movie."

As its reviewers eagerly pointed out, Barkley's memoir falls well short of any claim to the status of great literature; however, the narrative's value as a depiction of wartime experience, as a cultural and historical document, is much greater than its critics could (for obvious reasons) see in 1930. Because Barkley witnessed far more combat than the average doughboy—most members of the AEF fought in just one battle, the Meuse-Argonne, or in none at all—his book tells us, in much greater detail than the average firsthand account, what it was like to serve at the point of the proverbial spear. *No Hard Feelings!* shows us how "intelligence men," arguably the AEF's best soldiers, modified their tactics as they moved from battle to battle, how they became more adept at both reconnaissance and fighting. Barkley's treatment of the latter is perhaps without equal among American narratives of the Great War. His book abounds with information about World War I weapons, from Luger pistols to mustard gas, and what these weapons could do—did do—to human bodies. Only the battle scenes in Hervey Allen's brilliant memoir of his service in the Aisne-Marne campaign, *Toward the Flame* (1926), come close to matching Barkley's in terms of intensity and detail.

Yet for all its seeming ubiquity in the narrative, violence forms only part of the story that Barkley tells. Since the 1990s, a period that has seen a renaissance in scholarship on World War I, historians such as Mark Meigs and Jennifer Keene have reexamined the AEF as a cultural and political (rather than exclusively military) organization.[51] Within their analyses, the experience of combat, shared by fewer than half of the American soldiers who landed in France, is secondary; far more prominent are the cultural lessons that doughboys took away from their time as strangers in a strange land—lessons that tended to strengthen their ties to the United States. On this subject, no less than the subject of battle, *No Hard Feelings!* offers eloquent testimony. Indeed, throughout the narrative, Barkley is both a soldier and an eager, if usually misinformed, tourist. And in line with the behavior of most tourists (then and now), his glimpses into other cultures often only reinforce his American predilections and biases. Consider, for example, his initial impressions of France. Landing at Brest, he expects to see "sculptures scattered around in stone and marble," but instead he confronts a scene of (to him) shocking grubbiness:

> It seemed to me that everywhere I looked there were cow barns; and not even clean cow barns such as we have at home. The streets were paved with cobblestones. The women were more or less shapeless, clumping along in wooden shoes. They didn't look clean either.[52]

Like thousands of other doughboys, particularly those with middle-class backgrounds, Barkley is quick to equate France with dirt and poor hygiene. As the 4th Infantry moves inland, away from the seedy port city, his judgments become less severe. Detailed to an intelligence school near Paris, Barkley finds himself in a picturesque village, surrounded by "cherry orchards" and "forests" and inhabited by "kind and friendly people." Here, for the first time, he encounters the "charm of France."[53] But his foreign surroundings remain a playground for the American imagination. After helping to repel the German advance across the Marne, Barkley and his comrades discover an abandoned chateau, which they proceed to treat as a stage set. In one of the bedrooms, the Missouri woodsman breaks into a wardrobe, tries on a "fancy-dress" costume (complete with high hat), and play-acts in front of a mirror.[54] Floyd scowls at such finery; no American millionaire, he maintains, would ever wear such an outfit. Other sections of the estate inspire thoughts of romantic adventure. In the chateau's "long gallery," Barkley finds a miniature museum and delights in the exotic artifacts on display—"jeweled swords," "relics of Napoleon and his wars," and flintlock pistols that immediately remind him of duels that he has seen in picture books.[55] He wishes that he had some way to take these treasures home. In this scene, as elsewhere, France is less a living nation than a cabinet of curiosities—of potential souvenirs—unintentionally arranged for the doughboys' amusement or criticism.

However, the cultural insularity that so often characterizes Barkley's account sometimes breaks down, and touristy surface impressions give way to empathy and connection. Some of the best writing in *No Hard Feelings!* appears when Barkley encounters the stream of French refugees fleeing the German advance during the Second Battle of the Marne. The book presents war's human flotsam without a hint of sentimentality:

> Sometimes they passed quite close to us. But they hardly glanced up to look at us. Just watched the ground ahead of them to try to keep from stumbling. The worst thing about it to me was the queer sort of dead look on their faces. As if they couldn't see anything or feel anything any more.[56]

Other scenes portray moments of unexpected and often poignant cross-cultural interaction. Following days of savage fighting at Château-Thierry, Barkley and his comrades recuperate in a quiet village, where Jesse James attracts the attention of an elderly French couple who become devoted to him. Ironically, the old man identifies this Native American from Oklahoma with French antiquity, comparing the indigenous peoples of the New World to "tribes he'd read about in France thousands of years ago."[57] For him, Barkley's comrade is the noble savage of Chateaubriand and French Romanticism, and he weeps when James must return to the front. And then there is the remarkable episode near the end of the book, where, after having dispatched so many members of the German army (and with such evident enthusiasm), Barkley helps return a stolen Iron Cross to a German veteran. No hard feelings.

Barkley knew that his memoir had virtues that reviewers had failed to see. And he was not alone. In a letter to Barkley dated January 9, 1933, Major General James Harbord—the same Harbord who had created the AEF's gigantic divisions in 1917—wrote that *No Hard Feelings!* was "the best book I have seen on the War."[58] Harbord had considerable experience with war literature. In 1929, he served as one of three judges for an international war-novel competition, cosponsored by Houghton-Mifflin and the American Legion, and read dozens of manuscripts.[59] Reassured by fan mail from Harbord and others, Barkley pushed for a new edition and dreamed of a film adaptation of his book. But to no avail. In the midst of the Great Depression, his schemes became more desperate. On January 18, 1934, Barkley wrote to Mulcahy with a new idea. He had noticed magazine advertisements for Camel cigarettes that featured endorsements from Medal of Honor recipients. Here, he hoped, was a real opportunity to revive popular interest in his story:

> Now Mike you write to Camel. Tell them that you are my manager and that you have been authorized to submit my episode to them for their approval to be used as advertising material for their cigarette add [*sic*]. Give them the tank episode. Tell them that there were at least 5000 German rifle and machinegun bullets hit this tank [,] that each bullet strikes with a ton blow—that ten million pounds struck that tank in two hours and a half—enough nerve-racking noise on that steel tank to shatter the nerves or raise the hair on a Roman exicutioner [*sic*]—still my nerves are perfect—a fine rifle shot yet and still a constant Camel smoker with perfect nerves and a six inch chest expansion. Tell them I always smoke Camels for they don't jag my nerves. . . . I will furnish you with a photograph in full uniform painted by Howard Chandler Christy smoking a Camel. It is a marvelous picture with all my decorations.[60]

Like most of Barkley's earlier efforts at publicity, this one went nowhere, and by the time World War II arrived, he had made peace with his relative obscurity. He had also come to enjoy a more secure financial situation. In her eloquent afterword to this new edition of *No Hard Feelings!*, Joan Barkley Wells provides a portrait of her father in later life—his generosity and public service, as well as his role in the commemoration of American soldiers lost in the Great War. John Lewis Barkley never forgot them.

Ultimately, what is perhaps most impressive about *No Hard Feelings!*, a true lost treasure of American First World War writing, is not the epic scene in which Barkley earns his Medal of Honor (though no one who reads this book will ever forget that episode), but the haunting quality of his narrative voice, that of an innocent abroad who is simultaneously a human lethal weapon. Despite the number of editors who had a hand in the memoir—or perhaps because of them—that voice speaks expressively from the first page to the last and conveys the full range of emotions that war inspires in its participants, from disgust to exhilaration. Now that nearly a century has gone by since the Armistice of 1918, and the last American veteran of the Great War has died, it is well past time to hear what John Lewis Barkley, one of America's most courageous doughboys, had to say.

I

Training in Kansas

The old postmaster shook his head. He was sympathetic but firm. "It's no use, Johnny," he said. "There's no place in the army for a fellow who stutters as badly as you do."

There it was again! It began to look as if I wasn't even worth killing. The postmaster, who happened to be the recruiting officer in our little Missouri town, had known me all my life. He hadn't even given me a chance to get off the speech I'd carefully rehearsed.

I gulped down the lump in my throat. Everybody around me was going crazy about the war. I was under age—eighteen—but with as bad a case of war fever as the next fellow. Worse, probably. Because when America went into the war I'd made up my mind that for once I was going to do the same thing everybody else was doing. Ever since I'd learned to talk—or tried to learn—my stuttering had made a barrier between me and other people.

It hit me harder, too, because that morning word had come that one of our neighbor boys had enlisted and I'd heard my father say he "guessed the Barkleys were petering out." From Revolutionary days on, whenever America got into trouble there'd always been a Barkley in the fight.

I might have expected just what had happened. During the border troubles with Mexico I'd tried to get by a hard-boiled regular-army sergeant who was recruiting in Warrensburg. He'd turned me down cold because of that damned stuttering.

But Holden was my hometown, and the recruiting agent wasn't hard-boiled. I thought his having known me all my life might make a difference. Also, I hoped having been away to school would give me a chance to make him think my stuttering had improved. That was why I'd practiced up the speech.

And he hadn't even let me use it. It seemed to me I was up against a stone wall, and I got stubborn about it. My brother Doc and I both registered for the draft, but it was just a formality. He had never entirely recovered from a serious operation. We knew he'd be thrown out on the physical examination. And with two experiences to go by, it was easy to see what would happen to me.

Just the same I wasn't going to give up until there was nothing else to do. The Draft Board would be strangers. Not old friends like the postmaster, and not hard-boiled sergeants. I might be able to bluff them. And slim as the chance was, still I had a better chance than my brother. So when the summons came for him I kept after my father until I got him to use his influence and have my name substituted for Doc's.

I was pretty nervous when my turn before the Draft Board came. It started off all right. Physical examination, perfect. Eyesight and hearing, unusually good. But all the time they kept asking me questions that had to be answered. They got me rattled. After a while the words wouldn't even start to come out.

It was plain from the doctors' faces what they were thinking. Still I got up nerve enough to ask one of them who looked sympathetic if he thought I'd pass.

"Hell, no!" he said. "They'll never let you get anywhere." But he got up and went into the next room, and I could hear him talking to another doctor in there.

That was what saved me.

"God damn it!" the second doctor roared. "We're not picking orators. We're picking fighting men!" But even after my notice came to report at Camp Funston I still thought that when I got there and they heard me talk, they'd probably decide it had been a mistake and send me home again.

I didn't have many good-bys to say. There were my dogs, and my old horse (Charley), and my family, and a girl. She was the first one

I'd known who didn't laugh at my stuttering and she seemed pretty wonderful to me.

I hadn't any close friends. It's so much easier to go out to the woods with a gun and a couple of dogs than to try to make friends with people, at the risk of making a fool of yourself instead, every time you open your mouth. I'd spent more days alone in the woods than I ever had at school and a good many nights. Out there it was easy to forget that everybody laughed at me when I tried to talk.

Just before leaving for camp I got really engaged to my girl, with a ring and everything. My family thought she was fine, and I certainly felt grown up and excited about it. It was the most important thing that had ever happened to me. Except getting in the army.

It was the middle of September when we left for Camp Funston, and it was a mixed-up crowd we found on the troop train. There were several free-for-all fights before we got shaken down. I didn't mind those—I was used to fighting.

I can't remember when I found out that there's only one way to make a boy stop laughing at you. That's to fight him. And since I'd always been undersized, I'd had to learn how to move quick and think fast to keep from being beaten. I saw now that it had been darned good training. Also that I was going to have plenty of use for it long before we got to France.

It was at the end of one of those fights on the train that I met Tom O'Leary. I never got a word out of Tom about what he was doing out there in Kansas. He was four or five years older than I, and he came from Chicago. That's all he ever told me. But he'd evidently been hoboing in our part of the country when the draft caught up with him, and I always suspected that he'd found Chicago unhealthy for some good and sufficient reason.

Whatever was back of Tom's being there, he was all right. I'd have liked him anyway, even if it hadn't been for the special bond between us. We were the only men on the train who didn't have any decent clothes! Tom couldn't help it. He didn't own any except those he had on. But I was the victim of a recruiting sergeant in Holden who thought he had a sense of humor. It certainly shows how green I was.

The sergeant was very kind and thoughtful. He called me in the day before we were to leave and gave me a lot of good advice. Some of it was real, but most of it wasn't. Among the other things he told me not to take any of my ordinary clothes along. He said it was much better just to wear my farm overalls, since drill would begin at once and it might be days before we'd get uniforms.

I felt like a fool on the train, but after I found Tom it wasn't quite so bad. He looked worse than I did. The thing we minded most was being left out when the train stopped at a station and a lot of pretty girls crowded around with candy and fruit. They never knew we were there.

But one time it happened that we had all the luck. We'd stopped at a small town, and Tom and I didn't even wait to be overlooked when the girls started passing out their stuff. Tom was a really good acrobat and we amused ourselves by turning hand-springs on a plot of grass near the station.

We noticed a tall old man with a gray mustache and chin whiskers who'd been watching our stunts. After a while he came over and spoke to us.

"I am a veteran of the War between the States," he said. "I am glad to meet two real soldiers. I think I know a soldier when I see one."

We weren't sure what we were supposed to say to that, but he didn't wait for us to answer.

"There's one thing I learned in the hottest battle of my experience," he went on. "I'd like to pass it along to you. If you're ever caught under fire, or expect to be, fan out and *stay that way*. . . . If you gang together, or if you let the others crowd up on you, the grape-shot will get you for sure!"

We didn't find any grape-shot in France, but we found plenty of machine-gun bullets, and the old man's advice was just as good for one as for the other. I never saw a huddled group of our dead who'd paid the price for not fanning out that I didn't wish they'd been with us that day to hear the old man's warning.

Camp Funston was a dismal place—and *hot* that September morning when our train pulled in.[1]

Tom and I were assigned to Company G, 356th Infantry, a part of the Eighty-Ninth Division, which was just being built up.[2] They started us out at once on close order drill and calisthenics, and they gave it to us on a fourteen-hour-a-day schedule. It was pretty rough on new men, but Tom and I were tougher than a good many of them and in better condition.

I don't know where Tom got his endurance, but it's easy to see where mine came from. You can't spend all the time I had in hunting and fishing, in addition to helping with the work on a thousand-acre farm, and not come out of it with pretty good muscles and a lot of endurance.

As a matter of fact I didn't mind the drilling half as much as I did the monotony. It was a long time before we were really equipped, and it's hard to feel like a soldier unless you're fitted out like one.

We had other troubles too. The division that had trained before us had been gone long enough for the weeds to grow chest-high on the drill grounds, and the weeds were full of dust and redbugs.[3] But we drilled in them just the same until we'd knocked the weeds down and carried the redbugs off in our skins. That's something that wouldn't have happened if our officers hadn't been almost as inexperienced as we were.

The worst trouble of all was the sickness that broke out in camp. Measles, mumps, chickenpox, and a little of everything else. It got so that as soon as they hauled down one quarantine flag they ran up another one in its place.

But all along we were really learning the game of soldiering. That goes for officers and non-commissioned officers as well as for the men. We were all new together, except for a few old regulars about the camp, and we took them for models. We began to wear our clothes differently. It takes time to get the knack of wearing a uniform and making it look as if it belonged to you. Our talk was changing too. It was getting more like the regulars' talk.

Tom and I were "spoony" soldiers. That is, we were proud of looking like soldiers, and we'd have got on pretty well if we hadn't been too fond of excitement. When the monotony began to get on our nerves we had to think up some devilment to break it.

Once I got caught throwing out all the shoes I could find in my bunkhouse. They gave me an extra week's kitchen police duty, which I didn't mind; it meant enough to eat for the first time in several weeks. But I tried to help out some of the other boys by stealing things for them from the kitchen and got caught at that too. So they sent me back to drilling again.

All this time Tom and I stuck close together. He was about my size and build. He was quiet and soft-spoken enough when things suited him, but when they didn't . . . I'll bet he could have licked a cage full of wildcats.

The captain of our company was a parade-ground soldier. He hadn't much use for the runts—that's what he called the smaller men. Tom and I were runts and troublesome to boot, so naturally the captain didn't have many kind words for us. But the top sergeant was different. He was an old regular by the name of Meyerly. He called us "hell-raisers," always kept an eye on us, and let it go at that.

It was a couple of weeks before Christmas that I woke up one morning feeling pretty queer. Before I knew what was happening to me I'd been dumped into a pest camp with a nice case of measles. My tentmate had mumps, so I took that on too.

There were so many of us sick that we got mighty little attention. And the lieutenant who had charge of our particular part of the camp didn't seem to think it made much difference whether we had fire or bedclothes or food.

Finally a major doctor came around, with the Lieutenant and a nurse, to look us over. Sick as I was, I could see that he was excited.

And when they went on to the next tent, and found one of the boys in there dead, he went wild. It was hard to believe he was the same soft-voiced, gentle man who'd just finished examining me.

A month in the guardhouse wouldn't have been half as bad as the tongue-lashing that lieutenant got.

Shortly after the doctor's visit an ambulance came and took us all to the hospital at Fort Riley. We were made comfortable there, but by that time I was too sick to care.

It was just the time when influenza was sweeping the camp, and the men were dying like flies.[4] I knew that too. The hospital was so crowded that the bunks were only a few inches apart, and there was a Mexican in the one next to mine. He was pretty sick, but he never complained, and I got to like him.

I woke up one night thinking someone was trying to pull me out of bed. It was the Mexican. He was hanging over the edge of his own bunk and he had my left wrist in a death grip. His nose had been bleeding, and his bed was in a mess. I called the orderly, and they took him away.

I was worse after that. I woke up another time to find them putting a screen around my bed. Any soldier will tell you what that means.

However, I fooled the doctors and myself. By the middle of January I was back in camp again, so weak that I was marked quarters and did not have to go on duty. When my strength began to come back Tom took me in hand to help me catch up on drill, but we didn't get far with that. A call came from headquarters for a detail of men to go from each company to a scout and sniper school at Fort Riley.

I was surprised when I found my name among the eight selected from our company. I knew they were picking mostly college men— football players or athletes of some kind. It came out later that Meyerly had asked them to try me out.

I was the last of our bunch to go before the Board of Examiners at Riley. They'd passed only one man out of the other seven, and I didn't see how I stood any chance at all. The first thing we went up against was a board of psychologists. Those men seemed to know what I was thinking about before I did. They fired questions at me, and I knew they rated intelligence by the answers they got to those questions.

What I didn't know until afterward was how much short and pointed answers counted. I remembered when I was before the Draft Board in Warrensburg, and I had figured out that the way to do the least stuttering was to use the fewest words. So I tried to answer in one word if I could, and preferably in one syllable. I went through with flying colors. I could hardly believe my ears when they told me.

But before the medical doctors, where I wasn't looking for trouble, it was another story. They gave me a hundred percent on the physical examination, then they got to arguing over my stuttering. They tested my nerves. They tested them again. But I was desperate. I'd made up my mind not to get excited no matter what they tried, and they couldn't shake me. It had them puzzled, and they finally let me through.

But almost every time a bunch of new men came in they sent for me and examined me over again. I expected each time to be fired back to Funston, but that never happened. So I figured that someone on the board must be putting up a fight for me.

Our instructors at Riley were experienced French and British veterans, and regulars from the American army—seasoned soldiers all of them. And we were there for serious business: the business of learning how to get information about the enemy even if we had to go behind his lines to do it.

We were constantly being tried out in one way or another. As soon as the officers were convinced that a candidate didn't have the making of a good Intelligence man in him he was sent back to his outfit. Every day faces we'd known disappeared, and new ones took their places.

The Intelligence is called the eyes of the army, and there are three branches of the work. Observing, sniping, and scouting. It was all interesting to me. I wasn't satisfied to stop at the end of instruction periods, but was always tagging around after the old-timers and asking them questions.

In that way I learned about the Juramentado Moros who used to creep up on our sentinels in the Philippines and cut them down before they could make an outcry.[5] I heard stories of the German snipers who crawled through the Allied lines and picked off our men from the rear. I found out a lot about Gurkhas and Senegalese and Moroccans and their ways of fighting.[6] And I read everything I could get my hands on if there was anything in it that might be useful.

As observers we were taught to use field-glasses and telescopes, compasses, and maps. As snipers we were trained to fire quickly at indistinct or moving targets at unknown distances. This of course followed a drilling in ordinary rifle marksmanship which turned most of the men out pretty good shots.

Another thing we had to do was to practice seeking cover and firing from behind obstacles. A glint of sun on the muzzle of his rifle or on the lens of his telescopic sight has brought death to many a sniper, and it was dinned everlastingly into our ears that a sniper seldom lives to make more than one mistake.

The third branch of the service is scouting. The scout must go out to the front and work his way as far as he can toward the enemy, bringing back information of their movements. The observer, stationed in an observation or listening post, only has to telephone his information back or send it by a runner. The scout has to know many different kinds of wigwags and signals and also the Morse code.

In all this intelligence work you've got to advance to dangerous points or withdraw from them without giving away your movements by sight or by sound. So we were taught many tricks. How to make ourselves a part of the background by smearing clay on our faces and hands; by fastening grass and weeds to our clothing; by wearing baggy, nondescript suits of burlap and webbing. We were warned not to get anywhere near conspicuous objects in the daytime, and at night to keep away from weeds or gravel or anything else which might be noisy. We practiced finding our way in the dark without compasses. A compass is often worse than useless when it is deflected by the great masses of metal on a battlefield.

This sort of thing was somehow second nature to me. I'd always been terribly proud of the fact that Daniel Boone was some sort of ancestor of ours; I'd read a book mother had about him until the covers fell off. As a kid wandering around the woods along Scalybark Creek I'd tried to model myself on Boone. Pretending to be a pioneer cutting new trails through unknown forests was more fun than school. Now it began to look as if those kid games had taught me things that were going to be important to know if I ever got to France.

One of the first things a boy's got to learn if he spends much time alone in the woods is how not to get lost—how to find his way and tell directions even in the dark. That trick might be pretty useful if your compass was out of commission and you wanted to get back to your own lines. Many a sniper wound up his career as a prisoner inside the German lines because he didn't know it.

And an eye that's been trained to pick out a brown squirrel trying to hide in the top of a tree shouldn't have much trouble making out a sniper in a tree, camouflage or not.

As for guns, I'd been shooting some kind ever since my first old muzzle-loading double gun that rocked me from shoulder to heel every time I fired it. And when you consider the hours I'd spent lying motionless or trying to creep up on my game—like Daniel Boone—without a leaf moving or a twig crackling to give me away, it isn't strange that getting in or out of an observation post unseen didn't look as hard to me as it did to some of the boys who'd spent their time properly in school. Even my stuttering turned into a friend, for it came out that if I'd been able to talk like other people they'd have kept me there at Riley as an instructor in those things I'd practically grown up knowing. It might have meant never getting to the front at all.

I was mixed up in several fights while I was there, and missed Tom. But I remembered the tricks he'd taught me—how to duck to avoid blows and to throw my fists the way a mule throws his feet—and found them a great help. Tom had learned his fighting in a good school.

At Riley I had some adventures besides those fights. As long as I was at Funston I'd heard from my girl every day, and there had been plenty of letters from my family. I'd even had a furlough or two, with my father and mother at the train to meet me and a great celebration out at the farm. But we weren't getting any mail at Riley—it was being held at Funston. By the end of the second week I was pretty homesick. I knew everything would be all right if I could just get hold of my letters, so I decided to do a little scouting practice on my own.

There were chain guards around both camps, but I chose a dark night and went through the sentries. I got my mail and came back through the sentries too. Without a challenge. But it was almost daylight by the time I got into the barracks—and there were fourteen letters from my girl to read, besides the ones from my family. We spent that day firing on the target range, and I managed to squeeze in a letter after each of my turns at shooting without getting caught.

I was sorry when the training at Riley ended and I was sent back to Funston. The company had changed. The men were heavier looking. Their faces were leaner and harder. They stood straighter and moved quicker. Tom had become one of the best soldiers in the company. It was astonishing the way he could snap his rifle about. But he was still a buck private. His independence and his love of a fight had kept him in hot water.

They'd got him a great reputation among the men, though. I soon saw that we weren't going to be bothered—except by the first sergeant. He didn't think we were good for discipline. I'd gone back to my old tricks again, and after one of them he called me into the orderly room.

"Say, listen," he said, "I'm getting damned fed up on you and your kid ways. I've just about decided to kick a lung out of you."

By that time I'd learned something about the army game, and I knew that a non-commissioned officer who fought with a private couldn't do very much about it unless he licked the private. Meyerly was a lot bigger than I was, but I'd started fighting too young not to know that men aren't always dangerous in proportion to size. I decided to take a chance on it. So I said: "All right. If you'll hang your shirt with those chevrons on a nail, I'll be tickled to death to lick hell out of you."

He looked at me without saying a word. I don't know what he thought but whatever it was it made things different between us. We didn't fight and after that I was almost a model soldier. Unless breaking a rule would help Meyerly out.

Once when I was going on a furlough he asked me if I thought I could get a bottle of Scotch in with me when I came back.

His eyes twinkled. "If you let the damned M.P.'s get it away from you," he said, "I'll put you on kitchen police till the end of the war!"

"All right," I promised. "I'll guarantee to get off the train with your booze, but you'd better be at the station under arms. Then you can arrest me. I'm not so sure about getting by the sentries here at the camp."

I didn't drink myself, then—but I'd heard plenty of tales about the impossibility of getting liquor into camp. I spent most of my furlough trying to hit on a scheme that would work.

In Kansas City, on my way back to camp, I ran across a couple of other boys on furlough who were very low in their minds. They had two quarts of whisky, but they were sure they'd lose it on the train. By that time I had a plan, so I offered to take their whisky in for them. If I got it past the M.P.'s they were to give me one of the quarts.

When I got on the train at Kansas City I had my two bottles all ready. I knew that the military police had a regular system of search. There was a junction about twelve miles from camp, and no more stops after that until we got to Funston. The M.P.'s boarded the train at the junction, always at the rear, and worked toward the front. I was pretty sure I'd get by unless they'd changed their system. If they had I'd be sunk.

I went up to the front car when I got on the train and took a seat on the side that would be away from the station when we got to the camp. I'd made a cradle for each bottle out of buckskin-thong shoelaces and strong cord, then I'd tied a cord around the neck of the bottle and made a knot in the end of the cord.

The first part of my plan went according to schedule. The M.P.'s boarded the rear car at the junction. As soon as the train was moving, I raised my window and hung the bottles outside then closed the window on the knots in the cords. With the extra Pullman window pulled down too there wasn't a sign of anything suspicious.

The M.P.'s came through the train, turning things upside down. Literally. They finished their search of the car I was in as the engineer started whistling for our station, and just before we drew into the block at Funston they swung off the train. Still according to schedule.

When I was sure the last one was on the ground—on the side of the train away from me I opened the windows and pulled in my bottles. One of them went back to the boys who'd bought it, the other into my pocket. But the next step wasn't according to schedule. When I got off the train my sergeant wasn't there. I started across the road, pretty uneasy, my eye out for a sentry. I was looking for the challenge, but it scared me.

"Halt!"

I wasn't scared long. I knew that voice. It had bawled me out too many times. He'd been watching me from the darkness on the other side of the road. The voice came again:

"Who goes there?"

"The Man with the Bottle."

"Advance . . . with the cork out!"

I walked ahead of Meyerly all the way to the barracks, as if I were his prisoner. Several times the sentries held us up. It was always the same formula.

"Who goes there?"

"Sergeant with a prisoner," from Meyerly.

"All right. Proceed."

The sergeant was under arms. It looked perfectly regular as far as the sentries could see.

Inside the barracks I produced my bottle. "Well, I'm damned!" he said. "Just since yesterday they've doubled up the M.P.'s on those trains. And they had orders not to let a drop of anything get past them. How in hell did you do it?"

"That's for me to know and you to find out," I said.

I never did tell him, nor anyone else. As a kid I'd got used to playing a lone hand. I was finding that it was still fun. But Meyerly spread the news of what I'd done among his officer friends and from that time on my services were in great demand.

I pulled off the trick repeatedly without being caught, and as long as I was at that camp I never had any trouble getting furloughs. In fact they were urged upon me.

"Barkley," the sergeant would say, in a very worried tone of voice, "it seems to me you aren't looking quite so well. Don't you think a little trip to town might be good for you? I'll get you two or three days off if you say so!"

I'd like to find out what happened to that sergeant. If they ever let him get across I know he gave a good account of himself. He was a soldier, every inch.

2

Heading to France

There was a bulletin board at Funston where they posted our names as we were drawn from the division to be transferred to some embarkation point in the East. This was supposed to mean immediate service overseas. One morning Tom found my name there, but not his.

He made straight for the orderly room, and he didn't give up until he'd persuaded the major to have some other name taken off the list and his put on. He was terribly excited. When the crowded troop trains moved out of the station he said he'd bet we were "hell-bound for Siberia."[7]

We woke up the next morning to find that we were rolling through Arkansas. We seemed a long way from home already. The country was rocky and rough-looking and all the towns had names that sounded new and queer to us. About eight o'clock the train stopped in the railroad yards of some town. We all got out. There were dozens of girls and women with food and hot coffee and all sorts of things for us. It was our first treat, but from there on we had it all the way across the country. There wasn't a town where the people weren't fine to us.

We pulled into Newport News early in the morning on the third day. The train stopped, but we couldn't see a thing because of the thick fog outside our windows. Then a steamboat whistled. Voices yelled, "That's it!" and we all piled over to that side of the train. We thought we were going to be taken right from the train to the ship. When we moved on again we were a disappointed lot.

We traveled for another hour. The sun cleared away the fog. Then we found it wasn't land we were looking at any more. It was the ocean.

If you've been born and brought up in the Middle West, that's a thrill that comes once in a lifetime. Your first sight of the ocean. I'd often stood on top of a hill at home where I could see fields of corn, with the wind blowing over them, stretching miles in every direction. I used to wonder if their waves looked anything like the waves of the ocean. I saw now that nothing else in the world could look like the ocean.

We detrained at a small, crowded cantonment. We were quartered there, and Tom and I were assigned to Company K of the 4th Infantry.[8] We felt that we were much closer to the real thing than we'd been before. There were a lot of sunburned old soldiers fresh from service on the border, and others from the 15th Infantry, recently transferred from China.[9] We liked them all right, but we weren't sure we liked having them call us "Johns."

We were drilled three hours a day, and Tom and I showed up pretty well. It was all close order and that was our specialty. One morning we found our names posted on the bulletin board. We'd been picked out to be corporals. We went out back of the barracks to talk that over.

"Hell!" Tom said. "Whadda we wanta be corporals for? They'll put a squad o' bums on us. And what'll we hafta do? Run around after 'em like their mammies. See they take care o' their clo'es an' brush their teeth an' wash behind their ears an' keep their noses blowed. Look at 'em. No more respect for theirselves than if they was in a coal mine. Hell, no! We got troubles enough!"

I felt the same way. They were a hard bunch. They were a dirty bunch. They didn't care what they did. But how were we to get out of it? We let it be known that we'd rather not have the honor. But they were going right ahead to make us corporals whether we wanted it or not. We saw it was a case that called for measures. So we decided to go absent without leave for a few days; then there'd be nothing to do but reduce us.

We got past the guards that night and walked into town along the railroad tracks. The town was only five miles from camp and overrun with M.P.'s. But we found that the A.W.O.L.'s had an intelligence service all their own, just like a bunch of crooks. They all helped each other dodge the police.

They passed along news about the outfits too. Whenever we saw another soldier from the 4th Infantry we'd ask him what they were doing.

"Still just patrolling," he'd answer.

Then we'd find out if he'd heard anything about when they would sail. Of course we had to decide for ourselves how much what they had to tell was worth.

There were plenty of pretty girls and lots of liquor in Newport News. And Tom had had a run of luck at crap shooting. The fact that the saloons were closed to soldiers didn't bother us. There were as many bootleggers as there were M.P.'s. And they were equally on the job. All they asked was cash, and we had that.

The second day a couple of M.P.'s got on our trail, and we played hide and seek with them all day. Once we spent several hours in the shack of an old woman bootlegger. Another time we dodged into the best-looking house in the best-looking part of the town. And we were treated better there than we'd been in the shack even. The mistress of the house seemed to take a liking to us, or maybe it was just because we were soldiers. Anyway, she gave us a grand dinner and told us to come back whenever we needed a hide-out.

By the end of the fourth day our money was nearly gone, and we figured we'd been away long enough to be reduced, so we went back to the cantonment. The old-timers greeted us pretty solemnly. They told us we'd certainly be shot.

We laughed at first. Then they took us in to the company commander, who was a lieutenant. The lieutenant put us under guard and took us to the battalion commander, who was a major. The major sent us to the colonel. It began to look as if we *might* be shot.

But the colonel talked very kindly to us. He didn't really bawl us out at all. He just told us how sorry he was to hear that we'd disgraced ourselves and the outfit. That old colonel got us all worked up and ashamed. We told him we hadn't meant to desert or anything like

that. We said we'd only gone out of camp to tell our girls good-by.
Tom said that the girls had come all the way from Missouri just for
that good-by.

I'm sure he didn't believe us, but he pretended he did and sent us
back to our company. The only punishment we got was being kept
under guard for a few days. That colonel certainly knew his soldiers!

But it wasn't long before we wanted to get away from the camp
again. We knew we had a good chance of getting back without being
caught if we made our trips short enough, and from then on that was
the system we used. They hadn't said anything more about making us
corporals, so we had no object in being found out now. We'd break the
monotony of camp by a few hours in town, and no one would know
we'd been away.

On the first of those trips Tom and I were watching a big crap
game in a vacant lot. Suddenly someone hit me on the neck. "Hell!"
I said. "If *that's* the way you feel about—" and right then the fight
started.

Tom was with me of course. But the rest of them thought we were
trying to break up their crap game, and they all pitched into us. We
were having a pretty rough time. We weren't giving up. Not yet. But we
couldn't have held out long. Then suddenly the tide turned. Someone
had waded in beside us and in a few minutes the row was over. The rest
of the bunch faded away.

We turned around to see who it was we had to thank. We thought it
would be one of our friends from the company, but it was a man we'd
never seen before. He stood there looking us over. And we looked back.
He was something worth looking at. An American Indian. Tall, dark,
heavy-muscled, straight as no one but an Indian can be. He had all the
earmarks of a regular army man and he wore a sergeant's uniform.

We must have shown our surprise at seeing a stranger. "My name's
Jesse James," he said. "I liked your damned spunk. Who are you?"

We told him.

"There's not so much of you," he said. "But I guess you'll do!"

He went back with us to camp. After that it was three of us instead
of two. Of course we knew Jesse James couldn't be his real name. But

he didn't tell us the story back of it. And we didn't ask. When an Indian doesn't want to talk . . . he doesn't talk. And Jesse was almost a full-blooded Indian. He was three-quarters Cherokee. He did tell us that much. And he told us about his service in China. That was as far back in his history as he went.

He seemed to know a lot of people around in that part of Virginia, but he never said anything about them either. He broke out of camp one night, swam all the way across the river to keep some mysterious date on the other shore, and was back on our own side the next morning, drying his clothes. We never said anything about this, and of course he didn't. But if you've seen the width of the river there you'll know what a stunt it was.

Jesse made up for his silence about himself by the stories he told us of China. Some of these stories were probably true and some were lies. But they were always great stuff!

We learned a lot from him. He showed us new tricks which would be handy if it came to fighting with pistols and knives. He coached us on the target range, so that we began to pick up the finer points in shooting. He told us how to correct for light and wind; how to get in a quick shot between puffs of wind which might cause the bullet to miss; when to be careful to avoid a high shot.

Jesse had very little use for most of the men who'd been in China with him. I understood that. They were pretty generally riffraff. But we found out there was at least one exception.

Jesse had told us he had a friend he wanted us to meet. That's all he'd said about it. But I doubt if he could have told us anything that would have prepared us for Nigger Floyd.

He took us down to his barracks one day. Just inside the door we met a man Jesse knew. His name was Stew Ruford. I wasn't surprised by the name. The man was straight as a beanpole, but if ever a face showed that its owner had spent most of his life being stewed it was Ruford's. He was one of the men who'd seen service in China, and Jesse asked him if he knew where Floyd was.

"Sure," said Stew. He pointed over his shoulder. "He's back there shooting crap."

We stood at the edge of the circle of crap shooters and watched the game for a while. I've never seen anyone else like the man who was the center of the group. He was as dark as a Negro. His straight black hair fell down over his forehead. He had the longest arms I've ever seen.

He had the dice when we came up. He glanced at Jesse. Then he went on crooning to his dice. Rubbing them. Pleading with them.

"Come on now," he said. "*Nice* babies! Let's take some of this!"

When he'd finished his shoot Jesse spoke to him.

"Come over here a minute, Floyd," he said. "I want you to meet two damned good fellows. They're white Indians!"

Floyd stood up and looked us over. He was as tall as Jesse, and I've never seen anyone but an Indian as lithe as he was. Jesse told me afterward that he was part Choctaw and part Cherokee. He looked as if he didn't like us much. His eyes glittered at us from above his high cheek-bones. His lips stuck out. His mouth was wide. It had a queer way of twisting up at the corners.

"Indians!" he grunted. "Huh! How long you been in America?"

I hung on to my temper. "I don't see what difference that makes," I said.

He still stood there watching us. When he spoke not a thing about him moved except his lips.

"You look like pretty tough guys," he said. "Who's this other bird?"

Jesse answered. "Tom O'Leary."

"To hell with the Irish!"

That was too much for Tom. But Jesse held him back. "I want to speak to you by yourself," he said to Floyd.

They went off alone to the other side of the barracks. Jesse stood with his face toward us. We could see that he was talking fast. Several times Floyd looked over his shoulder at us, then turned to listen to Jesse again. After about ten minutes of this they came back.

Floyd spoke first. "Hell," he said. "I guess you'll do." He held out his hand. "Put it there. I'll try you out."

"That sounds all right," I said. "But suppose we don't measure up to suit you?"

"Then I'll knock hell out of you. That's all."

"I can tell you right now," Jesse said with a grin, "you'll be taking on a whole-time job!"

That almost started a fight on the spot. But Jesse stopped it. "Listen, Floyd," he said, "I've told you these are two white Indians. When I say it I mean it. They've fought everything in this camp. And they've wiped up with it. They're game to go A.W.O.L. with anybody. Any time. They're tried—and found guilty!"

"All right," said Floyd. "The A.W.O.L. part suits me. When do we start?"

I answered for the rest, "Any time you say."

"It can't be too soon for me. I gotta get out o' this camp," he said. "I gotta get damned good an' drunk. Before I left China Uncle Sam promised me I could go home an' see my folks in Oklahoma. He lied like a dog. Whadda we get? Nothin' but a damned kindergarten. Some fool's told these Johns we're goin' to sail soon. You can hear 'em cryin' all over the barracks. It's gettin' on my nerves. I feel like takin' a club and beatin' up the damned babies!"

"Well, don't do it," Jesse said. "They'll have something to cry about soon enough."

——◆——

Early in April we drew extra equipment. At one o'clock the next morning we were waked up and ordered to pack. Then we stood around until nine when we were marched up the gangplanks, and they didn't let us up from below decks until two in the afternoon. It was a good thing for the kaiser he couldn't hear what we had to say about him by that time.

When at last we got up on deck the shoreline was just a low cloud on the horizon. It was lucky for us that we didn't know how many of that company would never see America again.

As for me I wasn't very much bothered about what was ahead of me. I was only nineteen and I'd never really been away from home before. I couldn't think about anything but the distance that was getting greater every minute between me and the people in Missouri.

I didn't dare let myself think too much about home—I didn't dare think about my mother at all—until I was safe in my bunk alone in the dark. If Nigger Floyd had seen me then I'm afraid the trying-out period he'd promised would have ended on the spot. I was a long way from being a "first-class fighting man" that night. I was just a homesick kid.

We were on the *Great Northern*, one of the fastest in the service. But her speed didn't do us any good. We had to follow all sorts of roundabout courses on account of the U-boats, and on the sixth day we slowed down to keep close to a poky old scow which was carrying the 38th Infantry and the 7th Machine-Gun Battalion.[10]

If the Germans had been lucky enough to submarine that tub they'd have saved themselves a lot of grief later on. But as far as I know we were never in sight of a submarine. Our navy knew its stuff.

Most of the boys were seasick, but I wasn't. I got a real thrill out of seeing our little old *Great Northern* get down and buck the waves. When they let her have her way about it she raised a wave twenty feet high on either side of her bow. It was a great sight.

Jesse and Floyd and Tom and I stuck close together on the boat, but we began to have a little trouble keeping to ourselves. Jesse and Floyd were famous, and a lot of the boys wanted to gang up with us. There were only two we had any trouble shaking off. They were Mike—Michael De Angelo—a little Italian boxer and featherweight champion from Philadelphia; and Norosoff, an East Side New York Jew. [Norosoff's first name is never given in the text, and it does not appear anywhere in the John Lewis Barkley Papers—Ed.]

We kept them out as long as we were on the ship. Floyd told them there wasn't a chance in the world. He was especially rough on Norosoff.

He told him, "It's a club and it'd cost you more money to get in than you'll have if you live to be a hundred!"

But afterward, when we got into real service, it was a different story. Mike and Norosoff were both put in the Intelligence as runners, and they were two that you could always be a hundred percent sure of. Before long they were part of our gang. And no questions asked.

We never got much of Mike's background, but Norosoff told us that his father was a jewelry man. I suppose the jewelry store was a hock shop or a fence, but it didn't matter to us. Norosoff was all right. He turned out to be quite a character overseas. He never smoked, he never got drunk, he always had a smile. He was a little fellow, about my height, and he was one of the best runners we ever had.

The runner's job is to carry messages between headquarters and the men in the observation posts. When you gave a message to Norosoff you knew it was going to get through—unless he was bumped off himself. He wouldn't stop to talk to anybody. You couldn't make him talk.

"Godalmighty!" he'd say. "Howda y' know 't 'whole woild ain't blowed up before I get there?"

<hr />

It was on board ship that Jesse finally came through with the story back of his name. He'd been an orphan ever since he could remember, and had been brought up as a member of one of the most notorious bands of train and bank robbers in the Southwest. By the time he was fifteen the gang was being captured, one by one. It was taking the authorities a long time to get them all rounded up, but the young Indian was doing a little thinking for himself by now.

When he found out that there was one particular sheriff who was out to get him, and was warm on his trail, he decided the time had come to do something about it. So he went to the nearest recruiting station to enlist. He told them he had no parents and close relatives, which was the truth, and he bluffed about his age. That was easy, because it is hard to judge an Indian's age.

But when they asked him his name he had to think fast. He couldn't use his own and he'd forgotten to give himself another one. So he answered on the spur of the moment: "Jesse A. James."

"Well," the recruiting officer said, "you ought to make a grand little gunman for the army! Where do you want to serve?"

"Anywhere," the boy said. "Just so it's far enough away. I'm tired of this country."

"China ought to suit you," the officer said. "You do a little time here in the States and then we'll send you to China."

But Jesse passed the examinations and got shipped off at once to China with the 15th Infantry. He was there five or six years, and it was there he met Floyd. Floyd's history is a closed book to this day. I don't think Jesse ever found out anything about it.

⟫◆⟪

On the eighth day out we met a convoy of United States destroyers. We felt safer after that. But even so it was a great moment when word ran through the ship that land was in sight. There'd been plenty of those reports before. But this one was true.

3

Over There

It was around nine o'clock of a clear morning that I first saw France.[11] A line on the horizon, no thicker than a line on a sheet of paper. As we drew closer it rose out of the water. We began to make out shapes and colors. At last we could see grass and trees. They made me pretty homesick.

But if that glimpse of land had looked like home, the feeling didn't last long after we saw the harbor at Brest. Ferries, transports, subchasers, gunboats, grim old battleships—all riding at anchor. Big guns projecting from the rocks. Stone walls running far out into the harbor to keep back the waves in time of storm. Scavengers racing after our ship as we steamed into the harbor, trying to salvage all they could before they lost us.

It was my first sight of battleships and gunboats. They looked to me as if they meant business. I wondered how far it was to the front, and began to be on the lookout for signs of enemy activities. I hadn't any idea what signs of enemy activities would be like, nor of where Brest was in relation to the fighting. But I thought it quite possible that we might be fired on when we landed.

Nothing like that happened, but there were plenty of other unpleasant things. The only way to get from the ship to the land seemed to be a long flight of steps leading from the water straight up the side of the cliff. I couldn't even see the top of the cliff.

I said to Jesse, "They must have an elevator or something to get us up there. They surely don't expect us to climb those steps!"

But they did. With our sea legs and our sixty-pound packs and our thirty rounds of ammunition and our heavy rifles.

The first thing I saw when we got to the top was cow barns. I'd had a notion that European cities would look like the pictures of ancient Rome and Athens I'd seen in histories. I expected Brest to be a city with flowers and trees, and sculptures scattered around in stone and marble. I shouldn't have been surprised to find even the houses built of marble, with stately avenues filled with beautiful women. I'd mixed Egypt up in the picture, so that I was half-way looking for a pyramid or two.

But the first thing I saw when I got to the top of the steps was a group of cow barns. It seemed to me that everywhere I looked there were cow barns; and not even clean cow barns such as we had at home. The streets were paved with cobblestones. The women were more or less shapeless, clumping along in wooden shoes. They didn't look clean either.

Every now and then an ex-soldier, still in uniform, would hobble down the street on crutches. I saw a man who'd lost his arm. Then one who'd lost a leg. And when we passed another man with both legs off I began to feel a bit sick.

We didn't have a chance to find out whether the wine shops were as much of a frost as everything else. They marched us directly to the station. We'd expected to travel in something like the Pullmans in which we'd ridden from Camp Funston to Newport News. When we saw the size of the compartments forty men were supposed to be packed into, we just stood still and looked at each other.

The officers started trying to load us in. When our lieutenant had got twenty-five into one compartment he reported that it was impossible to get in any more. The orders came back: "Pack forty men in that compartment. And do it now." When it was over we were piled in there like a bunch of hogs. Forty of us, all with huge packs, in a space that wouldn't have been really comfortable for ten people.

The train didn't pull out right away, so we began to look around for something to take our minds off our troubles. Someone discovered a wine train standing on a track near by. Several of us slipped out with our canteens, but we couldn't find any way to get the wine out of the car. They were the usual kind in which wine is shipped in France—tank cars made of wood. So Jesse blew a hole in one of them with his forty-five, and the wine spurted out in a stream ten feet long. We filled our canteens.

Jesse and I didn't mind it much when we were placed under arrest. The arrest didn't last long and the fun we'd had was worth it, if the wine wasn't. It was my first taste of *vin rouge* and I didn't like it. It seemed bitter to me.

I thought: "My gosh! I've been through a French city. I've seen French women. I've drunk French wine. What next!"

We traveled three days and nights on that train. The scenery was pretty, when you could get near enough to a window to look out. But we weren't given any chance to forget that there was a war going on. When we pulled through towns we could see the platforms piled high with shells. Girls and women seemed to be doing all the work.

The engineer in our train had a good supply of liquor with him. I suppose that's why he bumped us around so much. But he never got so drunk he couldn't put her in reverse, slam on the brakes, then start ahead again. Some of the boys thought we were going straight to the front. After the first day in that train we all hoped we were and that the front wasn't far away.

We finally detrained at a little place called Bricon. I'd imagined a nice French village where we'd be quartered in houses, going outside to drill, coming home at night with nothing to do but run around and see the country. Bricon was another jolt. They turned over their cow barns for us to sleep in. And it seemed to me that the French must save every article of trash they'd ever had, and worship their manure piles.

We cleaned up the barns as well as we could, then we went down to look the town over. By this time the boys were pretty disgusted with life in France. To cheer us up a little we made a raid on the wine shops. When the officers saw that some of us were getting drunk they asked the French authorities to close the wine shops.

They did. Then we went scouting for the beautiful mademoiselles we'd been hearing about. There was only one really pretty girl in town, and a damned lieutenant was quartered in her house!

We had two days of misery in Bricon; then Jesse and I were drawn out and sent to an Intelligence school near Paris. There I found out that at least some of the things I'd been told about the charm of France were true.

The town where the school was was in a valley surrounded by hills and mountains. A canal ran through the valley, with cherry orchards sloping down to it on both sides. Back of these were forests and French government preserves of timber. It was a nice place. And we liked the people. They were kind and friendly to us.

Tom and Floyd had been left with the company, and we missed them, but we were kept too busy to mind it much. And after a while Mike and Norosoff came down from the company and joined us. That was where we really got to know them.

We met Sergeant Nayhone here too. [Nayhone's full name is never given in the text. He is mentioned at several places in the John Lewis Barkley Papers, but never with his first name—Ed.] Nayhone was a Syrian. He'd lived a long time in New York, but he still spoke like a foreigner. He liked being out in the woods and fields, and that made a hit with me. We used up a lot of our free time poking around together in the forests back of the town.

They worked us very hard at that school. We were under the best French Intelligence officers, and we went at everything as if we were in action. We reviewed all that we'd learned at home. Then we went on to things that were new to us. We studied all sorts of camouflage. We went through a course of instruction about the German army. That course covered uniforms and equipment, tactics and formation, methods of sniping and observing. We learned how to use their rifles and machine-guns and grenades. We were taught their points of strength and weakness.

They believed in being practical at the school. One of the instructors got a bunch of us huddled up close together one day to see a demonstration of grenade throwing. He called out one of the men and told him how to throw the grenade over the cliff in front of him—one long swing back, then forward with the arm stiff. The fellow brought his arm back all right. Then he let go of the grenade.

It landed square in the middle of us. When I came to, we were piled up like a football scrimmage. I was on top of another man—I'd been the first one to make the dive—but my face had had plenty of stepping on. When we found out that there hadn't been any explosion and that the officer was laughing, we knew what had happened. It was a trick to find out whether we were chicken-hearts who'd faint or fall backward instead of trying to get out of the way. The officer seemed quite pleased with the result of his little joke.

I tried very hard to learn that way of holding the arm stiff when the forward pass was made. I understood the reason for it. It was so you could throw a great many grenades without tiring your arm. But it was a trick I never mastered. Luckily I didn't seem to need it. I've thrown a bushel of grenades at a time, and my arm never gave out. I used to do it their way in practice at the school, but when I got into a real fight I went back to my own system. I'd grown up throwing rocks back in Missouri. I was almost a dead shot at rabbits that way, and when I got into action I found I did better with my old rock-throwing method.

Jesse and I went over everything together. He showed me a lot of Indian tricks that weren't taught in the school, but that I was glad to know later.

We were close enough to the front to hear the thunder of the guns, but it was not very loud. Several times enemy airplanes came over. Once we saw an air battle. The German planes were knocked down and several French planes were damaged. If it had not been for things like that it might have been peacetime, the valley was so quiet. But the only young men in the village were wounded soldiers.

We got to be great friends with the people in the village. There was one old man who liked to come out and talk to the American soldiers, and it was a crime the things we used to tell him. There were several boys who spoke fairly good French and they'd talk for us.

The first time the old man saw Jesse he spoke of his size and his dark skin. So, being very careful to let Jesse hear us—at the same time pretending to be afraid he would—we painted a picture of the Indian that was a classic. We told the old man that at home Jesse was a national figure as a bad man. That he was a terrible fellow when he was out on a hunt after wild boar or other game; everybody got out of his way when he was coming. We said he'd been known to eat little children who'd strayed away from home; and that when we saw him cleaning his rifle we all crawled into our billets. We advised the old man never to let Jesse anywhere near the town if he could help it. He went home stepping lively. Every now and then he'd stop in the road to look back. Then he'd shake his head and go on still faster.

During all this nonsense Jesse had been as solemn as an owl, taking in every word. But I never saw anything funnier than the expression on his face as he watched the speed that old man was making down the road. Jesse had rather prominent ears, but except for that he was a handsome Indian. He had a wide, slow grin that didn't seem to get into his eyes at all. That grin was doing full duty now, showing all his teeth. They were extraordinary teeth, even and very white. The only thing wrong with them was the gold one in the center of his upper jaw.

He didn't say a word. He was always quiet except when he was in a fight. But that grin stayed with him the rest of the morning.

It was in this village that I really got to know French people; I always felt differently about them after that. And it was here that I first made the acquaintance of a French "mademoiselle." She was a little peasant girl who wore funny long dresses and wooden shoes. She had a color like a wine-tinge in her cheeks. Her eyes and hair were beautiful. And her figure was graceful, even in her clumsy clothes.

At night I'd drop down to her house and she'd make me French salads. They tasted mighty good after camp rations. On Sundays we took long walks through the woods. Talking wasn't easy, but I had a French-English dictionary, and we managed. I even began to pick up a few words and phrases. There was one comfort. She didn't mind my stuttering. She thought it was part of the queer language I spoke, anyway.

Her mother took a great interest in me, but I didn't seem to make much of a hit with her father. His wife would cook up marvelous dishes for me, but he made it very clear that he thought I ought to pay for every egg I ate. That would have been all right with me; they were certainly worth paying for. But the trouble was that madame wouldn't take a franc for anything. And she scolded the old man about it until Jeanne would fidget and look unhappy and I'd be embarrassed even when I didn't know what it was she was saying. Anyhow, she went right on cooking for me.

Sometime in May we began to have a feeling that our days of preparation were nearly over. We'd find officers standing around talking to each other in low voices, or looking at maps and papers. There was a feeling of strain in the air. And one day the orders came through. We were to be loaded at once into trucks and sent back to our companies.

It broke me up to say good-by to Jeanne. She was a good kid. And knowing her had meant a lot to me. She didn't make it any easier. She cried and clung to me. I couldn't do a thing to comfort her. She'd said good-by to five French boys, and they'd all been killed.

"All!" she kept saying. "All gone!" I did the best I could. I kissed her; I tried to make her understand that I was promising to come back as soon as the war was over.

She lifted her head from my shoulder when I said that, and looked at me. The tears were still running down her cheeks.

"Non . . . non . . . non! They nevair come back!" she cried.

Then she was gone. I never saw her again.

—————◆—————

It was late in May when we got back to the regiment. We were assigned to the Intelligence section of the battalion now, but we were still attached for rations and quarters, such as they were, to old Company K.

We were glad to see Tom and Floyd, but astonished at the change in them. The whole outfit had changed while we'd been away.

The men were hard, quiet, and meaner than they'd been before. It paid to walk your way quietly. Most of them would fight at the drop of a hat. And drop the hat themselves. They knew how to fight too. I believe that the average soldier in that outfit could have whipped the average professional fighter of his size. And it wouldn't have taken him long to do it, either.

They'd had so much training in bayonet fighting and in hand-to-hand conflict that they were as hard as iron, and in their minds the change had been even greater than in their bodies. They moved with the ease and speed of cats; and they thought hard and fast in any kind of emergency.

Very shortly after our return, the officers began to speed us up. It seemed impossible that we could be worked any harder or any longer. But the drill *was* harder and the hours *were* longer. Inspection followed inspection. Our service of supply wasn't perfect yet, and many things in our equipment were lacking. But everything was put in as good shape as could be. Discipline was like our muscles. Hard as iron. We were fighting-fit, and knew it.

Rumors from the front kept drifting back, and they were very disquieting. The French were discouraged and pessimistic. Everywhere we heard tales of the great drive that was at last to carry the Germans to Paris. I don't think these reports affected us much, except to make us eager to get into the fight. But they did make me think more about home than I'd done before. It looked to me as if I was pretty nearly through with theories of war and pretty close to the practice of it. And that made me realize what it meant to have a home and a family.

In all the months that I was away from them I got mighty few letters that weren't cheerful. And that certainly helped a lot. They seemed to know what I'd like to hear. They told me the gossip about all the people I knew. They told about every-day happenings that mean home to almost everyone. They remembered to put in news of old Charley and my dogs, and to tell me if birds were plentiful or fish biting.

And of course there were the letters from my girl. It wasn't so good when she told about going to parties or the movies with other fellows, but I didn't really expect she'd spend all her time sitting at home. Only sometimes I wished I could be in on some of the fun.

The drilling was just about over now. We were marched back to the railroad one day and entrained. We had no idea where we were going, and we didn't care. We knew that this time we were headed for somewhere at the front.

And we were right. We were going to the Marne. The train carrying our battalion left Bricon on the evening of a day at the very end of May. All night we rode toward the front, with frequent stops for repairs or to let other trains pass us. Soon after daybreak next morning we were side-tracked to let a French train go by on its way back from the front.

That was our first sight of what the war might be going to do to all of us. Of what it would surely do to some of us. The train was a hospital train. Jesse and Floyd and I were standing in the open door of our car. We could look directly in through the windows of the other train as it moved slowly past us.

It was packed with men. Men lying as still as if they were already dead. Men shaking with pain. One man raving, jabbering, yelling, in delirium. Everywhere bandages . . . bandages . . . bandages . . . and blood.

It shook me up badly. And yet I couldn't seem to stop looking at it. After a while I pulled my eyes away, and turned around toward Floyd and Jesse. Those two Indians were standing there in the car door as straight and stiff as bronze statues. And as still. Not a thing about them moved except their eyes. They'd look at each other . . . then at the train . . . then back at each other . . . then at the train again. It was like a machine.

Floyd turned toward me. "Whadda *you* think, Barkley?" he asked.

I could hardly talk at all. "It's *hell!*" I managed to get out.

Floyd's lips barely moved as he spoke. "If it's as bad—" he said, "if it's as bad as I think it is up there—we gotta get shooting at those Germans. We gotta get shooting at 'em damned quick!"

Jesse seemed to think it was time to quit being serious. "Shooting!" he said. "You couldn't hit a flock of barns!" A remark like that was usually enough to send Floyd up in the air. He was a good shot at short range, but a poor one at much of a distance, and he didn't like to be reminded of it. It didn't keep him out of the Intelligence service, but it prevented his being used for observing or sniping, and it was a sore point. But he didn't pay any attention to it this time.

"That's all right," he said, "they won't always be a long ways off. Not if I have anything to say about it!"

Then we did a queer thing. At least it seems queer now, looking back at it. It seemed perfectly natural then, while that hospital train with its load of misery disappeared around a bend in the track and our own train went on again toward the front. We swore an oath—a solemn oath—that was to hold us together until there was no more need for it. We swore, each of us, to be on hand if the others were in trouble; not to let ourselves be sent back from the front as long as we had our legs to walk on; but to go back together if one of us *had* to go.

It was a pact. And it made us feel better. It was as if we'd begun to fight already.

We met another train filled with French soldiers passing through Troyes. Not so many wounded, this time, but a worn and discouraged-looking lot. Some of our men who could talk French called out to them, and they told us that the Germans couldn't be stopped. They were sweeping everything before them. They'd certainly go all the way to Paris. The war was over.

We heard that so often that we all recognized it. "*La guerre est finie!*"

We yelled back that the Germans would stop all right when they met us. But when we heard that they'd taken Soissons and were driving on toward Château-Thierry we weren't so sure.

The sound of cannon was in our ears all the time now. Some of the boys kept arguing that they ought to stop the train and let us hike the rest of the way. They were afraid the train would be captured.

"How they gonna know where the front line is now?" one of them said. "If the Goimans are comin' on so damned fast, what's gonna stop us from runnin' across the line 'fore anybody knows it? And if that outfit closes in on us, where the hell'll *we* be?"

As a matter of fact it looked as if the French trainmen were worried about the same thing. Certainly everybody was relieved when we detrained at Montmirail.

It was bedlam there. French refugees were swarming into town from one direction, and American soldiers pouring in from the other. We were told that part of our outfit, the 7th Machine-Gun Battalion, had met the enemy and been routed in disorder. Some of us believed the story. Some of us didn't.[12]

The next morning we moved out on foot along a beautiful broad highway, through Rozoy and Belleville, to the Grand Forêt. We were heavily loaded. And it was hot—damp and sweltering after a rain. Perspiration ran down into our eyes until we were almost blinded. It was a forced march, and they gave us very little rest.

When we did fall out by the road for a few minutes the officers would all get together in a bunch. You could tell by the expression on their faces, and by the way they studied their maps and nodded and pointed, that something serious was going on up there at the front.

In those short minutes of rest I'd look around at the country and think about the people who lived there. The road was lined with great trees. On each side were rolling hills, and patches of woodland that looked cool and shady, and green fields all divided up into little squares. Except that it was more "finished" it seemed to me a lot like the country at home.

We kept hiking and hiking. And as we drew nearer to wherever it was we were going we drew nearer also to something we'd had distant glimpses of ever since we left Montmirail. The French refugees in larger and larger numbers were struggling across the fields in flight from the battle areas ahead of us. At first it had been a group here and there. Now it was a steady stream.

There were women, old and young. There were children, of all sizes. There were tottering old men with long chin whiskers who looked as if they must be in their eighties. But there weren't any young men except wounded or crippled French soldiers who were being carried back by the others.

There were domestic animals of every kind. Many of the peasants were having a hard time trying to keep geese and milk cows and goats in line. One old billy-goat was giving a lot of trouble to his driver, a dirty little fellow with legs so thin they made me think of cornstalks. The goat was being very dignified; he was determined to go his own way and set his pace. He paid no attention to the boy, and he didn't seem a bit worried by the confusion around him or the guns growling behind him.

One old man was so feeble he had to be crowded into a cart that was already overflowing with furniture and bedding. A yoke of cattle was dragging the cart, and an old woman with a shawl over her head stumbled along beside it. She had one child by the hand and another clinging to her skirts. At the other side of the cart walked a pretty young woman with a tiny baby in her arms.

Behind this group came a little boy pushing a big wheelbarrow. Then a middle-aged woman and a young girl with three small children; all three of the children were crying. The girl would stop every now and then and stoop down as if she was trying to comfort them.

There was one old man who wasn't asking anything from anybody. He must have been seventy-five or eighty years old. But he was all alone, pushing a loaded wheelbarrow along, as spry as a cricket. And that wheelbarrow was making time! I wondered why they didn't have the old fellow in the army.

Sometimes they passed quite close to us. But they hardly glanced up to look at us. Just watched the ground ahead of them to try to keep from stumbling. The worst thing about it to me was the queer sort of dead look on their faces. As if they couldn't see anything or feel anything any more.

During one of our rests Sergeant Nayhone stopped some of these people and asked them what had happened up there at the front. Nayhone spoke seven languages. He had no difficulty making them understand his French, but he didn't get much satisfaction from them. They shook their heads wearily and said, "*Fini ... fini ...*" over and over. They were fleeing for their lives. That was all we could find out.

Floyd pulled at my arm. "What did that Frog say?"

"He said the war's over," I told him. "Over and finished. That there's no use for us to go up there now."

Floyd looked at me. "Well," he said, "I'm sure goin' up there to see for myself! I'm sure—Look yonder!" he pointed out into the field. "Ain't that a hell of a sight?"

It was a lame old peasant woman, driving her cow. She kept stumbling under the heavy pack she had tied on her shoulders. Once she fell and had a hard time getting to her feet again. Floyd watched her for a minute without a word. She hobbled on, trying to catch up with her cow, which had strayed off to one side. Then he turned back to us.

"My God!" he said, "it'd make your socks roll up and down like window-shades to look at it. I never saw anything worse than that in Oklahoma!"

He had such a look in his eyes that not one of us laughed.

"What are you going to do about it, Floyd?" Nayhone asked.

Floyd always carried a knife. He put his hand on the hilt. He said: "I'm goin' to grab that goddam kaiser by his whiskers ... and I'm goin' to turn him around ... and cut him four ways. Longways ... and crossways ... and sideways ... and deep ... !"

Again not one of us laughed. We didn't even speak. When we were taking up our equipment to march again Floyd pulled his bayonet out of its scabbard, which was fastened in his pack. Then he threw away the pack.

"I don't want this goddam stuff," he said. "I can't fight with all those blankets. Whadda they think I'm gonna do? Wrap up an'lay down? An' that cockeyed condiment can ... an' that damned pup tent. I was born an' raised in the woods. If it rains on me, I been rained on before!"

Jesse tried to make him pick up his equipment. But he wouldn't do it. "I got no use for it an' I don't want it. All I want's to get up there."

The march was over at last, and we made camp in the Grand Forêt. But the only thing that got any relief was our tired legs. Everything else got worse. Every few minutes there were bursts of machine-gun fire. It seemed to me they were just beyond us—down over the next hill. And there were even more refugees.

They didn't have that dead look the others had had. They were the hardier ones who'd stuck to their homes till the last minute. But now that they were finally driven out they were crying and wailing. They had only a few little bundles of clothing. They'd had to leave everything else. Some of them kept looking behind them as if they expected the Germans to be right at their heels.

About midday Jesse, Floyd, Nayhone, and I were called out of the outfit. A captain in the Intelligence Service took charge of us and several others. He marched us up the road, then led us off along a trail winding to the right. Finally we halted in a beech woods, and he told us to fall out and remain there. We were to take off our packs and strip to combat packs. Then he took two of our non-commissioned officers and went forward to reconnoiter.

Besides the regular equipment, I was carrying a Telescopic sight for my rifle, a heavy pair of French binoculars with a tripod to mount them on, a pistol, and about twenty pounds of ammunition for rifle and pistol. I discarded my entire pack and kept these. So I had only my observation equipment with the addition of my rifle, canteen, gas mask, helmet, Intelligence report blanks, and the clothes I had on my back.

The artillery fire had stopped, but the machine-guns were still banging away. We wondered if they were our guns and had a discussion about it. I consulted my map. Then I knew where we were. Just over that hill was Château-Thierry.

"If the Germans are driving into Château-Thierry," I said, "we know where all the people were coming from ... and I think those must be our machine-guns, because I saw them being rushed up on trucks ahead of us. They're probably trying to hold the bridges across the river at Château-Thierry."

"Well," Nayhone said, "whoever the guns belong to they're certainly raising hell!"

There wasn't time for any more discussion. A group of French infantrymen broke into the woods. They were retiring along the trail by which we'd come up, and they were completely disorganized. Many of them were in their shirt-sleeves, and most of them had thrown away their rifles. Those who weren't wounded were half carrying those who were. They were staggering, drunk with exhaustion. They didn't even look at us as they passed.

Close on their heels our captain and the two sergeants came back on the run. The captain gathered us about him and gave us our instructions. We were provided with small scale maps, and he had us locate ourselves on those. When we'd got our compass bearings he broke us up into details. We were to proceed directly up the ridge in front of us, go over the top of it, and establish observation posts on the slopes leading down toward the river. He would remain in the position we were now occupying, and we were to send our reports back to him there by runner.

We picked up the equipment we were taking with us, and started up the hill toward the sound of the guns. For months I'd heard, thought, lived nothing but war. And I hadn't known a damned thing about war. Now it had really begun for me.

4

Château-Thierry

J esse and I were the first sent out, each of us with a runner. We pushed over the ridge, then a short distance down the slope on the other side, to the edge of a cliff. I established my observation post in a clump of brush, and Jesse located his in a pile of rocks some two hundred yards from me. Between the two of us we could see almost everything in the valley, up to the limit of vision.

I hadn't really looked down yet into the valley on the other side of the river where I knew Château-Thierry must be.[13] I could see the men of our 9th Machine-Gun Battalion crouching behind their shelters of rock on the crest of the hill to the left.[14] There was never a moment's pause in their firing. I knew that sooner or later I'd have to look down at the place where their bullets were going.

I took a long breath—and looked. That rain of machine-gun bullets was splashing down on columns of moving men. Splashing down on them, but not stopping them—or hardly more than a natural rain would have done.

I knew that the French had already been beaten back across the two stone bridges that connected our side of the river with the roads leading down to it from Château-Thierry. I'd seen the last of them retiring over the hills to my left. Now long columns of men in gray moved down those roads. Onto the bridges. Almost across!

It was one of those days when the air is so clear it almost seems as if you could see far-away things more plainly than those nearer to you. We'd been ordered to study the German uniforms the first chance we got, and to find out how the officers looked and the noncommissioned officers. I had my binoculars ready, but it was several minutes before I could get myself to the point of training them on the bridges down there, and the roads.

When I did I found out that I was still pretty far from being a hardened man of war. The columns weren't stopped by the machine-gun bullets. But everywhere, as they came on, men were left squirming on the ground. I could see the officers quite clearly. They allowed no break in that steady stream. Every gap was filled up at once. And the column moved on. Moved on to certain death at the bridges. They were brave men, those German soldiers. I was learning that early.

When I couldn't look at it any longer I turned my glasses away, moving them slowly along the valley in front of me, then up the slope to the crest of the ridge opposite us. It was a beautiful valley, and it hadn't suffered much from shell fire. In the bright sunlight the water of the river sparkled, and the leaves shimmered in the breeze that was swaying the tree tops on the hill across from me.

And while I watched those swaying trees, on the crest of the ridge, I saw that there were other objects among them that didn't sway. They were four German batteries. There couldn't have been more than three thousand yards between them and our machine-gunners on the hill to my left. They'd blow the top of the hill to pieces.

Mike was the runner who'd been sent with me. I called him. My fingers trembled while I wrote out the position of the four batteries.

"For God's sake take this and beat it!"

Then I sat in my observation post wondering whether my first message would get through. Wondering where our own artillery was. Wondering how long it would take the Germans to get the range of the hilltop. Of course they knew exactly where that machine-gun fire was coming from.

Suddenly the four batteries went into action. I can see those guns yet, twisting around, looking for a target. They began to put shells over, and our machine-guns replied. But when it's machine-guns against artillery there's only one answer.

I looked back at the hill to my left to see where the shells were hitting. Just then, on the slope behind it, American artillery broke from the woods. They raced down the road, whipping their horses, and swept up the hill into position to fire. My throat felt sore as I watched and chills ran over me. It didn't look as if they were afraid of the outfit across the river!

But when they began to fire, their shots went wild. They didn't have the range of the guns—they were just firing in the general direction of the noise. And only a few shells, as if they were experimenting.

I felt sick. It looked as if Mike hadn't got through. Or maybe I'd made a mistake in my calculations and hadn't given the location just right. By this time the German shells were finding their mark. It wouldn't be many minutes before their work would be done.

Then with a roar all of our guns went into action. The earth trembled. When I turned to look back at the German batteries, our shells were falling all about them. Two of the guns had been turned completely around, and every one of them was out of commission.

Mike had carried his message through all right.

While our guns were still firing, the French artillery came up over the hill at the left. I heard afterward that they'd already started to move their artillery out of there, but when they heard of the stand we were making they turned and came galloping back.

While all this was going on, the men in gray, in mass formation, were still pouring over the hill and down the slope to the river, meeting at the bridgeheads the men still marching down the two roads from the town. They were trying now to force their way across the bridges by using trucks loaded with soldiers.

I saw our fire center on the drivers. Saw some of them fall from their seats as the trucks went out of control. Trucks were miring over the dead and wounded. The front wheels of one struck a pile of bodies and swung the truck about so that it completely blocked the bridge.

Men tried to climb over it. They were shot down. Then they began jumping into the river. In a few minutes they were swarming in the water. The river was full of them. But the machine-gun bullets were there too. Yet some of those men in gray actually fought their way through to our ends of the bridges, only to be brought down when they got there.

At last they began to fall back toward Château-Thierry. It was impossible for any troops in such a fix to get through. But they were falling back in good order, opening out into formations so as to lessen their casualties. German batteries which had been moving along the road leading down to the city turned about and galloped back up the hill toward the woods. They spread out as they did so as if going into firing positions.

The fire of our machine-guns began to slacken, and presently almost stopped. I heard afterward that many of our guns were red-hot. German observation groups gradually began to appear on the opposite ridge, and before long I saw one of their observation balloons on the horizon. I wrote a second message stating these facts, and waited as long as I dared for Mike. When he didn't come I started back myself. I hadn't gone more than two hundred yards when I met Mike. He was leading a signal corps telephone detail to my post and cursing them for their slowness. They were laying wire and moving as fast as they could under the circumstances. But it wasn't fast enough to suit Mike.

I told the signal corps men how to get forward to my position, and took Mike back to the post with me. I read the message to him, pointed out the details, made him repeat them.

"Jees!" he said. "Lemme go! I get it off my chest damn sight faster 'n you!"

And then I realized that it was a phone those men were coming up there to put in and that I'd have to stutter over it.

The other men in the Intelligence Service had got so they could understand my dialect fairly well. Floyd would get impatient every now and then and say: "Goddam it, Punk! Cut out that Chinese talk." The rest of them didn't seem to mind it. But what would happen if the captain answered that phone? I broke out in a cold sweat.

Just then the signal corps detail arrived and put in the telephone. I called back. Sergeant Nayhone's voice came over the wire. I was saved for that time. He said the captain was out inspecting observation posts and I was to talk to him. I laid out the copy I'd kept of my message and managed to read it off in pretty fair style. Nayhone O.K.'d the message and told me to be sure to keep in touch with him.

I called Sergeant Nayhone every little while and reported everything I observed. That wasn't much; the Germans were keeping rather quiet. Occasional groups of observers moving about on the crest of the river; a few bursts of shrapnel now and then. That was all.

I tried not to look down at the bridges, at the river banks, at the roads. The columns of troops were gone now. But there were plenty of men left. Only these didn't move. Except when they were twisted by pain, or crawled among the dead bodies in search of water or help.

I couldn't find anything that needed reporting to Nayhone, and for the first time I gave my eyes the relief of looking up the river to the right instead of down to the left.

I caught my breath. I couldn't believe it for a minute, with the things I'd just seen on my mind. It didn't look any more like war than the country at home. For a minute I had a feeling that I'd just waked up from a nightmare, and that this *was* home.

The river wound away into the distance. From the edge of the water, on both sides, smooth green fields sloped up to trees that covered the tops of the hills. Here and there a patch of woods meant a village. I knew that because a white church steeple rose from the center of each one, shining in the sun. There were other patches of trees that half hid old stone châteaux—at least that's what I took them to be. They had towers, and there were parks and walls around them. One had something that looked like a canal outside the wall.

The only thing unusual about it was that you didn't see anything moving. There weren't even any cattle in the fields. I knew that some of the people we'd been passing for days had come from this country, I knew that all the houses had been abandoned. But from this distance they didn't look deserted. Just peaceful and sleepy.

It seemed queer to see all the little hedges crisscrossing the fields when there wasn't any more need for boundaries. And the narrow, curving roads were queer, leading from village to village, with no traffic to move along them.

I liked the way trees that looked like our willow trees at home swept their branches down low over the water. And I liked the hills that rolled back from the river as far as I could see. I didn't like to think about shell fire raking that country.

Mike came back before long and stayed in my observation post with me. Just after that we were visited by the captain and two French officers. One of them could talk a little English, and he got very excited. He kept saying: "America . . . America . . . Vive l'America!"

That was fine. But I didn't like the careless way they were using my observation post. I knew what it would mean if one of those observers on the hill across the river got a glint of sunlight on the binoculars they were pointing so freely in every direction. I even got a little sore at the captain for allowing it. I found out later that he'd already planned to move me, and thought I'd be gone before the Germans could get my range. But I still think they were pretty reckless for men who were supposed to know the observation game.

There was another thing about those French officers that worried me. They kept saying it was "magnificent . . . magnificent"—just as if they couldn't see those poor devils down there on the bridges and in the roads. But I got to understand that better when I'd been in the war a little longer myself.

Nothing of any importance happened that afternoon, and shortly after dark we were established in listening posts down close to the river. I was about a hundred yards from the water's edge, and a little farther than that beyond the lower bridge. I stayed there all night, but heard nothing except the sounds of the Germans carrying away their wounded and dead from the bridge. In the morning we were drawn back to the wooded slopes, where we had food at last—and sleep.

This was the beginning of a deadlock that was to be something like a holiday for the rest of the troops, but not for the Intelligence men. We weren't returned to our various companies, but kept together in a group and sent out for observing or scouting whenever our officers thought it necessary.

Our captain called us together one morning and gave us a little speech.

"Don't be deceived by this apparent calm," he said. "This is the time when the Intelligence has its greatest opportunity. It's the time when we must not be taken by surprise. Before a big drive you will observe that it's always quiet. Right here something is bound to happen. The Germans are coming over on us again. You've been taught that the Germans repeat their actions. They do the same thing over again. That's Teuton. He doesn't change his methods. He lies quiet after a repulse, and waits for reinforcements, and gets ready to strike again. You must keep your eyes on those people every minute. Remember, they are coming across again! We've got to have information, and that's your part. We're depending on you!"

So in the daytime some of us were always in observation posts, and at night we were stationed in listening posts close to the river. As soon as it was dark our troops were moved down the slope of the hill toward the river, where they camped in the shelter of the freshly made shell holes. Just before daybreak they were withdrawn again to the protection of the woods on the other side of the hill. On the opposite bank of the river we knew that the Germans were going through the same maneuver.

But in spite of all our watchfulness, we couldn't find much to report. Once in a while, late at night or very early in the morning, we could see movements in their woods. Sometimes when that happened a soldier would get excited and fire his rifle across there. The next thing we knew machine-guns would be blazing away, in spite of the fact that both sides had orders not to fire.

And somebody would be killed before it could be stopped.

Later on the Intelligence men were given a certain amount of sniping to do, and Jesse and I usually carried out those details together. We had plenty of opportunity now to put into practice everything we'd learned at the Intelligence schools. The one thing the Germans didn't slow up on was their sniping. A good many of our men who went out on observation duty never came back.

We had to study the kind of camouflage we'd need in whatever post we had chosen. We had to move with the slow, smooth precision of wild animals; one quick movement might betray us to the glasses of the enemy's observers. If we were hiding in shell holes we'd have our rifles, our clothes, and our faces all painted with mud. At a thousand yards' range we could hardly be detected. But we had to remember that the mud on the surface of the ground is a different color from that at the bottom of shell holes.

After we'd located our target, we'd crawl out of our shelter to shoot. Otherwise they'd soon discover the spot from which the shooting came. It wouldn't be a shelter long after that. We'd lie perfectly still for a few minutes in the new position, then get the range and set the telescopic sights, and put the rifle out very slowly, close to the ground. We did this with as little motion of the arm as we could, and always had the rifle cocked before we put it out. Very, very slowly we'd ease down to the gun and fire.

It was my good luck that all this came natural to me because of the training I'd had in the woods. Sometimes I'd close my eyes for a minute, and then open them half expecting to see the banks of Scalybark Creek. . . .

After we'd fired at our target, we were supposed to lie there as if we were dead. It would usually take the German observers fifteen minutes to sweep the front with their glasses. Then they'd conclude that we'd already gone back to our holes, and movement was comparatively safe.

It was hard work—that sniping. And nerve-racking. Jesse and I had a bad habit of wanting to fire too often; it was easier than so many hours of just lying and waiting. But much shooting from a certain neighborhood was apt to bring on a burst of machine-gun fire, and Nayhone got after us about it. He said the captain's orders were to conserve ammunition, and not to shoot every time a target popped up. We were to pick officers, or to wait until a sniper had fired across the river at something on our side.

We tried. But it wasn't easy. I knew we were facing picked men. Probably the best there were in the German army. And the temptation to fire was pretty strong. Finally the captain stopped it. He sent for me. I went into his headquarters feeling a little worried; but he looked at me and smiled.

"Sergeant Nayhone tells me you're a bad Indian," he said. "You might be something much worse. But you must learn to take care of yourself. This going out there and blazing away like an amateur has got to be stopped!"

That captain was a psychologist. He knew the one word that would get under my skin!

Up to this time I hadn't really known whether I'd ever got one of the men I'd shot at or not. We weren't often in a position where it was safe to try to see if our shots had taken effect. The first time I did see what happened was pretty bad.

It was late in the afternoon, and I'd located a German observer in a hedge directly across from me. I was so sure of my shelter that I studied him through the glasses for several minutes. It looked as if he must have decided that all our snipers had gone in, or else he was very new at the game. He was making a wonderful target of himself above the hedge.

My glasses brought him so close that I felt as if I was face to face with him. And when he suddenly swept his glasses at me I jumped. It was just as if he was looking me in the eye.

It was the first time I'd had a target like this. Always before there'd been just a quick movement in the distance, the top of a helmet, or a glint of sun on glass or metal. This wasn't a target. It was a man. It made a lot of difference. And he was a brave man. I could tell that by the way he stood there, by the way he held his head. Perhaps he was young, and had a girl at home like mine. Or a mother who wrote him the kind of letters my mother wrote me.

I tried to stop thinking about it. He was an officer. There wasn't a chance of deceiving myself about that. And orders were orders. I worked myself out to shooting position. My slowness this time wasn't as much because of caution as because I hoped that he'd be gone before I got ready to fire.

At last I settled myself in position and looked again. He was still there. His head was clearly outlined against the sky. I cursed his carelessness. Then I steadied the trembling of my hand, took careful aim, and fired.

He lurched forward out of the hedge. I was certain the war had ended for him.

"Hell!" I kept saying to myself. "He'd have shot me if he'd seen me first."

But it didn't seem to help much. It was a long time before I went to sleep that night.

Gradually I got over that sort of feeling. There wasn't anything to do but to get over it. I couldn't stop sniping, and there were bound to be times when I'd have a clear view of the man I was shooting at. Even that first time I'd managed not to let the feeling disturb my aim. After a while I got so that it didn't disturb my mind either.

Jesse and I were always on the lookout for new observation posts, and one day we stumbled across the little graveyard at Blesmes. It looked like just the place for what we wanted to do. It furnished shelter, and it gave us a clear view of the slopes across the river. Some pretty active sniping came from over there.

Jesse settled himself in a stone water trough just outside the burying ground to the right, and I got down into a depression behind a big gravestone. There were trees and bushes and tall grass. It shows how green we still were that we thought they wouldn't look for us in a graveyard. We'd made only three or four shots when a shell exploded on the slope to our left.

A lot of shallow graves had been quickly dug for soldiers in this cemetery. They lay buried there in light coffins, with only empty brass seventy-five shells to mark the places. The second shell that came over exploded in the middle of these new graves.

The ground crumbled and burst open. Coffins were split into kindling wood. We didn't have to look at the bodies in this horrible resurrection. But we couldn't escape the stench. It exploded into the spring air. I was very sick.

I crawled back, as far away as I could get without coming out from the cover of the bushes. Jesse joined me, and we decided that the only safe thing to do was to wait there until dark. We couldn't get out of Blesmes without going across a certain amount of open country, and of course they'd be watching for us. I thought by the time darkness came I'd probably be so sick I couldn't get away at all, but I kept that thought to myself.

Just behind us was the open slope of a hill. We knew it was customary in French towns to put all the beehives in a common garden, each man's property marked so that he could gather his own honey when he chose. What we didn't know was the location of the bee garden at Blesmes.

Presently a shell hit the church in the square, and sent the cross from its steeple clattering to the ground. The next one smashed the water trough in which Jesse had thought he'd be so safe. The third landed in the middle of the open space behind us. And that open space was the village bee garden.

Snipers or no snipers we broke cover then. My gosh! Those bees were mad!

5

Our Gang

It was while we were on the Marne that our gang got together for good. We managed to get a lot of time off, and we spent most of it exploring the deserted villages and châteaux.

Nayhone was in charge of our group, so he had to stay out of the mischief the rest of us got into. But if he heard that we had been A.W.O.L., he would ask: "Have they come back?"

And if the answer was "Yes," that was all there'd be to that.

But there were two things Nayhone was strict about. He watched us like a hawk to see that we kept clean and in condition. And he was always on the war-path on the question of liquor. He was forever telling us to go and shave, or asking when we'd washed our underwear.

"Keep your underclothes clean," he'd say. "It may save you from infection when you get plugged. If you want to make good snipers, you've *got* to keep yourselves clean and your teeth brushed. You've got to get all the sleep you can. And lay off of booze. If you keep on hitting that booze, they'll pick you off as sure as you're alive!"

We knew he was right. Without liquor we could keep our minds clear; we could think faster and act quicker. But when there was only one thing that could make us forget how tired we were after a day of sniping—only one thing that could bring back courage for the next day—it was a good deal to ask us to give it up.

He didn't expect it, of course. He drank a little on occasion himself. But he knew the dangers we were exposed to in the "Suicide Club"— the name some cheerful soul gave the Intelligence Service—and he was going to keep us in condition.

He always wound up his little sermons the same way: "And remember! Never let me find a cootie on one of you men!"[15]

That wasn't so hard at first. The Intelligence men were kept in a camp of their own, and long after the men in the regular companies had been infested with the pests we still managed to escape them. We realized how fortunate we were whenever we ran into Tom. He was acting corporal now with the old company and not with us as much as we should have liked.

But every now and then we managed to get together, and Tom would describe for us just what cooties meant to the men they chose for their homes. We found out later for ourselves that he hadn't exaggerated it.

Aside from the cooties, Tom seemed to think it was a pretty good war. "It's a *hell* of a gr-rand fight!" he said. "Nothin' to do but eat an' sleep an' keep y'r eye peeled fer guns. What's the diff'rence from bein' home?"

We missed Tom in our raids on the neighborhood villages and châteaux. Nayhone was out, because of his responsibilities. Jesse and Floyd and Mike and Norosoff and I would usually go. Sometimes we took along another man or two, but not often.

It must have looked funny, as we set out together. The two tall Indians, and the three of us who, beside them, looked even smaller than we were.

Norosoff was a queer little chap, with a big Jew nose, light complexion, and curly black hair. He spoke a strange sort of lingo; Tom told us it was "Brooklynese." But he was a good soldier. When he started anything he finished it. When he saw anything he could do to help out, he went and did it. The fact that he didn't have to never stopped Norosoff. He'd volunteer. Time after time he carried Mike's messages for him when the little Italian was down and out. He was gassed once, but he always got through.

Mike was the light-weight prize-fighter type. He was five feet high; squattily built, but straight, with the black hair, swarthy skin, and thick red lips of the Italian workingman. His arms were unusually long and his movements never got over being like those of a monkey, in spite of all his military training. He could never make a parade-ground soldier. He kept time to the music all right, but he couldn't get away from the monkeylike swing in his walk.

He was kind to everybody, and good-natured. He was always looking for a bottle of wine—red by choice—but any kind of wine rather than water. If he came into camp with something hidden under his arm, you could be sure what it was.

"Hey, Barkley," he'd say, "da bigges' bottle a'wine I c'd find!" Mike was a good scout all right.

We found some great wine cellars in the deserted houses. Nayhone and the captain got pretty worried. The captain threatened us with every kind of punishment if we went down there in the old châteaux and "got all sopped up." And Nayhone told us that the captain's punishments would be carried out. "We don't know what'll happen here any minute," he wound up. "It'd be a hell of a note for those Germans to come over and find all of us cockeyed drunk!"

But shortly after that we unearthed a store of wine that was too good to resist. It must have been thirty or forty years old.

As Norosoff said: "You shake her up an' pop 'kaboom!' You drink too much—you fall down—'kaboom!'"

And Mike drank too much, and fell down, "kaboom"—after we'd got him back to camp. Of course the sergeant heard about it. He put Mike through the third degree to find out where he got the liquor and who was with him.

But Mike wasn't too drunk to stand by the gang. His answer to every question was the same. "My motto—see not'ing, hear not'ing, do not'ing, tell not'ing!" They threatened him with everything they could think of. But that was no good either.

"I'm Dago," he said proudly. "You line me up agains' da tree. You shoot me. You no make me squeal on my pals!"

The first few times we went out on our foraging expeditions we stuck to the villages. We'd go through the deserted houses until we found one that hadn't been much damaged by shells. Then we'd have a party. There were always a few dogs left in these towns, and quite a lot of pigs and chickens. The dogs were lonesome and usually made friends with Jesse and me. The pigs we left alone. But the chickens we fried. We had plenty of fresh eggs, too—and nothing ever tasted as good as that chicken and those eggs!

We did our cooking over fires in the fireplaces, but we always had to be very careful about the smoke. We knew that if our smoke went up against the sky we were more than likely to have a shell join our party.

That's what finally happened. We were in a little house in Blesmes, and we had an old hen in the pot over the fire, trying to cook it tender. Every few minutes we'd plug it to see if it was done. It took so long to cook that we got in a hurry and built up too much fire. There must have been smoke enough to make a perfect target. The first shell the Germans sent over ripped the tile roof off the house. Ceilings and plaster showered down on us. We got out of there as if the devil were after us.

After that we took to exploring the châteaux in the neighborhood. And when we came on the one just outside of Blesmes we knew we'd found our regular meeting place. It was the finest thing of its kind anywhere around there. I understand that a rich American has bought it and is living there now. None of us had ever seen anything like it.

There were long galleries, and big rooms, and grand furniture. It was all just as its owners had left it. The silver was still on the side table in the dining-room. There were dishes all laid over with gold in the cabinets. There were drawers full of laces and linens.

Most of the rooms seemed more like settings for a play than a place to live. But the bedrooms showed that people had used them. There were clothes in the closets and in the drawers. Men's clothes and women's; and signs of living all about. One dressing-table had powder spilled on it, and a tray of pins had been upset. It looked as if someone had dressed there in a hurry.

I used to like to stand in the doorways and look at those bedrooms. There were paintings of flowers on the walls, soft carpets, silk hangings everywhere. And the biggest beds I'd ever seen, with canopies over them and velvet curtains, and mattresses so deep and soft it made me sleepy just to look at them. The covers of the beds must have cost a lot—all lace and embroidery.

I wanted to take a chance on the Germans hitting the château some night and stay A.W.O.L., just to sleep in one of those beds. But I couldn't do it. I had to be back. I'd heard the captain ask too often about one of us who was away from camp.

"Where is so and so?" he'd say.

"I don't know," someone would answer. "Is he needed?"

"No. But I want him here. He's liable to get bumped off. And, anyway, does he know what minute I *may* need him?"

⸺◆⸺

One day we took another fellow with us to show him the château. That was the day we discovered the cellar in the basement, with the old wines and liquors. It was well hidden, but Jesse found it. After that we always made for the cellar first. We usually took a supply with us when we left and cached it in some place more convenient to the camp.

After we'd had something of a celebration in the basement that day, we went upstairs and began pulling the clothes out of the closets. We hadn't quite dared to disturb them before. They looked like fancy-dress costumes to me. I'd never imagined that the French "higher-ups" wore outfits like these. But they evidently did. One of the coats must have been worn a short time before. There was a letter in French in the pocket, and the date on it was only a few weeks past. I certainly would have liked to read that letter.

I got in front of one of the long mirrors and tried on the coat. It was some kind of swallowtail coat of the finest material I'd ever seen, but the trousers didn't seem to be with it. I'd still like to know what kind of trousers they wore with that coat. There was also a high hat—a stiff silk hat. I put that on. It was too small for me and Floyd knocked it off.

"That's a hell of a hat," he said, "even if it'd fit. No wonder this outfit ain't got nowhere. Spend all their time havin' a damned party, an' wearin' clothes like these."

"But this is the *rich* class," I said.

That didn't satisfy Floyd. "Rich class, hell! We got millionaire Americans in our outfit. Do you see 'em wearing togs like these? All you gotta do is go back to th' artillery. Watch the Frogs fire. They take a drink o' wine. Then they parley-voo awhile. Then they shove in a shell an' go 'Boom, Boom.' Then they sit down and take another drink. I don't know a damn thing about the rest o' the French army. But I know that's a hell of a way to fire a gun!"

I was trying to convince Floyd that the French had really been doing a little fighting in spite of their queer ways, and Jesse was helping me out, when we heard a commotion in the hall. Mike and Norosoff burst into the room.

After them trailed a woman, in a long lace and satin tea-gown!

"My God!" said Floyd. "Who's the fairy? Or have I licked up too much liquor?"

Then we saw the vision's nose. It was the fellow we'd brought with us, dressed up in some women's clothes he had found in the other rooms.

He was all rouged and made up, and he was strolling around in front of the mirrors looking at himself and posing. We found out then that he'd been an impersonator with a famous New York theatrical troop. He certainly was good. You'd have sworn he was a woman until you saw that nose.

"Well," said Jesse, "you make a fine woman all right. But suppose they shell this damned place and we have to run—wouldn't you be in a hell of a fix without your pants!"

"Oh," he said, "I'd grab up my skirts and run. Surely, even those awful Germans wouldn't shoot a woman!"

"Maybe not," Jesse said. "But you'd certainly look like hell coming into camp without any pants on!"

We found out afterward that we were quite safe there. The Germans were carefully avoiding the château in their shooting. They expected to be occupying that territory soon, and they wanted the château unharmed for officers' quarters. The wine cellars and the art treasures there were famous. They probably counted on moving those back into Germany.

On our first trip to the château I'd discovered a sort of museum in a long gallery, where there were cases and cases of guns and pistols and knives and sabers, that had been used long ago in French wars. The things I liked most were the jeweled swords, and the old single-shot pistols. I got hold of one with a hammer that struck down on a flint, or something which would throw a spark. I'd seen pictures of duels being fought; I thought of duels as soon as I saw that gun.

I used to spend hours studying those things and wishing there was some way to take them home with me.[16] There was one case full of relics of Napoleon and his wars. If they meant as much to the man who collected them as they did to me, I hope they were still there when he came back to his château, if he ever did come back.

One day a very grand-looking Frenchman came to the camp, and some of our officers went with him up to the château. After that they put bars over the doors and windows and quartered a bunch of our officers there. I guess the ones who got that billet were pretty glad. It stopped our visits to the upper floors of the château, but it didn't keep us out of the cellar. We raided it over and over again with the officers right there in the house. And we never got caught.

But Nayhone knew we were getting wine somewhere, and it worried him. He was a different type from the rest of us. Older and better educated and very much on the job. He wasn't at all good-looking; five feet seven, maybe, square-shouldered and short-necked. He had gentle brown eyes, set far apart, and was slightly bald under the wide hat he always wore. There was something queer about his speech—a sort of lisp—but you didn't notice that when he got going.

As I've said, he spoke seven languages. And it seemed to me he'd read everything that had ever been written. He knew Scripture, poetry, ancient history, old religions. Wherever we went he told us something of the history or legends of the place.

He got so wrought up after a while, about our drinking, that I tried to do better about it. The worst of it was that he blamed Jesse for what

I was doing—because I was such a kid. That made me feel pretty bad. I'd got so that I liked the wine now—or maybe the wine from the château was better than any we'd had before. But I eased up on it the rest of the time we were there.

All during this period a mail never came in without a letter from my girl. The letters from home gave a picture of what the war looked like to people so far away from it. I remember one from my older brother.

"I don't know whether this will ever reach you," he said. "I know things are getting hot. But I read in the papers all the time that when the American soldier strikes he never misses, so it ought to be over before long. If this finds you alive I want you to know that we are working like hell over here and are saving all we can. We have very little sugar. Hoover is economizing on everything.[17] The boys are leaving by the thousands. It looks like it's going to be a *hell* of a war. Everybody in Missouri is buying all the Liberty Bonds they have the money for— they're doing it all over the country for that matter."

<hr />

A series of moves now began all along our immediate front. The French were in command and seemed inclined to use battalions without paying much attention to regimental organization. Late on the night of the eleventh our battalion relieved a battalion of the 30th Infantry at Nogentel, a little town on our side of the river, but southwest from Château-Thierry.

About a week later we moved again, to a partially prepared position on our bank—this time to the east of Château-Thierry. Again we were relieving a battalion of the 30th.

The sniping and observing details began once more in earnest, and Jesse and I had to go back to work. Besides sniping and observing during the day, we had to accompany patrols at night. I learned to snatch a little sleep whenever the chance came my way. As for Jesse, he'd always had the knack of it. He could lie down and go to sleep anywhere, and under almost any conditions.

The Intelligence men had the worst end of things there for a while, but at least they escaped the trench digging and dugout building that was going on.

The last two weeks of June were peaceful enough. After the first emergency the French made less and less demand on us, and our own officers began to take over the routine control. Men and officers had lost their feeling of newness. They were confident, and eager to get into action.

The Intelligence group were kept fairly busy, but there never seemed anything of importance to report. Things were running smoothly with us now. We saw little of the captain or of the lieutenant who was our immediate commanding officer. Nayhone was exercising more and more authority over us. The outfit was beginning to function like a good machine.

Nayhone was the headquarters and administrative head. Jesse was the outside man; he directed the work of the observers and snipers. That captain and lieutenant knew how to make use of the unusual material they had in those two non-comms.

Near the end of June we began to get rumors that the Germans were about to launch another offensive along our front. The captain returned. A few days before the Fourth of July, the Intelligence group of one of our battalions attempted to get patrols across the river at two different points. Both attempts failed. The Germans had outposts almost on the banks. They were on the lookout and several of our men were killed.

Another week passed. A new enemy activity was unmistakable now. An observer reported a group of officers in the uniforms of a Prussian Guard division reconnoitering the German front. There was increased air activity over their lines. Their artillery began registering in. These things pointed to an organized offensive rather than to a surprise attack.

But our officers wanted to *know* which it was going to be. And they decided to find out.

On the afternoon of the tenth Jesse and I were called to battalion headquarters. There were ten or twelve other picked men there. None of us knew what it was all about.

The captain pushed aside the papers on the table in front of him and looked us all over before he spoke.

"I want five volunteers," he said then, "for a dangerous mission. I don't want anyone who has any hesitation about going. And I don't want anyone who isn't a good swimmer. This patrol has got to go across the river—and *get back!*"

Several of the men couldn't swim. That let them out. The rest of us volunteered. The captain selected Jesse first, and together they chose the other four. There was a fellow by the name of Wilson, another who cooked for K Company but whose name I've forgotten, and myself. The fifth was a man named Coske, one of our old soldiers from China. I'm not sure, but I think Coske was Polish. At any rate, he spoke German like a native—and hated them like poison.

The captain dismissed the other men. Then he told us what it was we were detailed for.

"You are to cross the river tonight," he said, "and you are to bring back a German prisoner. That prisoner must be in *reasonably* good condition. Good enough at least so that he can be made to talk. Remember a man who has been beaten half to death won't be of any use to us."

He laid out his maps and very carefully traced our route for us. Then he took us to an observation post on the wooded slope and pointed out the details on the ground we were to cover.

We returned to battalion headquarters, where the captain left us, saying for us to get what rest we could and warning us to tell no one of our orders.

We didn't talk much after the captain left. We just lay around and smoked. Coske acted pretty nervous—but not frightened. He was eager to go all right. He kept muttering to himself, and I gathered that he had some private grudge he was going to settle with the Germans. Wilson said something about wanting to do this in order to clear up his record. He was an old soldier too, and there seemed to have been a court martial or some kind of disgrace marked against him. He thought he could erase it if he got away with this raid. As for the other fellow, whose name I can't recall but who looked like an Irishman, he had nothing at all to say. He seemed perfectly satisfied, and spent most of his time sleeping.

We had supper that evening early, before the chow went out to the companies, then we returned to battalion headquarters. I wondered as we walked back whether I'd ever eat another meal. I asked Jesse if he didn't think we'd drawn a pretty rough detail.

"Well, I suppose so," he answered. "But somebody has to go and get one of those babies. It might as well be us."

A moment later he spoke again. "Don't be discouraged, kid," he said. "Remember those champagne raids on the château at Blesmes? It's a cinch if we can fool a houseful of our own officers, we ought to be able to fool the squareheads!"

I looked around at him. There was a grin on his face. The gold tooth was shining. I felt better after that.

We got back to headquarters to find the captain waiting for us, with a pile of weapons and equipment. He had us discard our regular equipment and take off our blouses and shoes. Then he fitted us up with black stocking caps, small French gas masks, and black tennis shoes.

We darkened our hands and faces so that we'd be harder to see in the dark. We wrapped our bodies with tape to make swimming easier and reduce the chances of our clothing catching on anything. Then the captain told us to choose our weapons. We each took two automatics and six extra clips of ammunition, and Jesse and I took trench knives besides. Coske picked out a trench club, and it was a wicked-looking weapon. I didn't notice what the others had.[18]

"Go through your pockets," the captain said. "Be damned sure you're not carrying anything that might give the Germans information if you're captured."

Jesse laughed. "Killed, you mean!"

The captain laughed too, and looked at Jesse. "That's the idea!" he said.

Then he led us out into the darkness, and down the slope toward the river.

6

Night Raid

At the edge of the river we found a French officer and a couple of French soldiers waiting with a boat. The captain gave Jesse the end of a wire with a little piece of rope attached to it. He took the rope in his teeth, slipped into the water, and struck out.

The captain whispered to me that Sergeant James was to land and pull the boat across with the four of us in it. I was to be in charge during the crossing; the rest was already arranged for.

When we reached the opposite shore we were to hide the boat, go out and get our prisoner, and bring him back to the boat. Another wire connected the boat with our bank of the river. Two tugs on this wire would be the signal to the French soldiers to pull us back.

By the time we'd got these instructions the wire had stopped moving. There was a little delay. Then it twitched, and the Frenchman who was paying it out grunted. "Bon!" he said. We got into the boat and lay down. Jesse pulled us across without a sound to give us away.[19]

The current had carried us so far downstream that when we landed we had to follow our wire some distance back before we found Jesse. He was standing in the water in the shadow of the bank. He'd been carried downstream too. We had to pull the boat along the river about forty yards before we found the point where the captain had told us a trail led up from the river bank.

We moored the boat against the bank there, and Jesse led off, up the trail. I followed him closely, with Coske and the other two behind us. I could feel my heart beating whenever Jesse stopped for a moment.

We had gone about a hundred and fifty steps when we heard what seemed to be a number of Germans coming toward us. We slipped to the side and crouched down in a little thicket.

The Germans marched past within ten feet of us. From our crouched positions we could skyline them. They were big fellows, with rifles slung on their shoulders. They were wearing little flat caps and had their helmets fastened to their belts. There must have been twenty or thirty of them, and they made a lot of noise.

They filed past us without a suspicion of anything wrong. We waited perhaps thirty seconds, then went ahead. Jesse placed Coske in front now. He was to stop the first German we met and begin to talk to him. While that was going on the rest of us were to slip up and knock him off. I followed Coske, and Jesse followed me.

We were a hundred or more steps farther along the trail when we heard someone coming again. But this time it sounded as if there was only one. We slipped off the trail to the right and left, leaving Coske to meet him. When the German was quite close Coske challenged him in his own language. While they were talking the rest of us were closing in on him.

He was completely fooled at first. But just as we were almost close enough to spring the trap Coske must have said something that made him suspicious. He jerked backward, and Coske jumped him. At the same instant I dived forward and caught his legs.

Somebody—it must have been Jesse—walked all over my back and kicked me in the face. But he got hold of the German too. By this time the other men were all in the mix-up, and we'd got our man down. He was a great big sergeant; he must have weighed over two hundred pounds, and he was full of fight. But five against one was too much even for him.

While he was on his feet he hadn't tried to make an outcry, but the minute we had him on the ground he began to yell. Jesse got him by the throat, and I put the gag on him—though he nearly bit my finger off before I succeeded. The others tied up his arms and legs. I heard Wilson cursing because he'd lost one of his pistols.

As soon as we'd finished trussing the German up, we started back down the trail toward the river. Jesse led off, a pistol in each hand. The rest of us followed carrying the prisoner. Coske and I had a leg each, and the two others had his head. They were to take charge of him if we ran into any interference. Jesse, Coske, and I were to shoot our way through if we could.

Our prisoner continued to struggle until Coske hit him a light blow across the face with his club. He told him in German to be quiet or he'd beat his head in. We made it back to the river without meeting anyone.

But while we were locating the boat that German got the gag partly out of his mouth and began to yell again. We all jumped on him at once, and he was pretty well beaten up before we got him into the boat. I heard Jesse whisper to Coske, "Easy with that club!"

I gave the wire two sharp jerks, and the boat began to move out into the river. But already we could hear the heavy boots of the Germans thumping around on the bank, and the click of their weapons. Then a machine-gun block cracked.[20]

From the opposite side the French were pulling for all they were worth. We must have been nearly halfway across when the first machine-gun bullets hit the water behind us. The second burst was also low. But the third was right on us. There wasn't a chance except to go overboard into the river.

"Jump everybody!" I yelled. I waited until my weight had taken me to the bottom of the river, then dropped my pistols. I figured that as I came back up to the surface the swiftness of the current would be carrying me downstream and out of the path of the machine-gun fire. I could hear the bullets "plopping" on the water. It was a funny sound they made. I didn't dare help myself along by swimming under water; it would be too easy to head toward the wrong bank.

When I couldn't stand it any longer I came to the top and got some air. I listened for a minute to the machine-guns to be sure which side they were on, and then struck out for our bank of the river. I must have been twenty-five yards downstream when I came to the surface and I was so nearly exhausted that I couldn't battle the current very well; I kept being carried still farther down. At last I made the bank, where there were some willow branches to cling to.

Back up the river automatic rifles had opened fire from our side, and there was a lot of shooting going on. But down here everything was quiet. After a while I recovered my breath, and began to climb the bank.

"Chuck! ... Chuck. ... What's that?"

The voice had spoken directly above me. Another voice answered.

"You're hearing things! What did it sound like?"

"It sounded like a damned Dutchman trying to pull something."

"Crow," said the one called Chuck, "bring that flare pistol here."

"Can't be done," said Crow. "The lieutenant took the damn thing up the river where that 4th Infantry patrol went across."

Somebody who hadn't talked before said: "It'd be a hell of a lot of use to him in a dugout. That's where he'd probably be in case of a fight."

I took a long breath, and called out in the friendliest tone I could muster: "Hey, Chuck!"

Chuck said, "Who the hell are you?"

"Barkley," I answered. "One of the 4th Infantry patrol."

There was a blank silence. Then Chuck said, "Come on in."

I climbed the bank. There were four men there from the 7th Infantry. And they had two automatics and two service rifles pointed straight at me.

Chuck was one of the riflemen. "Easy, brother," he said, "now talk."

That was all right. But one of the other men poked the muzzle of a forty-five into my ribs. That made me sore, and I said so.

Chuck sided with me. "*Wait* a minute!" he said. "What the hell are you trying to do, Grandstand?"

I told them my story as quickly as I could.

"I'm damned wet and cold," I wound up, "and just about all in. I'd like a cigarette and a light."

Chuck gave me a cigarette and a match, but he warned me not to light up until I got back where I wouldn't be seen from the river. Then they started me off in the right direction along a path. But I hadn't gone far before I met an officer and a private. The private covered me with his rifle while the lieutenant questioned me.

I was getting tired of having loaded, cocked guns pointed at me. I told the officer so. He said to the private, "Come to the order there." I told my story again, and they finally passed me. They gave me directions for getting into a path that would lead me back to the 4th Infantry.

I found the path without any trouble but had hardly started on it when I ran into a corporal and a private. I had to speak my piece again. My stammering didn't help matters either. And these stops were making me colder by the minute. My temper was getting pretty short. My attitude made the corporal suspicious. So he and the private turned around and went back with me to the 4th Infantry headquarters.

We found Corporal Rissey on duty there, and they handed me over to him as if I were a prisoner. I was mighty glad to get back to my own outfit, and said so in no uncertain terms.

Corporal Rissey took me down into the headquarters dugout. He was a big blond German-American from Iowa, and they kept him there at Intelligence headquarters because he spoke German.

There were a number of people in the dugout, the captain among them. But they were all gathered around a still figure stretched out on a table. The man on the table was evidently badly wounded. They were working over him and bandaging him, from head to foot, it seemed to me.

My heart jumped into my mouth. But it wasn't Jesse. It was the German prisoner. They'd found him still alive in the boat. His bonds had prevented his jumping, and German machine-gun bullets had gone through both legs. Another had torn his cheek open. But they thought he'd be able to talk when they got through with their bandaging.

I screwed up my courage to ask about the others in the patrol. Rissey answered: "You're the only one we've heard from yet."

The captain called Rissey over to interpret his questions to the German, and they got a good deal of information. The fight was all gone out of the big sergeant now.

He told his name and his rank. He said the outfit he belonged to would be relieved in a day or two and would be replaced with Prussian Guards. He said, "They"—meaning the German High Command—would attack about the middle of the month. He confirmed the rumors we'd heard that the Germans were bringing up many guns and great stores of munitions.

By this time I was shaking with cold. The captain noticed it and told me to go and take care of myself. I took off my clothing and wrung it out, then put my breeches and shoes on again. But Corporal Rissey took off his blouse and gave it to me, so I didn't have to put back on my wet blouse or undershirt.

I hurried out to the kitchen, where the mess sergeant fired up and cooked bacon for me, and gave me hardtack, cheese, and French bread. He boiled coffee and rustled me up some blankets.

I finished eating while my clothes dried beside the rolling kitchen; then I found a sheltered spot under a log near by and rolled up in my blankets, head and all. I was pretty sick about Jesse. But I was so worn out that I went to sleep in spite of it.

When I woke up in the morning I saw Jesse sitting on a rock, not three feet away. I thought for a minute it was his ghost, until he grinned at me. I was so glad to see him that I almost made a fool of myself.

He was wearing the same rig in which he'd gone on the patrol—even the elastic tape was still wound around his body. He had a blanket slung over his shoulders. His black hair hung down to his eyes, and the blackening on his face was all smudged. He looked funny enough to laugh at, only I felt a lot more like crying. So I jumped on him for not waking me up and telling me he was safe. The madder I talked, the broader he grinned. He knew what was the matter with me. He was a funny Indian!

While we were at this, the battalion commander came along, followed by a bunch of "dog-robbers"—our name for orderlies. When Jesse and I jumped up and saluted him, he demanded an explanation of why we were dressed as we were. Jesse told him what had happened. But evidently the major wasn't feeling well that morning, and he didn't care much for Intelligence men anyway. He gave us a mean bawling-out. He said we were a "disgrace to the outfit," and ordered us to go and get dressed.

We set out to find the Intelligence captain and our packs. Jesse finally located his, but mine had disappeared. I already had Corporal Rissey's blouse, so I returned it and borrowed his extra shirt. I managed to get a pair of shoes from Zelma Sisk, one of the boys from home.

We found out that we were the only ones of the patrol who'd returned. That didn't cheer us up much. After breakfast we got out to one of Jesse's caches in the woods and brought back a bottle of cognac. We were careful not to take much, though, as we didn't know when we might be needed. After supper that evening we saw the captain again for a few minutes. He hadn't slept for thirty-six hours and he looked about all in. He advised us to get as much rest as we could, because things would probably break before long.

7

Rock of the Marne

For a few days we did have a chance to rest. And then at twelve o'clock one night all our divisional artillery opened up. The French supporting artillery joined in and promptly at one o'clock, the whole skyline on the other side of the river crackled with light. It was as if a thousand electric storms had all broken at once over there above the German front. Our officers had moved us forward that afternoon. Our old positions were being torn to pieces.

It was bad enough as it was. The men just sat and looked at each other as if they couldn't believe it. Some of them packed cigarette papers or cleaning patches in their ears. Only an occasional shell fell into the woods where we were, but it seemed as if the noise and the shock alone were enough to finish us.

There'd been very little shelling in this vicinity before, and the woods had been full of birds and all kinds of small creatures. But when that barrage was over, the ground was littered with the bodies of crows and other birds, the skin of most of them smooth and unbroken. It was the shock of the concussion which had killed them. It killed the fish in the river, too. The thrifty French took advantage of that. They seined them out and had fresh fish to add to their bill of fare.

But we weren't thinking about food that night. Even where we were, many men were killed or wounded. And behind us, up the slope, the artillery was suffering terribly. The Germans weren't sending over any gas shells close to the river. They expected before long to be occupying that territory themselves, and they didn't want pockets of gas lying around. But they were using gas on the artillery, farther back. I suppose they thought it would have time to clear away before they got that far.

Almost the worst thing about it to me was the fact that they'd got the range on where the horses were. And they'd concentrated a special fire on them, both with explosive shells and gas shells. Wherever there were little open spaces, wounded horses staggered out of the trees, bleeding to death and screaming.

One of them came a little closer to us than the others. He was trying to find shelter, and his paralyzed hindquarters were dragging after him along the ground. I couldn't stand it any longer. I crawled up along the slope until I was so close I knew I couldn't miss him, and shot him dead.

Once there was a lull in the firing and we heard the furious ringing of a telephone, which evidently came from some abandoned post on the shell-swept slope behind us. A group of our officers was standing near us, and the captain of Company L who was with them called for someone to go back and answer it. I was the only Intelligence man there at the moment, so I volunteered. I could talk fairly well now over a telephone. The captain asked me my name, then he told me to go up there, get the message, and bring it to him.

The phone was still ringing as I worked my way toward it. It seemed to be in the center of a patch of woods. The heaviest German shelling was directed still farther back, but even where I was the woods were going to pieces. Shell fragments were shearing off branches and tops of trees, and whole trees were crashing down as if they'd been felled by an ax. I dropped to my knees and crawled.

Suddenly someone burst through the woods, tripped over me, and fell beside me. I pulled my gun on him.

"Hey there," he yelled. "Put that gun down!"

It was a voice I'd heard before. And just then a flash lighted up the woods. It was Stew Ruford. He didn't have any hat, shoes, or leggins. He'd been asleep in some snug dugout he'd found back there, and had just waked up to what was going on.

"My God!" he said. "Let's get out of here!"

"I can't," I told him. "I'm going to answer that phone."

"Well, I *ain't!*" he said. And he was gone down the trail, his unlaced breeches flapping about his legs.

I crawled on again toward the phone. A tree had fallen over it. It was whirring away in there under a heap of branches and debris. I pulled the branches aside to reach in to it and got a strong whiff of phosgene gas. I got my mask ready, and grabbed the phone.

"Hello!" I yelled.

Somebody answered and asked who I was.

"Barkley, of the Intelligence detail," I said.

Whoever it was on the other end started in to bawl me out for the long delay before the phone was answered. I butted right in.

I said, "If you've got any orders to give, make 'em snappy. If not, say so. I'm in phosgene gas."

That stopped him. "Tell your major to tell his men to stay in their dugouts," he said.

"Is that *all?*"

"Yes."

I reached down to put the receiver back, and a big shell splinter crashed through the branches. It smashed the phone to pieces and it came within an inch of getting my hand. The shell must have hit within thirty feet of me—the first one that had come really close.

I saw queer, jerky fires in front of my eyes. Then blackness. How long that lasted I don't know. When I came to myself enough to clap on my mask and back out of the pile of branches, I saw pieces of the shell driven deep into the earth.

The German fire in this section was heavier now than it had been when I came up the slope, and my mask bothered me in crawling. Once a chunk from a big tree fell across my legs and pinned me to the ground. It took me some time to dig and wriggle my way out from under it, and in doing that my mask was torn. I could smell the gas plainly down close to the earth. But close to the earth was where I had to stay, until I got through this torn-up area.

I got through at last and reported to the L Company captain. Then

I said: "If I hadn't been knocked out up there I could have got back a lot sooner."

For some reason it sounded queer to me. And then I realized I'd spoken without stuttering for the first time in my life. That dazed me. After a minute I decided it couldn't be so, that my brain was still reeling from the shock of the concussion out there. When the captain left to look for the major, I set out to find Jesse. I wanted to try it out on someone.

By the time I'd located him I had a long speech all ready; I reeled it off to him.

"My God," he said, "what's got into you? You're talking like a human being!"

So I knew it was true. And from that day to this I've talked like everybody else.

While I was telling Jesse what had happened to me, most of the men were digging themselves farther in. The whole forest looked unnatural. The air was thick with dust, mist, and smoke. And the ceaseless flickering of the guns made a weird light.

Suddenly, down the trail over which I'd just returned, a man came— running, stumbling, falling, running again. At the edge of our woods he bumped against a tree, then wrapped his arms around it and yelled that he was gassed.

We all knew him. He was one of our K Company officers, a lieutenant. The other officers were very quiet and steady, but this one had had a great habit of talking big before his battalion.

That lieutenant had gone to sleep like Stew, as he thought safely, behind the lines. Only he'd gone farther than Stew in disobeying the orders that we weren't to take off our clothes, and that our rifles were always to be at our finger-tips.

He had his gas mask in his hand, but no rifle. He was bareheaded. His O.D. shirt was unbuttoned. He had a Sam Browne belt hanging about his neck. But he had no breeches on.

Some of our 6th Engineers had moved up near us and one of their officers, a captain, came over.

"Grab that man, some of you," he said. "He's shell-shocked."

The lieutenant heard what he'd said. He began to yell louder than ever that he was gassed and shell-shocked. Several of us got hold of him and tried to pull him away from the tree. But we weren't having much success. The captain walked up and asked him where his clothes were.

"Back there!" he yelled, pointing up the slope. He was crying and pleading with us. "I'll give anybody a thousand francs to go back up there and get my pants! A thousand francs!"

The captain turned him over to two of the biggest soldiers he could find and started them back to the first-aid station.

The night passed somehow. I crawled into Jesse's dugout, and hour after hour we lay in the midst of that bedlam. After a while the artillery fire slackened a little—though it may just have been that we were getting used to it. At the same time the riverfront below us began to blaze with fire from rifles, machine-guns, and automatic rifles.

The rattle of small arms pierced the roar of the barrage. I heard distinctly the *talk-ah-talk, talk-ah-talk* of the Chauchat auto-rifles.[21] I could tell the sounds of the Chauchat and the Austrian whizbang better than any other weapons used in the war.[22]

About daybreak Mike brought us a message from the captain. We were to report to him at once.

Mike led us back some five hundred yards along the edge of a wheat field. We found the captain with most of the snipers, observers, and runners already assembled. He didn't say much, but he told us that our troops were being hard pressed; that the Germans were forcing a crossing of the river on a wide front; that he had orders to post all available snipers in advanced positions and to assist in every way possible in holding back the attack.

"I'm going to take you forward myself," he said. "After that it will be up to you to use your own judgment."

The rest of the order was routine—pick off officers or non-commissioned officers first, machine-gunners and runners next; avoid taking unnecessary chances. He checked up on our ammunition, then he led us across the field, up the ridge, and through the woods. The fight along the riverbank was continuous now. Both our brother regiments—the 30th and 38th—were finding the morning a warm one.

The woods were badly torn up and the going was stiff. We ran into gas and had to put on our masks. We had several casualties from shell fire, and two of the men either fell out from being gassed or got lost. There were thirteen of us when we started. When we made the open there were only six.

The captain halted us at the edge of the woods and pointed out the situation. It was still early in the morning, and the mist, smoke, and dust made visibility very poor. We couldn't see more than four hundred yards. The captain told us he wouldn't be far away. He was going back to see if he could find any of those missing from our detail. He sent us forward in pairs.

Jesse and I struck out directly for the river and took positions to the left of our 38th Infantry. This was holding a line along a road near the riverbank. A railroad also ran parallel to the river, and we got behind the railroad embankment. I could fire through a gap torn in the rails by a shell, and Jesse found a place about twenty-five yards from me, where he could fire between two metal ties that had been upended by shell fire.

On the opposite banks the Germans were swarming. Just to our right they were forcing a crossing by boats and pontoons. Many of them were already on our side of the river.

It seemed to me at first that Jesse and I were the only ones firing on that crowd. Then a couple of machine-gunners hidden on the slope above us chimed in. One good machine-gun and one sickly one, which seemed not to be working well. It would fire two or three rounds, hesitate for quite a spell, then pop two or three more. But the sound one was doing a land-office business. It was ripping off long bursts and landing them where they did the most good.

Jesse and I and the crippled machine-gun were working on the boats. The good gun was flaying groups of Germans on the far bank. But they went right on. I don't know how things would have turned out for us if a one-pounder on the slope hadn't come into the game just then.[23]

That one-pounder made all the difference. The Germans gave up the crossing. They pulled back along their bank and opened up on us. While they'd been trying to cross the river they hadn't paid much attention to us. They made up for lost time now.

Behind us the one-pounder quit firing. The sickly gun stayed gamely in the fight. But the good one went silent. The Germans had evidently got it. They couldn't locate Jesse and me, and we went on piling up our score. I had to wrap a bandoleer around my hand in order to hold my rifle. It was burning hot. The oil was boiling out of the woodwork, and it was smoking so that it interfered with my aim. I think in the first twenty or twenty-five minutes I'd used up two bandoleers and almost a third.

I dropped down behind the bank a moment to pour water from my canteen over the gun and through the barrel—and to take a little drink myself. The receiver screws had shot loose, and I tightened them as well as I could with my mess knife. I could see Jesse still pecking away at my right.

While I was working with my rifle, the Germans suddenly opened up on him with a machine-gun. Rocks and dirt showered all over him and he had to take refuge below the embankment. He ran to me, crouching low.

"Hurry up," he said. "Get her going. I've located that gun!"

We made our way up the railroad and found a new place to fire through. The gun that had come so close to getting Jesse was well up the opposite bank, and set rather high in order to fire over the tall weeds. It was still raking the track down there where we'd just been.

We both loaded our rifles with six cartridges and laid out two extra clips.

"Aim low, and give him hell," said Jesse. "Ready. . . . Go!"

There'd been three Germans at that gun. There were none there now, and we evidently ruined the gun; it didn't fire again. But our new position was not so good as our old one, because we could command less of the opposite bank.

"Let's go back," said Jesse.

We stayed at the old position until almost noon, when our ammunition was nearly gone. The battle was still on. The Germans moved steadily down toward the river from farther back on their slope. The water was filled with the wreckage of boats and pontoons destroyed by our artillery fire. Through the curtain of dust the noon sun looked like a smoky ghost of itself.

While we were trying to decide whether to go back and get more ammunition, the captain came along the embankment to us. He had Mike and a sergeant by the name of Clemmer with him. He'd just relieved a couple of snipers farther up the track; one of them was wounded.

The captain said he thought we'd done about all we could there, and might as well move back. That was all right with me. My head ached, my shoulder was kicked half off, and the Germans were using gas shells on the track.

We moved back up the slope through the woods. Every two or three hundred yards we had to put our masks on. We were perspiring heavily, and the eye pieces kept fogging up. In addition to that I wasn't any too sure about mine. It had only been repaired with a safety-pin where it had been torn the night before. That was as long a mile as I ever walked.

Our battalion was still in reserve, but when we got back to it we discovered that it wasn't rest we'd come for. The captain let us sit around for a few minutes; then he told us to go back to the dump and draw a new supply of ammunition. That captain was a wonder. He could carry on for days without rest and still be comparatively fresh.

Lieutenant Breaker, one of our K Company officers, was walking about among the men, kidding them along. He was a fine chap. Everybody liked him. I can see him now, talking to the fagged-out men, his brown eyes sparkling. His voice seemed to ring out and grip you. That afternoon was the last time I saw Lieutenant Breaker smile.

Presently the captain came. He gave us a cigarette apiece and said he wished he could get something for us to eat.

Things were happening fast that day along the Marne. The bridges had been blown up. Dead bodies were getting pretty thick even in the shelter of the woods. We could hear the 30th and 38th still at it, hammer and tongs. Our officers were ordered to assemble, and Colonel Dorey, our regimental commander, came around to speak to them.

He looked us all over closely as he passed us. He seemed so calm and confident that we felt a good deal better. But I doubt very much if the colonel felt as good as he looked that day.

After a short conference the officers returned to their men, assembled them by platoons, and began to issue orders. We were told that a thousand Prussian Guards had succeeded in making a crossing, and that it was up to us to take them on.

While we were listening, two stretcher-bearers came back through the woods and passed through our group. The man on the stretcher, with both legs blown off, was the engineer captain who'd helped the shell-shocked Looey the night before. Pieces of shell had torn him to pieces. But he wasn't unconscious.

"For God's sake!" he was moaning as they passed us. "Give me a drink of water. Or put me out! I can't go back like this!"

The stretcher-bearers disappeared in the direction of the first-aid station in our rear. The sight had put the men in a mean fighting mood, and they began to grumble at the delay. Then the major gave the signal. We moved out to meet the Prussian Guards.

We were halted when we'd gone perhaps a kilometer through the woods. Word had come back that our men up ahead had taken care of the Prussians. We were told to rest. Dead and wounded men were all around us; stretcher-bearers carried them past us to the rear; the guns went on roaring—but I went to sleep!

8

Counterattack

The following day our battalion was relieved from duty with the 30th, and we returned to the old position with our own outfit. Information, more or less correct, trickled in to us. The Germans had been stopped on the Third Division front, but had smashed through the French to our right and penetrated to a depth of several miles. American troops had attacked in the vicinity of Villers-Cotterêts and knocked the Germans loose from a lot of their earlier-won ground. We would begin a new attack as soon as the French had organized.

On the morning of the twenty-first, the French on our left attacked Château-Thierry and drove the Germans out, part of our regiment assisting them but not getting into the fight. That night we crossed the Marne, on a pontoon constructed by our 6th Engineers, and set foot on that territory across the river which we'd spent so many days looking at.

I knew the terrain so well that I was sure there was an enemy dugout not far from where we'd landed. I reported this to Sergeant Nayhone.

"All right," he said. "Pay it a visit and see what you can find. But use your head. The Germans have a pleasant habit of leaving mines in those places."

I found the dugout. But I also found something I hadn't looked for. There were still Germans in it. I could hear them talking.

I came away faster than I went, looking for someone to report it to. The first officer I met was Lieutenant Breaker. He ordered two squads of his platoon to follow him, and I led the patrol back to the dugout.

The lieutenant placed his men in position to command the dugout,

one squad armed with Chauchats, the other with rifles. Then he pulled
the pin out of a grenade and held it in his right hand. His pistol was
in his left. We were all still for a moment, listening. We could hear the
low voices of the men in the dugout.

Suddenly the lieutenant yelled, "Come out of there, you!"

A German voice answered in English, "We are prisoners."

"All right," the lieutenant said. "File out with your hands up or you'll
be dead men! Come one at a time."

They filed out in front of us, their hands in the air.

The lieutenant demanded, "Which one of you talks English?"

The one who'd come out first answered, "I do." He had almost no
accent.

The lieutenant turned to him. "Are there arms on any of you?"

At that instant another of the Germans dropped his arms, and drew
a Luger from his belt.[24] Almost before it was out, the lieutenant had
drilled him with his forty-five. I heard the safety go off on one of the
Chauchats; I was covering the fellow who spoke English with my rifle.
They were a badly scared lot of Germans.

The spokesman began to protest that the man had drawn his pistol
in order to surrender it. But the lieutenant stopped him.

"Keep your hands up!" he said. "We'll do the disarming ourselves."

A search proved that they'd all left their guns in the dugout except
the man who'd been killed. Satisfied as to that, the lieutenant and I
talked for a few minutes to the English-speaking German. We found
out that he had lived in the United States for fifteen years, most of the
time in New York and Chicago.

The German officers, he said, had told the men that the Americans
killed all their prisoners. But he'd assured this bunch he was with that
it was not so, that the Americans were good people and would treat
them well.

"But what are you doing in the German army after all those years
in America?" said the lieutenant.

He said that he'd gone back to Germany for a visit, had been caught
by the war and conscripted.

The lieutenant asked, "What year did you go back?"

"Nineteen-fourteen."

"You're a damned liar! You went back on purpose to get into it!"

It did sound pretty fishy.

The lieutenant dispatched two of his men back to regimental headquarters with the prisoners. I searched the man he'd shot. I took some papers and trinkets from his pockets to be turned over to the captain and cut off one of his shoulder straps.[25] He'd been drilled in the breast near the heart and had apparently died instantly. When I had finished, the lieutenant marched his detail off to rejoin the platoon, and I followed them.

There was some firing from rifles and light automatics going on up ahead where the Germans were trying to hold back the advance of our 1st and 2nd Battalions. But our outfits were moving right along. The German artillery fire was weak and desultory, and ours seemed to consist entirely of the heavies, which were shelling far to the German rear.

We were advancing through wooded country, and our movement was slow. Before daylight we halted and went to cover in the forest near Mont St. Pere. The night had gone by very quickly. The only sound of heavy firing was away off to our left.

It was two o'clock in the afternoon before the regiment moved out again. From the sound of things I gathered that the outfits to our right were heavily engaged. The rumors that reached us weren't so good, either. We heard that the French to the left had been stopped and that our outfits were catching flanking fire from the Germans on the French front. The German artillery was getting back into the game too. And ours was still being held up at the river crossing. But by the time the battalion halted I was too tired to care.

Chow had come up, and as soon as we'd finished that I looked up Tom and Jesse. I helped them empty a German canteen they'd found, then crawled into a shell hole with them for the night.

We resumed the attack next morning. Our 6th Brigade met strong resistance, and was checked. It had to dig in to hold what it had already gained. In order to aid it, the direction of march of our assault battalion—the 1st—was changed to the right and the 2nd Battalion took over the thrust toward Le Charmel. Our battalion closed up so as to support either of them.

The 1st Battalion made a determined thrust at a strong enemy position. But like the 6th it was compelled to stop and dig in. The German artillery was very active now, and the 1st suffered severely from its fire. The French on our left failed to get forward. And by midmorning the 2nd Battalion was stopped by a heavy flanking machine-gun fire from German positions in the French sector.

The 2nd Battalion had to stop its northerly movement and concentrate on the enemy machine-gun nests. It succeeded in knocking those out, only to have the German artillery fire come down on its troops.

The advance for the day was over. If ever an outfit needed artillery support, we did. But the river in the rear was still hampering our artillery brigade, and it could do little for us. In the meantime the whole regiment was being badly mauled. It was a great relief when we stopped for the day and dug in.

For Jesse and me that relief didn't last long. Before nine o'clock he was called back to battalion headquarters. He was to pick someone to go with him on a patrol, go through our front lines, penetrate as far as possible into enemy territory, and bring back all the information he could get.

He chose me. We passed through our front lines all right, and took up the approach on the enemy positions. When we'd gone a hundred yards in advance of our troops we began to crawl, and to leap-frog one another. By that I mean that each of us in turn would lie still and listen while the other moved forward for a short distance. We were moving over comparatively open ground. Fortunately the night was dark.

We had made about three hundred yards safely in this manner when we found that we were entering brush. We could do better on our feet there, so we stood up. Jesse had a shotgun[26] and a pistol; I had a pistol and a trench knife. With these in our hands we moved slowly and cautiously forward. Moved straight into three Germans armed with rifles and bayonets. They'd evidently been lying in wait for us.

I was in the lead, and the nearest one was lunging at me with his bayonet when I discovered him. There was no time to shoot. I struck his bayonet with my pistol, and swung my body away from him. But the bayonet point caught me on the right side, just below the ribs. It burned like fire as I tore myself loose. The German lurched toward me. I slipped to my knees and stabbed him in the stomach with the trench knife I held in my left hand.

In the same instant Jesse's shotgun roared. The German sprawled on top of me. I scrambled out from under his weight and jumped back. Twice more, with the speed of an automatic, Jesse's shotgun roared.

My side hurt, and it was hard to breathe. I could feel the blood running down my side. But when Jesse spun around after his third shot yelling, "High-tail it!" I was right beside him.

When we'd gone fifty yards without being fired at or followed, I told Jesse to slow down a bit; that I was hurt. We were running side by side, and he threw away his shotgun and caught my arm.

"How badly?" he said.

"I can't tell. But I'm bleeding fast."

"Put your hand over it," he said. "Stick it out a little longer. We'll make it, all right."

I pushed my pistol into my hip pocket, pulled up my shirt, and pressed my hand hard against the wound. We jog-trotted on another hundred yards, then slowed to a walk.

"Take it easy now," Jesse said. He dropped my arm and walked ahead of me toward our line.

About seventy-five yards from the edge of the woods Jesse halted and called: "Don't shoot! American patrol coming in."

Fifty steps more. A voice said, "Halt!" At the same time I heard the rattle of a Chauchat action.

We halted. Someone was approaching us from the right front.

"Get your hands up!" came the command. It was a sergeant from the 2nd Battalion and he had us covered with a Chauchat carried at the hip. Jesse told him our story.

"All right, James," he said. Then in a low tone to someone else, "Let them pass." He led us back through the line. "You won't be bothered any more," he said. "Good luck!"

Jesse had me by the arm again. "Stay with it just a little longer, kid," he said. "I'll fix you up."

We were in the woods now, and he led me down into a shell hole behind the shelter of a good-sized tree.

He struck a match. "Open your clothes," he said. "Let's see it."

The wound was just below the short ribs, two and a half inches long and half an inch deep.

"It's not so bad," Jesse said. "You'll be scarred up some, though."

I held the box of matches while he tore open a first-aid packet and bandaged me by the light of the matches. We didn't have our canteens with us, and I was beginning to feel faint and very thirsty. A soldier we met on our slow way back to battalion headquarters gave me a drink. But I was pretty well past noticing things by the time we got there.

At headquarters, Jesse made his report. Then they told him to go and take care of me. Jesse helped me into an old dugout, which had previously been occupied by both French and Germans. It smelled like it. I found that I was still bleeding. I asked Jesse if he didn't think we'd better see a doctor.

"Hell, no!" he said. "Don't you know what the pill-rollers'll do? They'll stick a tag on you."

He meant by that they'd send me to the rear, so I lay down on the cot, and Jesse went out. "I'll be right back," he said. "You're all right, kid."

I was thirsty again, and beginning to feel pretty sick. When Jesse came back he had a flashlight and some other things. He handed me a first-aid bandage.

"Grab that with your teeth," he said, "and hang on!" Then he washed the wound out, first with cognac, afterward with iodine. I almost tore the dugout down. But he held me and he got me bandaged up again.

Early in the morning Jesse waked me up. He and Nigger Floyd had been with me all night. Jesse fed me again—all the food there was. Neither he nor Floyd had anything to eat that morning; but I didn't know that until after I'd eaten it all. When I'd had my breakfast Jesse removed the bandages and looked over the wound again. Finally, he plastered a mass of tape over the whole side.

"*Now* you're all right," he said. "But I'd kind of favor that side for a few days." I stood up, and he pinned my breeches up to my shirt with nails. "You'll be better off with a loose belt for a while," he explained.

It was seven-thirty in the morning when orders circulated to the effect that we were to leap-frog the 1st Battalion and resume the drive toward Le Charmel.

The men were chilled from the night air and dampness. There was no food. But there was no grumbling either. We raked our little remaining equipment together and moved out. My side was stiff, and I felt weak and listless. Jesse cautioned me to take it easy. He'd received orders from the captain that the Intelligence men were to follow the assault companies and send all important information back to him or to Sergeant Nayhone at headquarters.

About eight o'clock our battalion passed through the lines of the 1st, and almost immediately came under fire. The Germans stiffened their resistance, and we made slower and slower progress. We were attacking through the Forêt de Fere. It was a large wood with clearings and made good ground for the Germans to fight a retiring action through.

In one clearing some of our fellows found all that was left of Major Nalle and his patrol.

The major's body had been stripped to the underclothing. Several of his wounded men had been shot in the head with rifles at short range. A boy we knew was lying stretched on his back, the whole side of his blond head blown in and one of his eyes lying on his cheek.

All day we drove on, never really coming to grips with the enemy, but harassed by artillery fire as well as by machine-guns and snipers. My side bothered me a lot, and Jesse made things as easy for me as he could. He got hold of half a canteen of schnapps for me somewhere, and I stuck it out. But it was tough going.

Orders came to halt at dark. There was very little water, and the only food we had was what we were able to salvage from the packs of the dead Germans. Jesse got blankets from somewhere. He shared those.

But he wouldn't touch the schnapps. He poured a little of it inside my bandages to reduce the chance of infection.

But it was a miserable night. Since we'd gotten into active service with the rest of the troops all Sergeant Nayhone's care and watchfulness had gone for nothing. By this time we had our full share of the soldier's pest.

As Jesse said, we were "as full of cooties as a coyote is of fleas."

By daylight we were at the business of war again. In front of us the Germans retired into a tall wheat field, and we followed. Immediately we came under a hail of machine-gun fire.

There was no safety anywhere. If we stayed flat on the ground we couldn't see to fire. And if we made the slightest movement the wheat betrayed us to the men at those machine-guns. At last our assault platoons were forced to lie motionless in the wheat and let the enemy's fire go unanswered.

The French were backing us up now, and they'd brought with them some of their Algerian troops.[27] They were black as coal, the fiercest-looking men I've ever seen. They had been trained by the French, and they were good soldiers. But they were terrible killers, and they never gave up their own ways of fighting. Their French uniforms were mixed with native finery. They wore bracelets on their arms for good luck.

The smallest of them must have weighed two hundred pounds, and they were all bone and muscle. They were covered with scars. Their faces were tattooed with cuts and slashes.

They entered that wheat field crawling. They were armed with small French rifles, and the knives they carried in their teeth.

They crawled straight through the field, paying no attention at all to the enemy's fire, and out on the farther side and disappeared. It must have taken them thirty minutes to catch up with the Germans. We could hear the steady *tat-tat-tat* of a machine-gun—then a sudden silence. One gun went out and then another and another.

I poked my head up and saw Germans running for the woods. The machine-gun nests had been cleaned out—every one.

When we came later on to the place where they had been, the

ground was full of Germans who'd been carved to pieces. But the Germans had put up a good fight.

All the Germans had their right ears cut off. An Algerian cuts off the right ear of the man he kills as proof of what he's done. Sometime later, when we'd come up with the survivors of that fight, I saw one Algerian with eighteen ears on a string around his black neck.

After this defeat the Germans fell back, organized a new line of attack, and opened fire again. Many of us were still in the wheat field, and German planes were flying over, dropping light bombs into the field. The bombs gave the exact range to the artillery, and they came into the game.

Things were pretty hopeless in the wheat field, and when Lieutenant Breaker took one of our support platoons and moved around a wooded ravine to flank the enemy, I crawled back into the woods and raced after his platoon.

As I caught up with the rear end of it a large German shell burst in the air at the head of the column. It killed or wounded nineteen men. The boy beside me drew in his breath as if he were choking.

"God!" he said. "It got the lieutenant!"

The non-commissioned officers took charge and the survivors of the platoon moved on. We passed the mangled body of Lieutenant Breaker. His face hadn't been touched and his eyes were wide open.

9

Relief

After the shell exploded the rest of the platoon forced its way around to a flanking position, but the outfits to the right and left failed to get forward. We had merely exposed ourselves to fire from three directions.

L Company had a little better luck. They reached a position where they could get at some of the Germans who were giving us the most trouble. We resumed the advance, but it was slow work. We lost almost all our officers, and we were more than a little confused.

When our company finally cleared the wheat field it was only to be pinned down at the edge of a strip of woods. A road ran along just there, and the Germans had it covered with machine-gun fire. A group of our men led by a lieutenant, the last of our company officers, tried to cross the road. The lieutenant dropped. The rest of the men dived back to cover in the ditch beside the road. A sniper's bullet had got the lieutenant, and the machine-guns then opened up. Mike and I were trying to drag the lieutenant back to cover in the ditch; several men ran out to help us. The machine-gun bullets began to spray around us; we gave it up and made for the ditch again.

We found one of our sergeants commanding what was left of the company. That sergeant completely lost his head. He sent a detail out to bring the lieutenant in. They were all hit before they got to him. And the fire they drew resulted in the lieutenant's being shot again, in the leg.

The sergeant ordered me to form another detail, go out in close formation, and come back with the lieutenant. I'd long ago found out the value of the tip given me by the old Civil War veteran at a railroad station back home. I asked the sergeant to wait a little while, then let me take Mike and go out alone.

"We'll get him in our own way," I said. "There's no use killing any more soldiers by sending them out there now."

The sergeant went crazy. He drew his pistol on me and repeated his order about the detail.

I pulled my gun too. "Detail, hell! You're nuts." He must have known that I was likely to shoot. "You'll wear stripes if you go out as I tell you," he promised.

"To hell with stripes!" I said. "They'll be a damned lot of use when I'm dead! As soon as this calms down, Mike and I'll go out and get him. Not before. And *not* with a detail!"

When he came at me with his gun, Mike took a hand in the argument. He covered the sergeant with his rifle.

"You damn lousy son of a bitch!" he said. "You shut your mouth or—"

The sergeant calmed down at that, and let us have our way about it. When we figured that the Germans had had time enough to shift their attention from the road, Mike and I wormed our way out and got back into the ditch with the lieutenant. There wasn't much shelter there any more, but we had nowhere else to leave him while we went on.

The bullet had hit the left side of his head and come out in the middle of *his* forehead. His brain was lying out there on his forehead but he was alive and he could talk. He was still alive when they found him there that night and took him back to the dressing station. I never knew what became of him afterward.

The Germans were raking the ditch now, and we had to scatter and look for cover wherever we could find it. Several machine-guns had spotted me. I doubled and twisted as I ran, and jumped like a squirrel in a hot cage. The air around me was full of cracking machine-gun bullets. At last I made a small hole at the edge of the woods.

The hole was shallow, and one of those gunners must have seen me drop into it. He laid his fire on the edge of the hole and almost buried me with dirt. He made a mess of my pack.

All the soldiers in that neighborhood were in about the same fix. There were several German guns which could sweep the ground and the road, and the fellow who had ruined my pack was located in a tree some two hundred yards down the road. He couldn't quite get us so long as we remained flat; but he had all the odds if we tried to move.

One of the men near me had seen what happened to my pack, and he called out to me.

"He didn't get you, did he, Barkley?"

He had a Southern accent and he pronounced my name "Bahkley." He must have exposed himself in calling to me. That German in the tree gave him a burst. He yelled as the bullets struck him. It sounded like a baby starting to cry. He was one of the nicest boys in our outfit.

I'd long ago forgotten my sore side. I gathered myself together, took a few long steps and a slanting dive, and lit in the ditch a little farther down the road, where it wasn't crowded. I took the German completely by surprise. I was under cover by the time he'd opened up.

I felt funny and warm all over—and big enough to tackle anything. I started down the ditch at a fast crawl. I passed Mike, and he caught my belt and asked me where I was going.

"Down there," I said, "to get the damned square-headed hell cat in that tree!"

"O.K.!" Mike said, and crawled after me.

We made good time down the ditch. When we figured that we were right across the road from the gunner in the tree we risked a look. We were nearly right. He was back about forty yards from the edge of the road, and he couldn't fire at us in our new position because of the trunk of his tree.

But another German gun, a heavy, had been mounted across a fallen tree a little farther up the road.[28] There was nothing to protect us from that gun. It was trained toward L Company, exactly in our direction.

The man on the heavy gun was not firing; but he kept swinging the muzzle slightly to the right, then to the left, seeking targets. I rubbed the tip of the front sight on my rifle with a bit of stone until it was bright. Dark sights are useless in the woods. Then I eased my head up to take another look.

I saw that a little farther down a shell had piled some debris along the edge of the road. I thought it would give me better concealment, so I crawled to it. I knew exactly what I was going to do if my luck held out: I was going to blow the head off the man at the heavy gun first, so that he'd be out of the game. Then I was going to settle with the man in the tree who'd killed the boy who called me "Bahkley."

I got my position carefully, and ruined the man at the heavy gun. Then I turned my old star gauge on the man in the tree.[29] His light Maxim hurtled down through the branches. It hit the ground and stuck there in its flash hider.[30] I issued "seconds" to him to make sure.

Just in time my eye caught a flash of movement. I saw that a big German was trying to man the heavy gun again. I killed or wounded him and another man before they gave it up. Then I fired two shots into the gun itself.

At that a group of Germans came up with another gun which they tried to set up. I don't know how many of them were knocked out before they gave it up too and abandoned the gun. It was getting a lot quieter in that neck of the woods!

Mike crawled up beside me and patted me on the back. "Good work," he said. "Atta boy!"

"Get down!" I said. "Quit grandstanding. . . . Look out there!"

A group of German riflemen had burst out of the thicket across the road. They tried to rush us, but we had the advantage. We sent them back again minus four of their number.

I started to crawl higher up the bank, hoping to see farther, and just then an eighty-eight hit the road almost directly in front of me. As it burst I half rolled and was half blown back into the ditch. A piece of shell cut my rifle in two at the small of the stock, and slit my sleeve from the cuff to the elbow.

I was half stunned, and my nose was bleeding. My face was packed full of gravel, and for several seconds I couldn't open my eyes. When I did I found that I was alone. Mike was gone.

I made my way back along the ditch and salvaged a rifle from the first dead soldier I came to. My eyes were clearing up by this time, and I risked a look across the road. I located another German gun, spoiled the gunner, then the gun. But while that was going on a German rifleman took a crack at me and ducked behind a tree.

I'd caught a glimpse of him as he disappeared, so I covered the place he had shot from and waited. Something told me that that German would be thick-headed enough to take a look to see if he'd got me. He did.

Suddenly to my left, L Company made a rush and crossed the road. Our crowd joined, and there was some dirty work there in the woods. But we didn't go back across that road.

I hadn't seen little Norosoff for a long time, but now I heard his voice calling for help. After a few minutes' search I found him. He was trying to bandage another fellow who'd had an ear torn off by a shell fragment. I helped him; then we had to leave the wounded man. The advance was on again.

That afternoon we took Le Charmel. There weren't many of us left.

The outfits to the right and left of us didn't come up. Once more we were the center of fire from both sides and the front. The Germans had not been driven out of a position they held in a château near Le Charmel, and they had plenty of machine-guns up there, on the higher ground. We were glad when at last darkness came, even though we believed it would bring a counter attack.

That attack didn't come. For four days we drove on, always under fire in the daytime, made miserable by hunger and lice at night. We were working with the 1st and 2nd battalions, sometimes side by side, sometimes leap-frogging one or the other of them. Our artillery had come up now, and the heavy fire was a great help. But repeatedly the French failed to hold; and the 110th American Infantry, which had been sent up to relieve the 7th, failed also.[31]

But the Germans were driven out of the château. We pushed them back across the Ourcq River and captured Ronchères. All this time we were without food except such as we could forage.

The first day my side was pretty painful, and I had fever. But Jesse and Floyd took care of me. They raided the countryside and got a little food and brandy for me from somewhere. Once Tom found a real supply of food hidden in a deserted house, and that helped a lot. The fever finally left me, but I was weak and shaken. It was all I could do to keep up with the rest.

We were all in a desperate condition by this time. The captain was gone; he'd been severely gassed the first night. Lieutenant Wyche had also been gassed and evacuated. Sergeant Nayhone and Jesse were running what was left of us. In the whole battalion there weren't enough officers left to run a company.

As for K Company, I am sure there weren't forty whole men left in it. We were weak with hunger. We'd had no chance to bathe or shave. We were being eaten alive by lice. But there wasn't any talk of quitting. The men who were still with the outfit were the roughest, toughest, and luckiest of the lot. I guess if it had been required of us we'd have hammered ahead until we were all dead. But late on that fourth day word came through that we were relieved.

Somebody said: "Relief? I've heard that word some place. What in hell does it mean?"

A lieutenant came down to us from M Company. He was a warm-looking officer and no mistake. He had a dirty overseas cap on his head and a splendid growth of whiskers on his face. His shirt and breeches were in rags. He was wearing an issue belt with a fancy German helmet dangling from it, and two pistols. The only other item of equipment he seemed to have left was his gas mask.

The lieutenant asked who was in command of K Company. Nobody answered.

Finally I stood up and saluted the lieutenant. "I'll take command of them if necessary," I said.

"Sure!" yelled Mike.

The lieutenant looked Mike over and grinned. Mike had worn his shoes and pants completely out, and had robbed some dead German of his. He was filthy as a chimney sweep, and his O.D. shirt was in ribbons.

But the lieutenant seemed satisfied. "All right," he said. "Let Barkley command. Fall your company in and follow me."

I formed the company and marched them off behind the lieutenant. He set such a good pace that it was hard for us to keep up. But by the time I'd got up my courage to speak to the lieutenant about it, we arrived at the rear of the battalion column, which was starting off very slowly.

"You won't have to move fast now," the lieutenant said. "Keep them together as well as you can."

We were the last outfit in the battalion on that march back. But we hadn't gone far when I found I had as many men behind me as I had in front. They kept falling out of the companies up ahead and falling in again at the rear of the column.

But they were never too far gone to hang on to what little equipment they had left. Every man of them had his helmet, gas mask, rifle belt, and bayonet. They were soldiers—I'll tell the world!

K Company stuck together. Somebody noticed the stragglers behind us, and we closed up and tried to make a march of it. I was proud of Company K.

Some of the outfits got a little food that night, but our company was out of luck. Our chow detail had run into mustard gas, and several of the men had died from it. We had to detour around the area in which they'd been caught. Nothing to do but tighten our belts and hike on. I know that we couldn't have covered in all more than ten or twelve kilometers. But it seemed damned long.

We spent the morning resting, back again at the Marne; and in the afternoon we crossed on the same pontoons we'd used eight days before. General Sladen, our brigade commander, stood near the southern end of the bridge and looked us over as we filed off.

He noticed Mike's German get-up, and asked who was in charge of the company. I saluted him and said that I was.

He pointed to Mike. "Have that man come over here," he said.

I ordered Mike to report to the general. He fell out, marched up to General Sladen, and saluted him. The general looked the little Italian over. "What man's army do *you* belong to?" he asked.

"American!" said Mike proudly.

"Where did you get those clothes?"

"I killed a Heinie to get 'em," Mike said. "Mine were *fini!*" Then he asked the general please to let him go. He was hungry and tired and about all through.

"You have done splendidly," the general said. "Splendidly. You may rejoin your command."

Mike snapped a salute at him and almost fell when he cut his hand away. He walked back to the company, and the general watched him with a strange expression on his face. It wasn't a happy expression. Next we passed Colonel Dorey, who was also sizing us up. He was still clean and trim. But he seemed to me to look at least ten years older than when I'd seen him last.

We were halted in the vicinity of the kitchens, and formed into chow lines. We had a big spoonful of brown gravy, a little cookie, and a third of a cup of coffee apiece! That was all we got. The medical officers were all over the place, and they arrested a K.P. who tried to put more in one of the men's plates.

Again that afternoon we were given those skimpy portions. But they waked us up in the night to give us a real meal, and in the morning we had another one.

After breakfast we were hiked back three or four miles to a little town and billeted in sheds and cow barns. Cow barns certainly looked good to us now!

Jesse had beaten the outfit back after the relief, and the first I saw of him was when he came looking for me with a "friend he wanted me to meet." The friend turned out to be a pill-roller sergeant who unbandaged my side and removed the scab. The wound was healing nicely from the bottom, and he dressed and rebandaged it. It was several weeks before the tenderness went out of it, but it never really bothered me any more.

Shortly after this we were loaded into French trucks and driven some thirty kilometers back to Courboin. The trucks were driven by slant-eyed Annamese.[32] The trucks had no springs, and the drivers had no idea what a steering wheel was made for. I'm sure the truck we were in didn't miss a hole or a rock between Courboin and the Marne.

A French sergeant or corporal was supposed to be in each truck, with the driver, but the one who should have been with us was missing. We passed one place in the road where a long truck train was moving over the hills. After that we ran across several trucks all smashed up in the ditches, with the boys being laid out and given first aid.

Just after we'd seen one of these we came to a long grade and our truck rocked like a cradle over the torn-up road. Floyd had been getting madder with every mile. Now he got tough. He kept shoving his hands in his pockets, then taking them out again. He set his helmet on one side of his head. Then he took it off and set it on the other. He glared at the back of the driver's head. His hair hung down in his eyes. His lips stuck out. His eyes glittered.

He got his gun out in one hand and his knife in the other. We struck a particularly vicious hole, careened to one side, straightened out again.

"Lemme get at that goddam son of a bastard!" muttered Floyd. "I'll shoot him as sure as he's a goddam Chink!"

The driver couldn't understand what he was saying, but he looked around to see what the excitement was. Floyd said something in Chinese. Slant-eyes nearly fell out of his seat. The truck lurched wildly to the left. Floyd pushed himself up close to the driver's seat.

"God darn you!" he said. "You straighten her up in that road an' keep her straight. And watch what you're doin,' or I'll shoot the heart out o' you!"

The man didn't understand the words, but he understood the look and tone. For miles Floyd sat there with his eye on the driver, gun in one hand and knife in the other. I couldn't see that it improved the Chink's driving.

Late in the afternoon we passed another wreck. The boys were all laid out waiting to be taken to the hospital. And just at that moment Floyd caught the Annamese trying to take a shot of dope. He knocked it out of his hand, and never took his eyes away from him again. Things were more uncomfortable than ever after that. These fellows kept themselves doped up all the time, and they were worse without the dope than they were with it.

Finally Jesse took a hand. "Come on back here," he said. "Let the poor Chink alone!"

But Floyd was iron. "If he don't drive this truck right," he said, "I'm gonna cut his heart out!"

And he stayed there, knife and gun ready, until we stopped at Courboin for the night.

We had a French sergeant with us when we went on the next morning to a little town whose name I've forgotten. We were there three days. They gave us medicated baths and deloused our uniforms. After the bath we smelled like a dog hospital. And when our uniforms came back there was so little of them left that some of us had to wear blankets to piece them out. The new major turned us out for what was supposed to be inspection, gave one glance at our uniforms, and dismissed us. The next morning we had new uniforms and equipment.

We were moved into another village, where we got replacements until we were built up almost to full strength, part of them new men from the Middle West, and part our own men returned from hospitals.

We heard two encouraging bits of news. Our 1st and 2nd divisions had met the Germans near Soissons and beaten a lot of fight out of them. And General Pershing was planning to assemble the American troops and handle them as an army. Those of us who'd gone through the Marne were mighty glad to hear that.

After a while we settled down to the old fourteen hour a day drilling. But it was all open order and offensive warfare stuff, and we were glad of that. Most of us, as soon as we began to feel a little fit again, wanted to get back into the fight. And we hadn't any notion of being on the defensive!

You could never forget there was a war going on because of the sound of the guns. In the daytime their rumbling was very clear. At night the flickering of their flares over the front was like an electric storm on the horizon, but the sound of the firing we sometimes lost unless an unusually heavy barrage was going on. Then it was like the rolling of thunder; and the whole sky would light up red, as if there was a big fire.

We never knew how many troops were engaged, or how the fight was going at those times. Our officers would come out and watch and listen and talk among themselves about it. I remember one time when, except for that far-away rumble, the night was so still it seemed to me almost to be holding its breath. All night long, a goat kept bleating somewhere. There was no sound from the cows in their barns around us; but every little while a horse would nicker uneasily.

I couldn't sleep that night. I kept thinking, "At home . . . when it's as still as this, and the animals are restless . . . it means a storm."

But it didn't mean a storm here. Only that storm of death.

Suddenly I wanted the clean, pleasant comfort of my home. I wanted never to hear the thunder of cannon again. I wanted never to see another man die.

10

Rest

I got to know the French people better than I had before while we were getting this rest. We were quartered in several little towns close to one another, part of the time in pup tents and part of the time in the villages themselves.

Most of the richer village people had moved in nearer to Paris. But a lot of the peasants who'd left their homes when they thought the area was to be overrun by the Germans were drifting back now. And hundreds of refugees from the country closer to the front had come there for shelter and help.

Between the American soldiers and the refugees, the natives of the villages were rather crowded. But they took us all in, and they were kind to us all.

I liked one funny old town, with its narrow streets and stone houses. Mike, Nayhone, and I paid a visit to the cemetery, and we got a jolt when we saw the dates on some of the stones. One of them was so old that even Nayhone was surprised. We could hardly get Mike away from it.

He kept looking back and saying, "Jees! I wonder where dat Frog is now!"

It seemed to me the graveyards in France were always in the most beautiful place anywhere near the town. The natives kept them well too. It was queer to see here in this old burying ground, with its weathered stones, the little crosses and seventy-five shells that marked the soldiers' graves. There were so many of them, and they were so new.

On our way back to the village square an old man stopped us. He had long white hair and chin whiskers; all his front teeth were gone. He looked seventy-five or eighty years old, but there was plenty of life in him yet.

He kept slapping me on the back and jabbering something. But I didn't know a word he was saying. I asked Nayhone; he'd begun laughing.

"What's this damned Frog talking about?" I said.

Nayhone began to roll French at the old man. The old man was tickled to death. He began to slap Nayhone's back and pointed to his stripes, and talked and waved his arms around.

Nayhone told us what it was all about. The old fellow had seen in the paper an account of our machine-gun fight with the Germans at the bridge across the Marne. He was trying to tell us what he thought of the Americans.

We left him jumping up and down and yelling, "Vive l'America," or something like that.

Nayhone laughed. "That old Frog's gone cuckoo," he said.

Most of the people seemed to feel the same way about Americans, even if they weren't quite so excited about it. Nayhone told some of the villagers that Jesse and Floyd were the only real, original Americans. Then they were the particular heroes. There was one old couple who fell hard for Jesse.

They came up and spoke to us one day when Nayhone and Jesse and I were sitting on the steps of the little fountain in the center of the square. They sat down beside us, and Nayhone told them all about the Indians, and about Jesse's being a great chief. They would nod their heads and say, "Qui . . . oui!" in a breathless sort of way. And always after that they called Jesse just "The American."

They stayed there for hours while Nayhone reeled off stories about the Indians. And Jesse sat like a statue of one, put up there to decorate the fountain!

The old lady never interrupted. Just sat in her white dress, nodding her head and saying, "Ah! . . . Ah!" under her breath. But the old man would break in and chatter so fast that Nayhone would have to say, "Wait a minute. . . . *Wait* a minute!"

The old man knew all about bows and arrows; he said they'd been used in his own country in ancient times. And he understood about the Indian tribes, too; he compared them to the tribes he'd read about in France thousands of years ago. They had a great talk. And from that time on the old folks adopted Jesse. They tagged around after him, and tried to persuade him to stay at their house.

But he couldn't do that. Those two Indians seemed to have decided that it was their business to look after me. They'd got themselves billeted in a barn with me, and I could hardly go anywhere without one or both of them going with me. If one of them was staying behind, he'd go to the barn door with us, and he'd say to the one who was going with me: "Stay with him. And bring him home drunk!"

It wasn't so easy to come home drunk. Our officers had asked the French to close the town to us, so far as wine was concerned. We were allowed to have beer, but it was pretty weak. Nayhone was glad of it. But not Floyd and Jesse. They finally took the matter into their own hands.

We organized a raid on a nearby town—just the three of us. At the edge of the village we met a little mademoiselle, and Jesse undertook to tell her what we wanted.

"Comprez?" he would say, and hold his hand up as if he were drinking.

After a while she caught on. "Oui, oui!" she said. She took us into a little shop and we paid her for a lot of wine. She had to go out somewhere to get it. While she was gone we looked around the basement; there was a barrel in the corner. Jesse pulled the plug out of the spigot and smelled it.

"My God," he said, "this is cognac! She'll never dare to sell it to us. Find a bottle to put some of it in."

The only thing we could find was a two-gallon keg. "Fill it up," Floyd said. "You two fellows go back up there an' get the wine. I'll climb out through this window in the basement. Meet you later!"

When Jesse and I got upstairs and looked out of the window, Floyd was three hundred yards up the road toward our town and he was making time. We took our wine and slipped some extra money under a paper to pay for the cognac. Then we set out for home. We had to be very careful. The officers were on the lookout for bottles and broke every one they found.

We knew where to look for Floyd. We had a cache in a grain field near our barn, in which the supply had been running pretty low. We took a few drinks to celebrate. Then we were foolish enough to go up into the town instead of going to bed. We ran into Nayhone, and he knew right away what had happened.

He turned around and followed us. Finally we stopped, and he jumped on Jesse. He gave him hell! Floyd and I had had just enough to make us laugh at everything. But Jesse stood and listened without the trace of a smile.

"Damnation, James!" Nayhone said. "If we're going to keep this Intelligence together we've got to cut out booze. An Intelligence man has got to keep his mind clear and his eyes open if he don't want to get bumped off. You know that. Why do I have to keep telling you?"

Jesse stood there, at attention, clicking his heels and saying, "Yes, sir . . . yes, sir." When Nayhone quit talking, Jesse came up with a salute and about face—very military—just as he would to an officer.

It made Nayhone mad. "That goddam fool," he said: "I don't see what in hell he means!" He swung on his heel and went back into town.

Of course Nayhone was right. Liquor seemed to have no effect on Jesse, unless it was to steady him, but most of us couldn't carry it like that.

Once, when Floyd had had a little too much of our cognac, he decided to trade off his pack with somebody. He made the trade, and came home wearing the undershirt he'd found in the new pack.

But, he hadn't used judgment in choosing a man to trade with. The new undershirt was much too small. He stood up in front of the doorway talking to Jesse and me about something else, and all the while he was loosening his blouse and tearing at his undershirt.

Every few minutes he'd say, "This goddam thing's too tight under the arms," and go right on pulling at it and talking about something else.

He finally had it all in shreds and yanked it out from under his blouse. "There's the damned thing!" he said. "I don't want it." He threw the shreds away. And the next morning when he'd sobered up, it was to find he hadn't a shirt to his name.

But things like that didn't happen every time we took a drink. And if there'd been anything really interesting to do we probably would have followed Nayhone's example and let liquor alone.

The Y.M.C.A. tried to help.[33] But they were like Floyd in his trading; they didn't always use good judgment in the men they picked to mix up with a bunch as tough as most of those boys were after a spell at the front.

There was one time when our pay was held up, and no one had any money. I saw a box of chocolates and another of beautiful red apples down at the canteen—and they certainly made me hungry. I went back to see if I could raise any money. The Y man had told me the apples were a nickel apiece. I ran into Mike first, and gave him the news about the apples.

"I only got three or four cents," he said. "We gotta borrow the rest."

I managed to get a little money, and Mike came back with a little too. Then we met Norosoff, and he wanted to go in with us. Norosoff was very saving. I never saw him when he didn't have money.

"I'll put in my thoid," he said. "You see what you can do."

By that time I had what would be about sixty cents in American money, so I went down and told the man at the Y that I wanted a dozen apples. I handed over my money. He looked at it and then at me.

"We've had orders to raise the price of the apples," he said.

I started to argue with him, but he wouldn't listen. Then I told him what I thought.

I said, "It's a damned shame to change the price in fifteen minutes. I think it's the bunk, and you're a damned liar!"

"How dare you say anything like that!" he spluttered, and lunged toward me. He was a big fat man.

I picked up one of the apples and hit him in the cheek. It mashed the apple into cider. He didn't get up right away, and I took my dozen apples and walked off to look for Mike and Norosoff.

Before long I was called up before the major. It had been reported to him that I had knocked out a Y.M.C.A. man.

He looked pretty stern. "This damned outfit," he said, "is trying to put it over on a man who's doing his best to help us out. They're raising money out there, and doing everything they can. But go ahead. I'll listen to your story. What made you do it?"

When I finished he took a chew of tobacco. He chewed and chewed. I could see the muscles of his jaw move. At last he spoke.

"In a case of that kind," he said, "I hardly know what to do." His eyes twinkled. "I'll have to put you under arrest . . . on the records. After that, I guess we'll kind of forget about it."

The old fat Y.M.C.A. man saw me walking around next day and he was furious. He stopped the lieutenant in the street to complain.

He told his story. Then he wound up: "That lowdown ornery soldier ought to be in jail instead of strutting around here! He ought to be in Sing Sing—that's where he belongs. Unless Sing Sing's too good for him! What kind of discipline do you call this anyhow?"

That lieutenant was a wiry, snappy-speaking chap. "You seem kind of mad at Barkley," he said. "The way you talk, you don't seem to like Barkley very well."

He waited a minute while the Y man fumed. Then he turned around and went on.

Some of the French Blue Devils were billeted near us, and some Italian troops who had been badly shot up fighting in the Alps.[34] We used to go over and try to talk with them, but we never got very far unless we had Mike or Nayhone with us. Mike had a great time telling the Italians about America. They asked him all sorts of questions, mostly about the chances for making money.

"You'd be surprised," Mike told them. "You oughtta come over in God's country and see!"

Camp was pretty monotonous. Once in a while there was a little excitement when German airplanes flew over the camp and dropped propaganda, trying to break up the war.

"What are you doing in Europe?" these papers would say. "Why don't you stand on your constitutional rights? The capitalists in Wall Street are putting you over here. They are putting you over here for money!"

The officers were fussed about it, and we had orders to burn any of the papers the moment we got hold of them. But the soldiers just laughed at them.

"What the hell do we know about Wall Street?" some middle-western boy would say. "We came over here to fight. Let's go!"

Once I saw two Swedes standing there reading one of the papers. "Maybe it bane truth," one of them said. "But what the hell? It's yoost their side of it."

Toward the latter part of the summer some of us in the Intelligence began to be kept busy instructing the new recruits who'd been picked to fill up the gaps in the Intelligence Service. There were plenty of gaps. Even the best snipers and observers get careless—and one moment's carelessness is enough sometimes.

These new men weren't all promising material; many of them had had no training and couldn't understand the French maps. You're useless as an observer unless you know how to use those maps, just as you're useless for sniping unless you're an expert shot with the rifle.

We worked all day and almost all night trying to whip those boys into shape. They were smart, handsome fellows, but they couldn't seem to get their minds on their work. I suppose they'd been picked for the Intelligence Service and put into it whether they wanted to go or not.

There was one boy who told me he was from the University of Kansas. I could see from his face that he wasn't following a thing I was saying about the maps.

"You've got to buck up and show some interest," I said to him. "You've got to realize that this Intelligence Service is the best work and the highest position in the American army. You must have the stuff in you. If the officers hadn't thought you were a hell of a good soldier, they wouldn't have put you here. It's important work. But it's dangerous work. There's no blinking that. It's damned easy to get bumped off. And the only way to make a success of it is to *learn these maps.* We're likely to be called up to the front any day. If you get up there and don't know a cockeyed thing about this, where are you going to be?"

He broke down and cried like a baby.

I didn't know what to do. "Well," I said, "it's just too bad! What can I say to cheer you up?"

"Nothing," he answered. "Nothing!"

I tried again. "What in the hell are you crying about? Don't you know you're alive?"

"Yes," he said. "But I don't expect to be long!"

I gave up then. I said, "Well, you're probably all right. And I wish you all the luck in the world. But you're a total loss as an Intelligence man."

I took the matter up to the lieutenant. He was an old hand at this work, but he'd had very little actual experience. He was a book warrior, and full of theories.

He heard me through; then he asked, "How long have you been up here?"

I said, "Long enough to wear out several pairs of socks."

"None of that sarcasm!" the lieutenant snapped.

"Well," I said, "as man to man, we might as well face the fact that that fellow will never make an Intelligence man."

"Just what kind of man do you want?"

"Anybody who has a little sense and has got over crying about home!"

"He'll get over that all right. I like him and I'm going to keep him."

After that the lieutenant had his eye on him, and told Jesse and Nayhone to see what they could do with him. Nayhone was encouraged when he first saw him—but the trouble began as soon as instruction started.

Nayhone reported to the lieutenant: "You can't do anything with that baby. If you don't want to send him back we'll just have to keep him around here for an ornament. No use to try to teach him anything. He's batty and he's getting everybody crazy."

But the lieutenant told Nayhone to try again. That time the fellow just broke down and bellowed.

"For God's sake, be good!" said Nayhone. "All I'm trying to do is to tell you how to save your life!"

He went right on crying.

"Listen," Nayhone finally said. "You can learn this stuff if you want to. Now get to hell out of that bawling, and get to work."

"Oh, God!" he said. "I can't . . . I can't—"

After a little while they put him back in the line and he was killed in action soon afterward. A soldier who happened to be near him told me about it.

"It was queer about that guy," he said. "He didn't even try to take care of himself. We were under machine-gun fire, advancing on a little bridge. We were trying to take it in squad formation. All of a sudden he ran out there right into the machine-gun bullets. He didn't even lie down. Just acted like a crazy man. He was killed instantly. Riddled with bullets. It certainly was queer about him. He was a good-looking guy, too!"

———

Summer was nearly gone. We were getting very restless as fall drew near. The outfit was fighting fit again, and an outfit like that gets nervous if it's kept inactive too long.

One day I found Floyd looking for me. "Punk," he said, "where's Jesse?"

I told him I didn't know.

"Huh!" he said. "You'd make a hell of a poor chief if you didn't know where your Indians were! Go an' see if you can find him. I been hearin' things."

When I turned up at our barn with Jesse we found Floyd getting his pack together. "Marchin' orders," he said.

We didn't believe him at first, but soon found out it was true, and we began to pack. I was going through my pockets and among other things I took out some letters from my girl and my mother's picture.

I showed it to Floyd and he took a photograph out of his pocket and held it out to me. "What you think of this squaw?" he asked.

"She's a good-looking Indian! How did *you* ever come to have a girl that pretty?"

"Huh!" he grunted. "Where's your girl's picture?"

"I haven't got any."

"I'll bet she's ugly as hell!"

"No, she's not. But say, how'd you ever get a good-looking girl like that?"

"Well, these women are kinda funny," he said. "You gotta give 'em a pair of shiners once in a while if you want 'em to think anything of you."

"Listen! You never blacked *this* girl's eyes!"

"Sure! I knock hell outta her. That's the reason she likes me!"

"My gosh!" I said. I couldn't get over it. "That's no way to treat a woman."

"Hell, Punk!" he said. "You just don't know your stuff!"

Before they loaded us into the trucks we looked up some of our French neighbors to tell them good-by. Jesse's two old friends couldn't bear to see him go. Jesse always made a hit with old people, children, and dogs.

Floyd noticed what was going on. He said, "Why the hell's that old Frog followin' you around?"

"Oh, he always does whenever he sees me. It's some of Nayhone's stuff. He told them a lot of yarns about Indians."

"Why don't you punch him in the nose?"

"I don't want to hurt the old man," Jesse said.

"But damn it," said Floyd, "the old bird's dotty!"

When it came to saying good-by, the old man caught hold of Jesse's coat, and his wife cried. Jesse asked me what the old man was trying to say. I wasn't sure, but I'd begun to pick up a little French and I made a stab at it.

"He thinks he'll never see you again."

"Hell! Is that all!" Jesse said. "You can't kill a good Indian. I'll come back and see you!"

But the old man was still crying and holding on to Jesse's coat. He had a hard time getting away.

Floyd made out he was disgusted. "What's the Frog cryin' about?" he kept muttering.

Floyd was afraid someone would know how it got him; he was trying to cover it up by pretending he didn't like the old man and being a little more hard-boiled than usual.

Just before we piled into the trucks I saw one of our men saying good-by to a little French girl he'd seemed to be very much in love with. She was crying, and he didn't look any too happy himself. He was patting her shoulder and saying he would come back soon.

When he said that, she only shook her head and cried harder. She said the same thing Jeanne had said to me. "Non! Zey nevair come back. I nevair see you again!"

And she was right. That boy's name is on K Company's roll of gold stars. I saw him go west in the Argonne, less than two months later.[35]

At last we were bundled into the trucks and got away. It was the middle of August when we started. We traveled by truck, by train, and by foot. We halted for a last short period of training and for the distribution of supplies, which were coming through much better now. It was the fourth of September when we entered what all the old-timers knew was the last lap of our journey toward the front.

At Vaucouleurs, General Pershing reviewed us, but I didn't see him. We rested a day or two, then resumed the march.

It was all night marching now. By day we halted under the shelter of forests, and were ordered to keep well under cover. The last night's march was made in a pouring rain and a confusion of traffic. Scores of other outfits were moving, mostly American.

The sound of guns was drawing closer all the time. It was the beginning of the big drive at Saint-Mihiel.[36] Our last halt was in the Forêt de la Reine. We were trying to settle down for the night in the dripping woods when the roar of the guns suddenly grew much louder.

We'd landed back at the front just in time for the opening of the Saint-Mihiel barrage. It was the Marne barrage all over again. Only bigger, and better!

II

Saint–Mihiel and the Argonne

The Saint-Mihiel barrage began at twelve o'clock. It was amusing to watch the faces of our replacements. They were a dumfounded lot. We'd hardly received orders to get our packs and lie down, when another order came through that we were to move. I supposed this meant business, but it didn't. We only went three hundred yards farther up in the woods because some of the long-range artillery had selected our camping spot for their guns. The guns were heavy, and they wanted a position near the road where they could move out at short notice.

I was lying in the woods in a pup tent with Floyd and Mike when those long-range guns opened up, right on top of us, it seemed to me. We were very tired, and I was nearly asleep when the first gun went off. The concussion knocked the tent down on top of us.

Mike jumped up. "What t' hell—" he spluttered. The gun went off again. And again.

Floyd rolled over on his other side. "Say I gotta get some sleep. You guys quit talkin', will you?"

I lay down, but there wasn't any sleep for us. There were twelve of those guns, a few hundred yards from us, strung over a quarter of a mile. We set up the tent again, and we stretched a blanket over the top of it. We had a candle in one of our packs, and Mike got two or three more of the fellows in there for a game of pitch.[37]

Before daybreak, orders came to pack and move up. Our division had been placed in reserve, but the attack was gaining ground so fast that it was necessary to keep the reserve moving forward in order not to lose touch.

Years of warfare had blasted the country we marched through; there wasn't a blade of grass anywhere. The earth looked like soil I'd seen in Texas. It was dark on the surface but a yellowish color where the subsoil had been thrown up out of the shell holes, or excavated for trenches. It was rich soil but as stripped of life as a desert.

Uprooted trees were lying everywhere. They looked like skeletons. Some of them had been partially covered with earth, so that they were just old snags sticking up. Hour after hour we passed barbed-wire entanglements, abandoned dugouts and trenches, and shell holes. The shell holes grew fresher as we went on.

Everywhere there were cannon wheels, ragged old shreds of metal, wire with straggling weeds growing up around it, rusty duds, battered helmets, ruined guns.

Burial parties had been careless, or shells had plowed up the graves. Little crosses, with helmets fastened to them, lay here and there; white splinters of bone; occasionally a skull; everywhere the odor of dead things.

When we passed out of the French areas and over the ground held for years by the Germans we found the same old signs but with a difference. Seventy-five duds, where there had been seventy-sevens, coal-scuttle helmets instead of the little ones the French wore, Mausers and Maxims in place of the Chauchats and Hotchkisses.[38]

The only things that were just the same were the bones and the skulls.

Once we passed over a little ridge that commanded the whole valley. Spread out down below were thousands and thousands of troops—American troops—halting and marching. Ambulances, artillery, trucks on the roads. Prisoners moving back.

It looked to me like pictures I'd seen—like some old-time battlefield.

But our battalion moved on, in brigade formation; I knew it was real all right. We began to pass the prisoners. More and more of them all the time.

For several days we were marched and countermarched; it wasn't until the afternoon of the seventeenth that we were loaded into trucks and deposited late the next day in a woods near Verdun.

The fall rains had begun, and it was muddy and raw, but not cold enough yet to be really hard on us. The waiting was hard. The German air forces were active, and we had to keep close to cover. Sentries were posted at all times to observe for these enemy planes, and the roads were camouflaged. The feel of big things was in the air.

On the afternoon of the twenty-third we were assembled and Major-General Buck, who had relieved Major-General Dickman late in August, talked to us. He'd come to us from the First Division, and he had the reputation of being a first-class combat unit commander.

A platform had been put up, and we broke formation in order to get the men as close to it as possible. Jesse was right at my elbow. We liked the way General Buck looked, and we liked his voice. He began by telling us that he was proud to be connected with the division; that he would consider it an honor to lead such troops into battle.

I don't remember his words, but we understood him to mean that he was going to do that leading into battle in person. Whether he said it or not, that's what he did, even at the cost of being relieved of his command. General Buck was a *first line* officer.

He said we were going against the enemy at one of his most critical points—one that he had held for four years.[39] We would find the enemy positions there a mass of wire and machine-gun nests; his defenses were re-enforced concrete backed by massed artillery. The general made the case mighty strong as far as the enemy was concerned.

Then he gave us the other side of the picture. We were going to mass guns in front of those enemy positions—hub to hub, row after row. We were to have at our disposal every tank and specialized instrument of warfare that could be procured. We were to win the fight that was coming, regardless of the price we would have to pay. No matter how hard the enemy fought, we were to fight harder.

"It's not the first test of your mettle," he ended his speech. "You've faced the enemy at his best before—and you've beaten him. You can do that again. You've *got* to do it again!"

General Buck won every man there with that talk. Even Jesse was impressed. No one said anything until the crowd had broken up, then I asked Jesse if he didn't think it was a good speech.

"Speech, hell!" he said. "That was *orders!*"

⮞◆⮜

The next ten days found us moving most of the time, but still in reserve. We passed through Montfaucon in a driving rain and spent four inactive days southeast of there, with artillery and machine-guns making it hot for us.[40] The 3rd Battalion came through well enough, but the 1st and 2nd took some sharp punishment.

The greenest of us knew we were now going into a big battle. Guns rumbled and machine-guns and rifles barked all night and all day.

The enemy air service was active and bold and very successful. Their reports were so accurate that as the days passed the German artillery fire grew more and more deadly.

On the last afternoon of inactivity for us, the mail came in just before chow call. I had a letter from my mother, and several from others in the family. And I had one from my girl. I put the rest in my pocket and tore that one open.

"Dear Jack," she began, "I'm going to make this very brief and to the point."

And she did. She thought a lot of me, but I'd never get out alive anyway, so it wouldn't make any difference to me. She was going to marry the boy she'd been going places with, to try to keep him from having to go into the army.

I went down to supper. I tried to drink some coffee, but I couldn't down even that. I threw my "slum" into the garbage can and went back up to camp.[41]

I was all alone. The rest of the boys hadn't come back from supper. I walked up and down for a while, then got out my rifle and started cleaning it. The telescopic sights and instruments had to be kept in good shape.

After a while I began to curse.

The boys came back and started a black-jack game. They wouldn't give me any peace, so I finally got in the game. I didn't know whether I was winning or losing. I threw down my cards and walked over to my tent.

Norosoff was sleeping in the tent with me and when he came in he knew something was wrong.

"What's the matter?" he asked.

"Nothing. I just want to go to bed."

"I'll go too then," he said.

But I couldn't lie still.

Finally Norosoff sat up. "Listen," he said, "you can't kid me. Somethin's eatin' you. What is? Bad news from home?"

"Yes. But keep your mouth shut about it."

"Sure," he said.

He lay down again, on his back. I was lying on my side. I felt a little better when I had told him.

All he said was, "Gee, that's tough." And then, after a while, "Maybe you ain't got this thing straight, Barkley. Maybe it ain't so bad when you know about it."

"I got it straight all right," I said.

———◆———

That was the morning of the third. On that day our regiment went into action, supported by tanks and artillery. We drove the Germans from Woods 268. But all that day and the next, the 1st and 2nd struggled to take Hill 250. The tanks outdistanced the troops and penetrated the enemy's lines without destroying them. Both battalions were pretty badly shattered.

The Germans had held this ground for years. They knew it down to the smallest furrow. They had countless machine-guns, and our troops were exposed to flanking artillery fire, and had very little support from their own artillery.

There were a lot of peculiar things going on. Everybody began to be disgruntled. Our battalion was held out as a brigade reserve after we'd taken Woods 268; we were punished all the time, but we weren't allowed to do anything about it.

The 79th when it fought over this area had been forced to leave several German strong points still in working order, and the machine-gunners and snipers were making things pretty unpleasant for us.

Twice Jesse went to battalion headquarters and tried to get permission to push out some of these snipers. It was refused. So we knocked them off without authority. But there was a gun of fairly large caliber concealed not far to our left front, and we hadn't been able to place it. It was still being served and it was doing a lot of damage to our front-line troops. We could hear it roar every now and then, and about dusk I happened to locate its flash.

I went back and reported the matter directly to the major. Sergeant Nayhone was busy and bad-tempered besides. I didn't find the major in a very good humor either.

When I'd told him of my discovery, he snapped, "There's a hell of a lot of things going on around here I don't understand!"

I knew that one of the things was what had happened to him when we moved into that position. He'd been assigned to a certain dugout, and when he tried to move in he found it was still occupied by armed Germans! His dog-robbers who were with him beat a retreat, and the major cleaned out the dugout singlehanded.[42]

He seemed to be thinking hard for a few minutes, then he gave me my orders. "Get a patrol together," he said. "Take some grenades. Go out there and put that gun out of action."

He went with me back to the company, where we picked a detail of five men. He put them under my control and repeated his orders about silencing the gun.

"Kill the outfit," he said. "Don't come staggering back with them.

We don't want any prisoners. We haven't got any men to send to the rear with them. We're up against a fighting outfit, and they'll kill you if they can. Get them first!"

It was pretty dark by this time, and we weren't in much danger from distant fire. But the terrain was still alive with small groups of Germans, and our own troops were almost as dangerous; they were apt to shoot first and ask questions afterward.

The men in the detail were all riflemen. We had four grenades apiece, and I told them to follow me in single file, doing everything they saw me do. They were to crawl when I crawled, stop when I stopped, and so on. The gun fired twice while we were on our way to it, and we saw that it was a 105 Howitzer.

It was located in a large excavation with a fairly high bank thrown up on our side. Poles had been put up over it, and some of the camouflage was still on them.

When we were near enough to hear several Germans moving about the gun and talking in low tones, I called my patrol close and gave them their orders. Two of them were to go around to the left, two to the right, the other one with me. We would avoid the side toward us. The high bank would skyline anyone who tried to get over it. When I fired my forty-five we were to throw a grenade apiece into the gun hole—and we were to be sure to hit the hole! When the grenades went off I'd fire another shot, and we'd rush the position.

I took my man with me, and we started out first. Before we'd reached our positions, somebody behind us kicked an old German helmet and started it rolling. Instantly a Luger began to spit, straight at me.

I ducked low. "Take 'em now!" I yelled, and made for the hole, firing at the flash of that Luger.

I had covered half of the ground, had fired one clip and reloaded, when several grenades burst in the hole. Some of my gang had heaved their grenades when I yelled, and not one of them had missed the hole.

It was good work. We finished it up with a grenade apiece, and after that everything was quiet. One German crawled out and we saw him get away, but we didn't risk a shot for fear of hitting one another.

When we rushed the hole we found two of the gunners apparently dead. The other one made a movement toward us as if to throw something, and one of the patrol ran him through with his bayonet.

When I reported to the major, the first thing he asked me was whether I'd disabled the gun. I had to tell him that I hadn't thought of that after we'd gotten rid of the men who were firing it.

"They probably can't bring up a new gun. But I don't see what's to prevent some new gunners from sneaking out there and firing it as long as it's in commission. I guess you'd better go back and take the breach-block out of the gun."

Well, it had been bad enough the first time, but to go back out there alone with those men we'd just killed . . . I'd never had quite such a creepy feeling in my life. But the responsibility had been mine, and the oversight was mine. I couldn't ask someone else to share whatever risk there might be in finishing up a job I'd left half done.

I could hear my heart beating when I got into the hole again with the gun. I couldn't find any way to get the block out, so I packed the barrel for about two feet with rocks, working from the muzzle out and driving them in tight with a pick handle. I found the clearing rod leaning against the carriage and threw that away.

I don't suppose it took me more than thirty minutes to spike the gun. It seemed a lot longer. You could hardly move out there—inside the hole or anywhere around it—without stumbling over dead Germans! As I crawled down into the hole I noticed one of them lying half in and half out. I'd just started work at the gun when he gave a moan, and then began making a snoring sort of noise. It sounded as if he was regaining consciousness. And yet I knew that he was dying. I knew it from the gurgling in his nose. I'd heard that sound too often by now to make any mistake about it.

I went over to see if there was anything to be done for him. But he was so badly shot up he was past any kind of help. Somebody had emptied a forty-five into him. He was just about where the man who'd fired his Luger at me would have been. It was probably my forty-five.

When I was sure I couldn't do anything for him I went back to the gun. I don't know whether he was young or old—I didn't want to know. All the time I was working there, the snoring kept on. I knew he was dying . . . and I wished he would hurry up and die.

By the time I'd finished jamming the gun I was shaking with chills and my muscles were sore.

When I got back to the battalion there was a lot going on, and pretty soon I forgot about that damned snoring.

I looked everywhere for Jesse, but couldn't find him. Finally Mike told me he had moved out ahead with the major to reconnoiter. Mike also told me the reason for the excitement.

The battalion had been released. At last orders had come through that we were to move out to the attack. We were to start at once, under cover of the darkness. Our orders were to take Woods 250.

John Lewis Barkley in 1919. (Courtesy of the National World War I
Museum Archives, Kansas City, Missouri)

German shoulder straps collected by Barkley and other Intelligence troops. (Courtesy of the National World War I Museum Archives, Kansas City, Missouri)

Shoulder straps taken from German snipers killed by John Lewis Barkley. In a letter to Mike Mulcahy, Barkley explained that the strap on the right came from "one of the quickest snap shots ... I ever saw—he rained terror on everybody." (Courtesy of the National World War I Museum Archives, Kansas City, Missouri)

John Lewis Barkley's comrades in Germany, 1919: William Floyd
(left), Jesse James (rear), and possibly Mike D'Angelo (right). Note
Floyd's Distinguished Service Cross and the dark ribbon on James's
sleeve, presumably the insignia for a battalion "Intelligence man."
(Courtesy of the National World War I Museum Archives, Kansas
City, Missouri)

John Lewis Barkley (right) and an unidentified comrade in Germany, 1919. Barkley's scalp still shows signs of his mustard-gas burns. (Courtesy of the National World War I Museum Archives, Kansas City, Missouri)

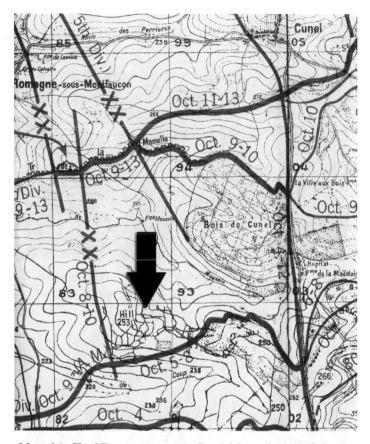

Map of the Third Division sector near Cunel, Meuse-Argonne Offensive. The arrow marks the approximate position of the abandoned French tank that Barkley occupied. Note Hill 253 and the Bois de Cunel, important landmarks mentioned in Barkley's account. (Courtesy of the American Battle Monuments Commission)

View to the northwest from Barkley's position. This is the ground that the Germans were crossing when Barkley opened fire on them from his tank. (Courtesy of John Bratt)

View to the north from Barkley's position. Note the edge of the Bois de Cunel, the woods from which the Germans advanced. (Courtesy of John Bratt)

A French F17 Light Tank. Manufactured by Renault and used by both
French and American forces, this two-man vehicle carried either a
Hotchkiss heavy machine gun (as shown) or a 37mm cannon. Note the size
of the aperture containing the gun and its swivel mounting. Barkley's tank
was without its armament. The resulting foot-square opening left him
terrifyingly exposed. (Courtesy of the National World War I Museum
Archives, Kansas City, Missouri)

John Lewis Barkley in the 1930s. (Courtesy of the National World
War I Museum Archives, Kansas City, Missouri)

John Lewis Barkley and Bradley Kelley, fiction editor for King Features, New York, 1930. (Courtesy of the National World War I Museum Archives, Kansas City, Missouri)

John Lewis Barkley and William Floyd (right) at the 1946 Regular Veterans Association Convention in Denver, Colorado. Barkley was not, technically, a Regular in the U.S. Army; the organization invited him to join as an honored guest. The Convention marked the first time that Barkley and Floyd had met in person since 1919. (Courtesy of the National World War I Museum Archives, Kansas City, Missouri)

Barkley (second from left) in later life at the Liberty
Memorial in Kansas City, Missouri. (Courtesy of the National World War I
Museum Archives, Kansas City, Missouri)

12

Killers

It was apparently to be close fighting, so I exchanged my rifle for a sawed-off shotgun. I had my pistol too, with about thirty-five rounds of ammunition in clips, my trench knife, and two grenades left from the raid on the gun.

Our battalion moved forward slowly with frequent halts. We were trying to make no noise, and we couldn't have made any speed if we'd wanted to. It had rained so heavily that the ground was a slippery quagmire, and it was still misting. Our orders said two of our companies were to assault the woods; the other two were to constitute the support.

Suddenly a heavy rifle and automatic rifle fire opened directly ahead. I heard somebody yell "Let's go!" and we ran straight forward. At the same time the Germans on the right end of the line opened up on us with dozens of machine-guns.

The company on our right was having a tough time making the woods, but it was putting up a good fight. There was a lot of hand-to-hand fighting going on. I crowded up behind them, and just as I did so a party of the enemy rushed them. They closed in to meet the attack, firing from the hip.

In the mix-up that followed one of our own crowd swung his rifle back over his head to meet an oncoming German, and the rifle got me across the side of my helmet. It only knocked me out for a moment; almost immediately I was back on my feet. But my shotgun was gone. And there was too much going on around there for me to spend time looking for it.

The fight swayed farther to the right. I saw a chance to get into a better position, and started to run across a little open place toward the woods. Halfway across I fell headlong into a hole. The wind was knocked completely out of me, and I cracked my hip against a machine-gun which was mounted at the side of the hole.

As I turned over and sat up someone else slid into the hole. He stepped on my left hand. His boots were German boots, and as I moved he made an exclamation in German.

My pistol was still in my right hand, and I fired three shots as fast as I could pull the trigger. He fell toward me and pinned me against the machine-gun. He was lying across my chest, and just as I'd succeeded in rolling him over my legs and getting to my feet, another fellow lit beside us.

He had evidently been running. He came in head first just as I had. I pushed my gun into his back. But when he yelled, in perfectly good New York English, "Where in hell's the rear?" I took it away again. He didn't wait for an answer. He scrambled out of the hole, and disappeared in the darkness.

I was alone in that hole with the man I had just killed. I made sure that he was dead, then I tried to get him up onto the ground outside. I struggled until I was dripping with cold sweat. But it was no good. He was a heavy man, and so limp that I couldn't get a hold on him.

I knew it would be suicide to crawl out myself and pull him over the edge. The hand-to-hand fight was over around there, but parties of Germans were still prowling over the battlefield. I could hear them talking at different times in the night. A number of machine-guns were raking the field every once in a while, and now and then I heard the whine of a sniper's bullet.

I looked over the machine-gun in the hole where I was, but there was no hope of using it. The block had been removed and the breech cover bent, so that a new block couldn't be inserted.[43]

There was nothing to do but stay in that hole—and keep the German there with me. I pushed his body into a corner in a sitting position and wedged his heels into the dirt so that his legs would take up as little space as possible. Then I got as far away from him as I could.

Whenever the noise of firing died down, the night all around was filled with cries, groans, curses. In English. In German. In languages I didn't know. Cries for water, for help, for death. Once I heard one boy ask another if he had any chewing-gum. I wouldn't have minded having a little myself.

Another boy babbled over and over for hours it seemed to me, "What is this war? What's this war for? What is this damned war?"

A faint lightening began in the sky where the sun ought to be. Then I heard a man kicking his way slowly through the brush quite near my hole. He was calling in low tones, and the words were German. I eased myself up the bank on the side toward him, my pistol ready in case he was headed my way.

I'd hardly got him located to my satisfaction when someone rushed him from the brush to his left. I heard what sounded like a blow, and the German gave a frightened cry. After that it was quiet.

In the morning I found that he'd been bayoneted straight through from side to side, just below the ribs. He was a big fellow—an officer. He'd evidently been trying to get some of his men together. It was Nigger Floyd's bayonet that had got him.

Floyd, as I've said, wasn't good on long-range shooting, but at this kind of close fighting he was hard to beat. He liked to get into a position where he could tackle his man hand to hand. And he was always around when a raid of any kind was in prospect. In action, he usually carried his trench knife in his teeth, like the Algerians. And they weren't any more dangerous than he was.

The dawn—it was a very foggy dawn—came at last. Now I could see what I'd only had to listen to before. But at least I wasn't going to be alone much longer.

I peeped over the edge of my hole. I could make out blurred shapes through the mist, but I couldn't be sure whether they were trees, men, or guns. It grew lighter, and the fog lifted some. I saw then that there was another hole a little way to my right; a man in it had his gun trained directly on me.

A long time I sat still, watching him. Then some sound made him turn his head, without disturbing the aim of his gun. The movement gave him away. It was Floyd. I called to him and he answered.

He asked me if there was room for him in my hole, and when I said yes he started crawling over to it. He had the Luger of the German officer he'd bayoneted and his silver pocket flask. It had had schnapps in it when Floyd took it—but it was empty now.

He asked me if I'd searched the German I'd killed, and I said no. I didn't want to. So he did. He didn't find anything of much value or interest. The Luger and the extra clip of ammunition he turned over to me.

I felt I'd stayed in that hole as long as I could, so we decided to make a break for some of our own troops. We had to go very cautiously. We could see Germans moving around just inside the woods—we knew them by the shape of their helmets; it was still too dark to make out the color of their clothes.

I took a rifle from a dead American to replace my lost shotgun. He'd been shot through the side, and he looked as if he was sleeping until you noticed the bloody foam on his lips. He was lying close to a young German who had a bayonet stuck through his body just under the arm and out through the other shoulder. There was a clear trail in the mud where the American had crawled over to him, and there was an American canteen gripped in his hand.

More or less fighting began again as the light grew stronger. Once a grenade burst right behind us. It tore open Floyd's pants and blew him full of dirt, but not a fragment hit us. Soon we began to run into groups of our men. They told us orders were circulating that we were to police the woods. We learned why there were so few of us. The Germans had thrown a barrage behind us that had shut off our support companies.

No one had any news of Jesse, but someone told us that Sergeant

Nayhone had been knocked out by a shell early in the engagement. We couldn't get any line on how serious it was.

We managed to salvage a little food out of a German pack, and as we made our way slowly to the right our men became thicker and the Germans fewer. Tom was the first of our own gang we came across, and he told us which way to look for Jesse.

Tom had a Luger. He waved it at me. "I got one o' the damn things too," he said.

When we found Jesse he told us he was going out on a scouting expedition and wanted us to go along. A new officer, Captain Smith, had been brought up and was commanding the part of the battalion which had succeeded in getting into the woods.

Jesse told us he was a fine chap. He knew his business and he was trying to get the men together and organized. He wanted to know just where they were and what shape they were in.

But when we asked Jesse if he'd talked to Captain Smith about this patrol, he said: "No time. I'll tell him about it when we get back."

Our troops held only the edge of the woods, while the Germans in considerable numbers still held the rest of it. They had us ringed about from the interior of the woods with a thin line of riflemen. These were serving as observers of our movements and as a screen, so we couldn't know what was being done by the larger bodies of troops back of them in the woods.

Jesse's plan was to penetrate that screen and find out what was going on behind it.

When he got through explaining it, Floyd stood and looked at him. Then he said, "Say, are you shell-shocked or plain crazy?"

"Well, if you birds don't feel like going, it's all right with me. I'll get somebody else," Jesse said.

It was a wild scheme, but I had a lot of confidence in Jesse and I didn't much care what happened. "I'm with you. How about it, Floyd?"

He said: "All right. Might as well get ours now as any other time. Let's go!"

We were each armed with a rifle and a belt of ammunition. Jesse had three forty-fives; Floyd had a forty-five, a Luger, and his trench knife; I had a forty-five and a Luger. We had our pistols stuck into our waistbands where they'd be handy. We made this more comfortable by tucking our blouses inside our breeches.

Jesse had worked the thing out carefully. We'd got almost through the screen of observers when we came upon a German sentry only a few yards to our right. Floyd was closest to him. He signaled to us to stop. Then he crept up on the German and stabbed him from behind with his trench knife so quickly that there was no cry, and no noise, except the sound of the heavy body falling.

All through these forests were small open meadows, then trees again, with rather thick undergrowth. The undergrowth made it hard to go quietly. But as the light got better the fighting warmed up, and the firing helped to cover up any noise we might make.

Every now and then we could see the Germans moving about farther back in the woods. They were evidently organizing to stop our troops from advancing farther.

In a little hollow we came upon the bodies of an American sergeant and six privates laid out in a row. It looked as if they'd been disarmed, lined up, and shot. Their uniforms had been badly torn and the pockets ripped open by those who'd searched them. Jesse and Floyd looked at each other. Neither one of them said anything.

But I knew these two Indians well enough to know that scene meant trouble for the next Germans they ran into.

I hadn't liked the way Floyd treated prisoners, nor his little habit of helping himself to anything he could find on the bodies of the dead Germans. He had a collection of wristwatches, some of them worth a lot. One of platinum must have belonged to an officer of high rank. But as we kept on running across sights like this—and worse—I didn't mind what Floyd did so much.

We went on again. We were making our way through a patch of bushes, Jesse and Floyd a few steps ahead and to the right and left of me. We found ourselves suddenly in a little clearing—hardly ten feet from the center of a column of Germans: four squads of riflemen, and two squads of machine-gunners carrying two heavy Maxims, all set to go into action.

They had halted there and they seemed as surprised as we were. Floyd was the first to open up. He dropped the machine-gun officer, who had whirled around directly in front of him. Then Jesse chimed in with his pistols, and I got three Germans with three shots from my rifle. It was too slow. I let the rifle go and yanked out my pistols.

By the time the Germans had really waked up to what was going on, we'd had time to pepper them with shots and dive back into the thicket. They sent bullets cracking after us, and a flock of grenades. But we dodged the bullets somehow, and the grenades burst behind us. I lost my helmet when I stumbled once, but I didn't stop to pick it up.

The firing started something in that part of the woods. Rifles and machine-guns were cracking all around us. We were getting back toward our own troops now, but the woods seemed full of Germans.

Jesse got separated from us as we fought out of the thicket into more open woods. We could see him a little way to the left. Floyd and I ran over a group of Germans who'd been killed by our shell fire the day before. We grabbed a Mauser and a belt of cartridges apiece as we ran.[44]

The fire now got so heavy that there was nothing for it but to drop into shell holes. I felt pretty naked down there with my head bare, and wished for a minute I'd taken one of the German helmets. But I knew that would have made me a target for American fire, and I knew what their marksmanship was. I thought I stood a better chance with the Germans.

After a while Floyd called to ask me if there was room in my shell hole for him, and said he was coming over. I stuck my rifle and head up over the edge of the hole while he came crawling toward me, pushing his rifle before him. A German sniper, running back from the direction of our lines, stopped and took a shot at Floyd, which splashed the dirt in his face. I got the German before he had time for a second shot, and Floyd tumbled into my hole, safe.

I'd been hearing a light Browning cracking away down near where

I thought Jesse must be.[45] A Browning meant he was among friends. We decided to go over and join him. We made a dash for it, and just as we neared a shell hole Jesse popped his head up.

"Duck!" he yelled.

But there was no place to duck. We had to keep on going while the bullets kept up with us. We tumbled into Jesse's hole. It was so small it would hardly hold all of us.

Jesse said, "Some damned Heinie has got hold of a Browning."

"He got me," Floyd said.

Floyd had been hit in the left arm. We pulled off his blouse, and Jesse slit the sleeve of his shirt. The bullet had gone through the fleshy part of the arm without striking the bone. With proper care it shouldn't be a bad wound.

Jesse started to bind up the arm with a first-aid bandage. He said: "We ought to get some iodine on it." But Floyd only said: "*Tie that knot and get through with it!* I suppose it'll get stiffer than hell. Somebody'll pay for this!"

We could tell from the sounds our advance were getting close now. We could hear the "crack" of the Springfield bullets and the "plunking" of the rifles.

Jesse put his helmet on the muzzle of his rifle and held it up above the edge of the hole. In a few minutes we heard a trampling of feet. Then a voice yelled: "Hey, James! What you doin' in there? Gold-bricking?"

"Keep on north a couple o' hundred yards. You'll find out plenty soon how much gold-bricking we've been doing!"

They passed us, and we crawled out and headed for the rear, looking for someone to report to. There was a steady roll of rifle fire deep in the woods now, and German prisoners began to trickle back. There were too few of us there to send anyone to guard these prisoners and many of them had merely been disarmed, given a kick in the pants, and headed toward our rear. There was nothing to prevent their picking up arms and doing a lot of damage if they chose.

We got back, however, and reported to Captain Smith. Then we set out again for the front lines. We'd discovered that the closer you were to the Germans the better off you were. The rear lines were being heavily shelled and chances were considerably better up with the snipers and machine-guns. On our way up we ran across Tom. He had a bandaged left hand and we asked him what had happened.

"I picked me a tough one!" he said. "But I ain't hurt very bad."

That was all we could get out of him.

"What you fellows goin' to do?" he asked.

Jesse grinned. "We're goin' up and run this damned war to suit ourselves."

Tom said, "Wish I could go, but somebody's gotta stick around and take care o' th' damned rookies."

"Well, that's what you get for bein' a corporal!" Jesse said.

When we'd pushed on up a little farther Mike overtook us. Someone had told him we were headed for the front line, and he wanted to join us. As usual he had a shotgun—his favorite equipment.

Jesse said, "You can come along. But don't belly-ache if you get killed."

We had come now to the point where the Germans were contesting every inch of ground with a storm of light machine-gun and rifle fire. They were using snipers too, and our men were falling right and left.

We kept gaining ground, but always at a stiff price. The new men were suffering most; they tried to hurry things too much. The old-timers had learned how to go slow and make their fire count. There was a lot of bayonet fighting.

Early in the game I stumbled on the boy who'd left the little mademoiselle crying when we set out from our last training billets. He was fighting for breath and his face was twisted with pain. He was too far gone to know me, and I saw that he was past help.

We were free lances in that fight—Jesse, Floyd, Mike, and I. We ranged up and down the line wherever the hunting was best. We were under no one's orders. When one of us had lined up on some German crew he'd pass the word. If the nest was within long range of Mike's shotgun all four of us would bombard it. On the singles, we worked as individuals. It was a damned busy morning.

They were certainly killers—those two Indians and that little Italian. I didn't realize until afterward that I was a killer too.

13

No Hard Feelings!

About noon our two support companies got across the open, and preparations were made to resume the attack. The next objective was to be another woods still farther north, the Bois de Cunel.

While the reorganization was going on we had a chance to get some rest. We slept until two o'clock in the afternoon, when Mike woke the rest of us up. Floyd's arm had stiffened. Jesse took a look at it and said it seemed to be all right. Floyd set his teeth, flexed it a few times and said it would do.

We found that a lot of work had been done. The wounded had been gathered up and carried to the south edge of the woods to wait for darkness when it would be safe to move them farther back. The 2nd Battalion had come up and was to attack with us. The officers had been redistributed, but we were getting back fast to the old Marne conditions and there weren't nearly enough to go round. Many of the platoons were commanded by sergeants.

Sergeant Nayhone was out of it, for how long we didn't know. When Jesse reported to the battalion commander he was put in charge of Intelligence details. He turned the administrative end of things over to Corporal Rissey, who was better qualified for it than he was. He paid no attention to Floyd's protest at this.

Floyd took it out in grumbling to me. He'd always been suspicious of Rissey because he'd been brought up in a German-American settlement and spoke German like a native.

I said, "Cut it out. Jesse knows what he's doing. Rissey's a damned good soldier."

Floyd said, "If I catch him pullin' any funny stuff it'll sure be too wet to plow for him!"

Jesse got together all the snipers he could find and distributed them along the battalion front. Word drifted along the line that Old Man Buck and General Sladen and Colonel Dorey had all been up there to look us over. That bucked us up. The Third Division was officered by real men, and it helped us a lot to know it.

We hopped off about four. But we hadn't hopped far when we saw that it was no use. Our artillery were giving us everything they had, but you can't make a siege gun out of a seventy-five, and the Germans had prepared those positions to hold. We were exposed to the bombardment from the Bois de Cunel, and to withering machine-gun fire from a hill the Germans still occupied on our left.

Before orders finally came through to stop the attack and return to cover in the woods, I'd had time to get myself into a mess. While we were in the worst of the firing I snatched up a helmet and put it on in place of the one I'd lost the day before. I felt considerably safer. And as long as the excitement was going on I didn't notice anything wrong. But when we'd settled down in the woods again I suddenly waked up to the fact that my head was tingling and itching.

It wasn't cooties. I knew what they felt like. I took off the helmet and sniffed at the inside of it. The helmet had been splashed with mustard gas.[46] I tried to wash my head with water from my canteen. It didn't do any good. The top of my head and the back of my neck where the helmet strap had touched burned worse and worse. I began to look for Jesse.

He was back near battalion headquarters. But he was in worse shape than I was. He'd hopped off with one of our first waves and been driven into a shell hole by machine-gun fire. The shell hole had gas in it, but there wasn't any other place to go. He put on his gas mask but the eye-protector part had been split by a bullet. His eyes had been pretty badly burned. He could hardly keep them open, and the tears were running down his cheeks.

He said, "I'll be all right in an hour or two. I didn't stay there long. I ducked back here to the woods the first chance I got."

Floyd was there too—in a bad humor. He said his arm was giving him thunder. We had a council of war to decide whether to report to the pill-rollers.[47]

Jesse settled it. He said, "Damn it, we can still use our legs. If we tell 'em what's happened they'll pin a tag on one of us sure as hell!"[48]

So we sent Floyd back to the pill-rollers to get as many first-aid bandages as he could. He told some cock-and-bull story about needing them for the company, and while they were getting the bandages for him he stole an eight-ounce bottle of iodine. Inside of thirty minutes he was back with his loot.

There wasn't much to do for Jesse. He said, "I don't need anything but a whale of a lot more quiet than you birds are putting out!"

So I went to work on Floyd. He took off his blouse, and when I got the old bandages off his arm I found it pretty badly swollen. I wiped it off first with a piece of bandage soaked in iodine. I was trying to be careful and not hurt him.

He said, "Don't be so damned chicken-livered, Punk. Get a little of that panther blood in where it'll do some good!"

He gave me directions how to push a twig through the wound and work it up and down, while I poured iodine in until it started to come through on the other side. The job made me sick, but Floyd never moved a muscle except to squint his eyes a little and stiffen his jaw. When I had the arm all bandaged he patted me on the shoulder.

"Pretty good, runt! Damned if you won't make a soldier when you grow up!"

Then he had me sit down and hold a first-aid compress tight against my eyes while he gave me an iodine shampoo. I'd rather have all my teeth pulled than go through that again. When he said I could take the compress away it was wetter than it had been to start with.

Jesse had his eyes opened and was squinting at me. "How's he coming?" he asked.

Floyd grabbed two or three hairs and pulled on them. "They're getting tighter already!" he said.

I had to laugh with them in spite of the fire on the top of my head.

Jesse took what was left of the iodine and painted streaks across my face. He stood back and looked at his work, then at Floyd.

"I'll be goddamned if I don't believe he belongs to the old tribe!" he said.

I knew those two Indians well enough to understand that that wasn't just a joke to them.

It was growing dark by that time, but there was still work to be done. Men were so scarce that Intelligence men and even officers had to pitch in and help. We were put on details to help to take care of the wounded and organize the position for better defense.

After a couple of hours of this Mike brought me word that I was wanted at headquarters. By that time I was in such misery that I had half a mind to hide out. But I knew what Jesse and Floyd would say to that. I reported for duty.

I found Sergeant Nayhone back. When he'd been knocked out by the shell the day before, he'd gone so dizzy that he tore off his mask and absorbed quite a bit of gas. He looked pretty sick now, but he was very much on the job. I found out later that he'd walked out on the medicos. He was needed too much to be spared from headquarters long.

I wasn't surprised to find several new officers about the headquarters dugout. Officers were like passing shadows with us now. It hardly paid to try to get acquainted with them. But one of these new ones came up and asked me all sorts of questions about the ground around there, checking my replies off on the map. He was a slenderly built, snappy fellow. I gathered that he was the new Intelligence officer and that he was testing me before sending me out on some duty.

Nayhone was waiting while he did this. Finally the officer nodded, and Nayhone began giving me my orders. They were sending picked men into our most advanced rifle lines to secure information about the present state of the German front. Nayhone pointed out the locality I was to work on and told me to get as far forward as I could. I was to report back not later than midnight.

Outside, I borrowed Mike's shotgun and a belt of shells. I was tired and hungry, and the top of my head was so sore I had to walk with a stiff back to keep my helmet from shifting its position. My mind flashed back to Major-General Buck's talk that day behind the lines. He'd said something about fighting harder than the Germans, no matter how hard they fought.

"I guess there's no use belly-aching about it," I said to myself. "The Old Man meant what he said. He takes his chances with the rest of us!"

I plodded on. I found our front lines about as hot a place as I wanted to be in. The Germans had been fed up on surprise attacks and didn't propose to have any more for a while. They were shooting flares and sending out patrols all over the place.

The German front line was so close that I couldn't get forward any farther than our own lines. Until nearly midnight I crawled up and down, trying to find an opening. But it was no use. The two lines were so close that we could hear the Germans talking. Some of them could speak English.

"Hey, 4th Infantry!" they would yell. Then they'd curse the 4th Infantry and the American army and President Wilson. They had a pleasant little habit of punctuating these remarks with grenades or bursts of machine-gun fire.

It was easy to tell that the men opposite us were fresh troops—not winded and broken down as we were. They were picked troops. The best of the German army was being thrown against us in that sector, and we were so exhausted that if you gave us half a chance we'd fall asleep before we hit the ground. We could go to sleep as soon as we got out of range of artillery fire. We hardly minded machine-guns any more. We were so used to them.

I went to sleep once in a little patch of woods and woke to find it all blown down.

But we weren't too tired to answer those Germans in their own kind of language. Whatever they had to say about President Wilson we matched with the things we said about the kaiser.

They got hold of some of our names. One German kept yelling at a Polack in our outfit who had a name that sounded like Kolchak to me.

"Hey, you Cupjack!" the German would yell. "Pring dose krenades over here!"

Then he'd laugh and turn loose a burst of machine-gun fire.

His talking and shooting gave away his position. As soon as he was sure where the German was, Kolchak crawled over there and shot him with his Springfield. He had to kill another one with his bayonet, and he came mighty close to getting killed himself. But he made it back to our line.

Shortly before midnight I ran across Floyd. He'd found a little bread in some German's pack and he gave me a piece of it.

"Say, Punk, how'd you like to be down in good ol' Missouri, sittin' at your mother's table, eatin' a nice, fat roast chicken?"

"For God's sake, can that stuff!" I said.

It made me feel funny. There we were half sick, half starved, sleepless, and lousy. And somewhere in the world there were beds, and food. ... I left Floyd grinning, and crawled on.

It was almost twelve o'clock when the call came along the line that I was wanted at headquarters.

I found the woods about headquarters as lively now as the front lines I'd just left. The shells that had been going over our heads in the last two or three hours had been landing here. I had to ask around before I could find headquarters. The one I'd left early in the evening had been blasted to pieces.

I located Nayhone at last in another dugout, alone. He reached for some maps to show me what he wanted me to do. At that moment a heavy shell lit just beyond the dugout and burst. Something came sailing down the entrance. The candles went out. On the outside a terrible racket began. Sergeant Nayhone lit the candles. The thing that had come down the dugout entrance was an arm in an O.D. sleeve.

One of our new men came running down the steps and knocked it out of Nayhone's hand. He was a handsome fellow, with a fine build. But his eyes had a funny, dazed kind of glare in them and he was making a horrible noise in his throat, half howling, half moaning.

He had a helmet and a gas mask in his hands. He dropped them when he saw us, and headed straight for me. He jammed me back against the wall in such a way that I couldn't use my strength against him. He was clutching the breast of my blouse with both hands. He had the flesh in his grip, too.

"Good God!" Nayhone said. "What next? . . . Get out of here!"

But the fellow clung to me tighter than ever. He was trembling, but he was crushing his hands down so hard it brought tears to my eyes. He didn't want to hurt me; he wanted me to help him, but he couldn't say anything—just kept up that crazy howling.

Nayhone's nerves were shot anyway. He didn't look at us. He said, "For God's sake, throw him out!"

I told the sergeant I couldn't handle him alone, and while Nayhone went to the door of the dugout I reached up and began to rub the back of the man's neck and his forehead. I couldn't do it as hard as I wanted to because of his arms, but it seemed to me he loosened up a little and his eyes lost some of their glare.

If I could have rubbed his back in a way Jesse had showed me I believe I could have helped him. But there was still foam on his lips, and he was still moaning, when a big blond soldier came down the steps in answer to Nayhone's call.

He was a new man, too, of German descent. He looked a lot like some of the men we'd just been killing. He seemed very calm and capable.

"What's wanted, sergeant?" he asked.

The shell-shocked soldier let go his hold and slid down to the floor in front of us. He put his head down in his arms and began to cry.

Nayhone pointed to him. "Take this man out," he said. "This is battalion headquarters, and there's work to be done!"

"He's pretty quiet now," the big blond said.

But Nayhone said, "Take him out!"

The man bent over and tried to talk to the fellow on the floor. When he saw that it had no effect he picked him up in his arms and started toward the steps.

He put up a fight when he knew he was being taken outside. He bit Blondy's hand. I started to help, but Nayhone ordered me back. He called some other men, and they carried him away, fighting and moaning. I was in a cold sweat from head to foot.

One of the men came back. "What shall we do with the coo-koo guy?"

Nayhone was white and trembling. "I don't know!" he said. "But if you don't let me work, you'll all be dead in another twenty-four hours."

The man went out. But all the while I was down there with Nayhone others kept coming down to report that there was a crazy fellow running loose up there and raising hell and what should they do about it?

Nayhone gave them orders to try to get him back to a first-aid station. But they couldn't do anything with him. He finally got away from them and wandered off toward the enemy's lines. I suppose he was killed. We never knew.

Nayhone took a deep breath and said, "Pull yourself together, Barkley." He told me that he had orders to post me for observing on the northeast slope of Hill 253.

I looked at him. I said, "That's in the rear of the Jerry line. And the place is lousy with them!"

"Ring off, I know what I'm talking about," he said.

"Maybe you do. But I'm not so crazy about getting information that I'm ready to go and ask the Germans to give it to me."

That riled him. "Good God Almighty! Can't you get it through your head that this is serious? The Germans are massing along our front. The 7th hasn't been able to get up. There's a gap between us and them. We've got to have information!"

I said, "Well, I don't see how getting a gap blown in me is going to get it for you."

I was pretty sure by that time that he hadn't had any orders about the thing at all. That it was his own idea, putting me up there in that particular observation post. It made me mad all the way through.

I said, "If you want to bump me off, for God's sake do it here! You can say I went crazy and attacked you, like that guy that was just in here."

He came down off his high horse then, and admitted it was his own idea. But he pointed out to me on the map just how serious the situation was.

He said, "The aviators haven't been able to find out a damned thing. And we've got to have information. You can see for yourself there's no way out. Somebody's got to go."

He held out his hand.

"I know you'll do the best you can. . . . And no hard feelings!" he said.

I shook his hand. "All right," I said. "No hard feelings! But write a nice letter home to my folks. . . ."

14

Valor Above and Beyond

Nayhone sent someone after a signal corps he'd told to wait near for orders. In a few minutes they came in, a corporal and two privates. Nayhone outlined to us what we were to do.

As we got away from the dugout we circled well around to the right. The signal corps men said the wire they were using was fine French wire and had to be laid where it would be out of the way of traffic.

As we crossed the valley it seemed to me that the firing was less general than it had been. But over toward Cunel the rifles and machine-guns were still clattering away. It sounded as if the gap between us and the 7th was about half a mile wide.

When we reached the spot we were headed for, on the northwest slope of Hill 253, I told the signal corps men to lie low while I reconnoitered for an observation post. I found a shell hole that seemed a good place. It was in a fringe of trees just outside the forest proper, and the top part of a tree had been blown down across it.

The corporal installed my phone and fixed it so that the bell wouldn't ring. There would be a slight buzz instead. I tested it. Sergeant Nayhone answered. I told him I was all set.

He said, "Good! Don't phone anything not of major importance. You're too close to them. They might hear you."

The signal corps men shook hands with me and wished me luck. They pulled out. It was two-thirty by my watch.

In a few minutes Sergeant Nayhone called. He told me he would call at short intervals all night to be sure that our connection was not broken, but that I was not to reply unless he asked a question or I had something to report. Instead of replying I was to scratch the mouth-piece with my fingernail. I was not to ring him unless I had to, and I was to make all reports in code.

About three o'clock I could hear the Germans moving about in the woods to my right, almost at my back, as I faced Hill 253. They seemed to be shifting farther to the left. This would bring them into the woods that covered the hill facing me to the right. The valley was narrow here. I could distinctly make out their commands and hear the clatter of their equipment and sounds of digging.

When I reported this to Nayhone I heard him chuckle.

Nothing much happened the rest of the night, and the worst part was my struggle to stay awake. I was knee-deep in mud. There were dead bodies around which smelled as if they'd been there considerably more than one day. There were no comforts provided with my seat behind the scenes.

I was pretty nearly light-headed from hunger and lack of sleep. Every now and then I tried rubbing my sore head, hoping the pain would wake me up. But even that didn't always work.

Once at least I must have passed out. I had the receiver clamped to my ear and was awakened by a voice repeating my name. I answered.

"Can't you ring me oftener?" I asked. "I'm damned near all through!"

Whoever was on the phone said, "Stay with it! You're doing excellently!"

I asked where Nayhone was. He told me the sergeant had collapsed and that they were working on him.

I heard another voice say, "We'll have to spare the sergeant all we can or we'll lose him."

Nayhone was one of the cleverest Intelligence men on the entire front. I could tell from their voices that they were mighty anxious about him.

Daylight came. I found it was a little easier to keep my eyes open now that there was something to use them for. Right away I saw why Nayhone had picked this post for observation.

It was on a ridge almost connected at an angle to the left with Hill 253. From their hill at my right the Germans would have to march down through the valley straight across my front, and up the slope of Hill 253, in order to get at our troops who were spread out along another hillside back and to the left of me and behind the crest of 253.

From my position on the highest point of the ridge I could see in every direction. The woods that concealed the Germans were very close. The valley was even narrower than I'd realized in the darkness. Behind me and to my left the tree-covered ridge ran back to the headquarters in Woods 250, from which I had come. To the right of headquarters, as I faced that way, and in the distance I could see Cunel.

Somewhere between our Woods 250 and Cunel the 7th was posted. Cunel was still German territory, linked with the hillside facing me by another ridge, which made a curving line around the far side of Hill 253.

The woods directly back of me had been full of Germans when I had taken up my position. I could see now that these had all been shifted around to the left and were being organized there on the top of the hill, probably for an assault on Hill 253.

The trees on their hill covered the whole slope down to the valley, but they weren't very thick or very large and I could discover a good deal by watching the officers as they moved about among their men. It gave me a fair idea as to their exact location and I made a rough estimate of their numbers.

They were doing no firing, and the movement was carried out with so much caution that I was sure it was a surprise attack they were planning. They hadn't figured on such a stunt as Nayhone had pulled off in posting an observer up there almost inside their lines.

When I had these things worked out I reported to headquarters. Nayhone was on the job again. I knew by the sly chuckle at the other end of the line that what I had told him was good news. I started to ask a question.

"What the hell!" he broke in. "I'm asking the questions. When I get through, if there's time for any more I'll let you know!"

After that there were several hours when nothing happened which seemed important enough to report, and I had plenty of time to think about the danger I was in. There wasn't anything so far as I knew to keep a German sniper in those woods at my back from discovering I was there. But after a while I got so tired and sleepy I stopped worrying.

There was no firing except from a few machine-guns near Cunel. There was only an occasional distant rumble of heavy artillery. The planes which were up, both over our lines and the Germans', seemed to be there for watching rather than for fighting. Several of our observation balloons hung above Montfaucon, and the German balloons were up well back of their lines. The balloons looked lazy.

But I'd been too long at the front to be fooled. The 79th and the 5th had taken this terrain once, and had been repulsed.[49] Now we were trying to take it back again. They had smashed through the woods back of me out into the open, and the hillside was covered with American and German dead. The American soldiers' packs had been ripped open, and thrown away empty. Everything of value had been carried off.

They had evidently tried to hold their formation as they burst from the woods, and had been met with machine-gun fire from the opposite hill. They were lying now in wave formation. Some of them must have rolled and twisted as they died, but not enough to disturb the outlines of that wave.

Near my shell hole most of the dead were Germans. I was tempted to crawl out and see if I could find food or something to drink in one of their packs.

I didn't want to use up my own supply. But the risk of being seen was too great. I settled down again to fight my fatigue; it was making me as numb as if I'd been doped.

About noon a couple of German machine-guns began to fire from the woods well to my right. They were firing over in the direction of Cunel. Presently the 7th began snapping back. I chose that moment to pass out completely.

The thing that brought me back was hearing a voice in the receiver clamped over my ears. The voice was saying, "I wonder where the hell he's gone now!"

I answered. It was evidently one of our new officers, and he was pretty hard-boiled.

"You're in a hell of a poor place to take a nap!" he snapped. I told him I'd try to do better.

He asked me if I'd seen the air fight to my left. I hadn't. He said one of our planes had been knocked down. I knew from the way he talked and from his excitement about the plane that he was new. A plane getting knocked down was nothing to the old-timers. They'd lost interest in everything but a real "dog fight."

I asked him about Nayhone, and he told me he was asleep. He repeated the remark I'd heard before in the night that "the old sergeant was nearly gone. They'd have to look after him."

Early in the afternoon the enemy artillery started firing in the neighborhood of Cunel. Our guns began to answer. The one-fifty-fives were shelling the German rear over the hilltop to my right.[50] I began to wake up then. I always got over being sleepy when there was something going on.

A little later my phone buzzed. "Be on your toes!" said Nayhone's voice. "Stay with your phone as long as you can!"

Over around Cunel the German artillery fire kept increasing. At the same time movements among the Germans in front of me indicated that they were getting ready for action. While I was reporting this to Nayhone, the German artillery opened heavily against Woods 250.

"Stay with it as long as you can," Nayhone said. "Take care of yourself. If anything—" The phone went dead.

I knew what had happened. The line had been cut by shell fire.

I figured that that let me out as far as observation was concerned. But it didn't tell me what to do next. I could run the risk of being seen by snipers and work my way back into the woods. From there I could probably get safely back to headquarters. Or I could stay and do a little sniping on my own account when the Germans began to come out from the shelter of the woods. I was sorry I didn't have a machine-gun.

I studied the ground, trying to make up my mind what to do. Some seventy-five yards farther out on the ridge, and in a perfect strategic position, was a light tank that had evidently been abandoned in the fighting several days before.[51]

From the way in which dead German bodies were scattered around it, I figured it out that the tank must have burst from the woods behind me and surprised a considerable group of Germans. It looked as if the tank crew had killed thirty-five or forty before they were finally knocked out.

I couldn't help thinking what I could do if I had a machine-gun out there in that tank. But there were seventy-five yards of open ground between me and the tank, and the sun was shining straight down on the ridge. I gave up speculating about the tank, and concentrated on what I actually might be able to do.

An old Intelligence man at the school had told me once to pick up a German machine-gun block the first chance I had and always to carry it with me. There were usually plenty of guns left behind in fought-over territory, but the Germans made a practice of throwing away the breech-blocks. Without this block the gun is useless. It is a little thing, but the firing device is in it.

I had learned about the mechanism of the German guns at the school, and had been carrying one of those breech-blocks for weeks. It had been worn bright in my hip pocket. It hurt when I sat down, and when it seemed to me I was getting a calloused place from it, I'd change it to another pocket.

I had spotted a light Maxim and a few boxes of ammunition not very far from me among a bunch of dead Germans. There were several shell holes at the edge of the woods, and I decided to try to make it to one of these, getting hold of the Maxim and some ammunition on the way.

If I got by without being picked off by a sniper, I could make things interesting for the Germans for a while. And I'd be under cover of the woods where I could duck if things got too hot.

The Germans were beginning to appear now, moving around in considerable numbers all along the edge of their woods. They looked like Jagers to me—a good fighting outfit made up of men from thirty to thirty-five years old, usually heavy-set and strong.[52] They were carrying a lot of material; grenades, heavy machine-guns as well as light, and machine-gun ammunition.

I worked my way out of my hole and back toward the pile of dead men where I'd seen the machine-gun. I made a good target, but there seemed to be no snipers on the job. That meant I had a pretty good chance of getting back safe to headquarters if I made a run for it now.

I had reached the gun I was making for. I had my hand on it when our artillery opened up on the woods all around there with smoke shells. In thirty seconds I was cut off from the Germans on the opposite hill by a screen of smoke.

All of a sudden I saw what I could do under cover of that screen. I grabbed the gun and all the ammunition I could carry and raced for the tank. When I was inside it, I looked the gun over. It was minus a breechblock, and the water-jacket was nearly empty.[53] Otherwise it was in good condition, and it had an extra barrel lashed to the water-jacket. I snapped my breechblock in and tested it. It worked.

I was in the firing compartment of the baby tank, which was large enough for two men, a machine-gun, and ammunition. The gun was gone, and the only thing left of the men who'd been in it was a bloody leather helmet on the floor.

I went outside again. I found the doors to the driver's compartment open, and closed them. Then I set to work collecting boxes of ammunition. I kept one eye on the smokescreen.

Quite close to the tank a bunch of German machine-gunners had been killed before they'd had time to make much of an impression on their ammunition. And they had been well stocked. There were piles of boxes that hadn't been touched. It looked as if there had been a reserve supply located right at that spot.

I worked fast, for I didn't know what moment the smokescreen would lift. When I had more than four thousand rounds inside the tank I began piling the boxes up just outside where I could reach them from the door. As I found out later, they were piled in such a way that whenever I pulled out a box another one would fall over toward me. That was just a piece of luck. It would have been pretty bad if they'd happened to tilt away from me instead.

I took a good look at the screen. It was thinning, but I still had a few minutes left. I ran back to where one of our boys was lying. I don't know how he came to be there. All the others I'd seen—American or German—had been dead for several days. This was a Seventy-Ninth Division man, but he had apparently been killed only the night before, and his pack and belongings hadn't been touched.

When I'd passed him on my last trip to the gun with ammunition I'd noticed that he had a loaf of French-issue bread tied to his pack. I couldn't remember now when I had had anything to eat, and the sight of that bread had made me so weak with hunger that I decided it was worth the risk to go back and get it.

That bread stopped the growling in my stomach for a while, but it made me more conscious than before of my thirst. I had about four inches of water left in my canteen, but I didn't dare to drink it. I'd seen too many boys use up their last drops of water. I didn't know how much worse I might need it later. There had been water in my shell hole, but we never touched water in shell holes. If it had been gassed—and it usually had—it killed you.

I set up my gun. The firing port had been cut for a French gun on a tank mount and was larger than necessary for the one I had. That meant a chance for bullets to come in around the opening. But there was nothing I could do about it except be careful how I swung the turret.

I emptied several boxes of ammunition, hanging the belts over the sling in the turret which the gunner uses for a seat, and threw out the empty boxes. I shoved my gun out the firing port, inserted a belt of shells, and turned the turret so that the gun was pointing toward the place I'd last seen the Germans.

I dropped one belt over my left shoulder, and pulled the gun back into the turret, so that the tank would look as it had before I moved in. Then I peeped again through the gun port.

The screen was nearly gone, but a haze partly hid the woods on the hill across from me. I took a look out of the turret door, back toward our lines. No one was in sight. Shells were still bursting in the neighborhood of Woods 250. I could see a little sky now through the haze. I closed the turret door.

I wondered why our artillery fire had stopped. Afterward I found out that they had run short of ammunition. They were having a pretty hard time just then, struggling through the mud with heavy guns and trucks. They were dead-tired. But they didn't stop struggling. Later in the day I had proof of that.

When I'd made all the preparations I could think of, I settled down in the tank to wait for the Germans to start moving out of the shelter of their woods. The air was clear again, and I could see quite well through the port.

I tried not to think about anything. My legs felt wobbly. I hoped if there was any God, he'd give me the breaks.

Then I forgot everything, for through my port I'd caught a glimpse of movement at the edge of the woods.

I watched while the Germans marched out into the open in a formation resembling our squad columns, sending up several flares as they came. They were moving diagonally across my front toward the crest of Hill 253. The nearest column must have been less than two hundred yards from my tank. I estimated that there were between five and six hundred men all together, a battalion made up of four companies—vigorous and fresh.

I turned the turret very slowly, to keep pace with their progress. I waited until their rear elements had left the woods and started up the slope of Hill 253. By that time the leading elements were beginning to spread out.

I had them where I wanted them. My fire would rake them directly from the flank. If I didn't fire into the ground . . . or too high. . . .

I took a long breath, worked the barrel of my gun out through the port, picked the direction of fire that promised the greatest results all the way across to the farther flank, let out a little breath, laid the gun waist-high on the man who was closest to me, and eased down on the trigger.

15

Scarlet Fields

The surprise seemed to paralyze the Germans for a moment. They huddled together, and looked desperately about in every direction. They couldn't understand where machine-gun bullets, at such short range, could be coming from. Then they saw the tank and started ducking for cover. But there was no cover in the open field for most of them, and they were some distance from the woods.

I took advantage of their surprise and confusion. As fast as I could relay the gun I fired burst after burst of ten to fifteen shots. I finished one belt, and jammed in the one I had on my shoulder. I finished the second belt with long bursts. The German who had carried that gun had her beautifully adjusted. She fairly purred.

As I inserted the third belt I heard the gun gurgle; I knew that I'd have to go a little slower. Rifle bullets were beating a steady tattoo on the tank now. They couldn't do the tank any harm, but they could come in through the opening around the gun. And my ears were catching hell. It's calculated that each one of those bullets strikes almost a ton blow.

Before I went into action I'd located a group of officers. I found them again after a moment's search. There was no cover where they were, and they'd thrown themselves on the ground.

If my gun had been on a line with them they'd have been pretty safe where they were. But the gun port was five feet above the level of the ground. I trained the gun on the ones in the center and gave them a long burst. I got two. The rest scrambled up and started running for the woods. On the next burst I bobbled. By the time I was lined up again they were close to the woods.

I gave them a burst for good-by and got the slowest. He was a big fat fellow. One of the others stopped to try to drag him in, and a bullet got him too.

While this was going on, the Germans left on the slope of the hill had had time to get machine-guns, light and heavy, pointed in my direction. The fire upon the tank was so heavy it seemed to me as if it must melt.

Tanks are cone-shaped, and made so that bullets can only bounce off or shatter into fragments. But it sounded as if a thousand trip-hammers were battering against the metal. And when I swung the turret back to return the fire from the hill, I wished that hole in the turret hadn't been so big.

I didn't dare to fire as fast now as I had at first. My gun was getting pretty hot. I had used up the better part of two belts, and seen a number of German guns go out of commission, when the rattle against my tank redoubled. The Germans back in the woods on the hill to my right had set some guns and opened up on me.

I hoped they didn't have any tank rifles.[54] A tank rifle shoots a long bronze-colored bullet. This doesn't glance off or shatter into fragments; it goes right through the tank. Even without a tank rifle things were getting a little uncertain. Several bullets came in through the port.

I stopped every few minutes to let my gun cool off and to open up boxes of ammunition. But the gun was beginning to boil and smoke. I poured all the water from my canteen into the jacket. The water boiled back in my face and over my hands. It nearly scalded me. But I kept swinging from the Germans on the hill back to those in the woods. This way neither crowd had much time for thinking.

One fellow in the woods was getting pretty accurate aim on me. Once he landed a burst squarely around my port opening, and two of his bullets came in. He was under cover of the woods where I couldn't get back at him.

I shifted my attention to Hill 253. Ever since I'd started firing from the tank, I'd noticed a queer thing. There was no machine-gun fire coming from our lines. But from some point back about a thousand yards to my left I kept hearing a rifle being fired, very temperately and slowly. If I happened to be looking at the slope of the hill at the same moment when I heard that report, I saw a German out there tumble on his face.

All the rest of the afternoon that methodical firing went on. I couldn't figure it out. I watched for a while, between my own shots. Then I swung my turret back toward the woods.

Sometime in the afternoon a patrol of about twenty headed my way, carrying two light Maxims and a lot of grenades. They got halfway across the little valley. I knocked over one of the men armed with Maxims, and went after the other. They dodged from shell hole to shell hole, and kept on coming.

The fellow with the second Maxim was slowed up a little by the weight of his gun, and I finally got him. But by that time one of the other men had recovered the first gun and had got into a position not more than seventy-five yards away from me. The Germans in the woods opposite ceased firing so as not to hit their own patrol.

That fellow with the Maxim used his head. He started firing straight at the barrel of my gun. If he had hit it he'd have put the gun out of commission. I whirled the turret toward him. He was a brave man. He stood up in his shell hole and, with head and shoulders exposed, he tried to beat me to getting a burst home.

The odds were all on me. I swung the sights just below his gun and fired. I was sorry. But it had to be one of us.

In the meantime the rest of the patrol had crowded up and were working on me with grenades. But those old spud-mashers didn't do the tank any more harm than hailstones on a turtle's shell.[55] If they could have got close enough to throw a whole bunch of grenades together, they might have put the tank out of business. But I didn't mean to let them get that close.

I wasn't having much luck with them, however, and I was getting pretty worried about the men back on Hill 253, when a shell from a

German seventy-seven burst right in the middle of the patrol. That patrol got away from there in a hurry!

I swung the turret to look for the seventy-seven. Another shell burst below me, but farther up the slope toward me—much closer. They were raising their elevation. I tried to locate the flash of the gun, but the opening in the port was a small place to look through.

The third shell fell short of the tank, but not very far. The fourth sailed overhead and landed beyond me. But on that fourth flash I'd located the gun. It was in the edge of the woods at the far end of the valley—some six hundred yards away from me.

Before I could get my sights placed there was a terrific crash—on the tank, in the air, inside the tank. A sharp blow against my chin—a ringing in my ears—and blackness.

I couldn't have been out long. I woke up strangling. There was a heavy weight on my chest; it was a box of machine-gun cartridges. I fought that off. I was still strangling. I found myself grabbing at my throat, trying to get my shirt open. I tore off all the buttons. I heard a gurgling sound, and saw that it was blood.

I thought I was dying. Then I discovered that the blood was coming from my nose. But I still felt stifled, and I was getting weak from the loss of blood and the heat in the tank. I wanted water and air. But I'd long ago emptied my canteen into the gun barrel, and the only air was outside the tank in a rain of German bullets.

Then I realized that the bullets had stopped beating against the tank. I threw open the turret door and put my head and shoulders out. I felt better right away. The flow of blood stopped. And I saw why there were no more bullets coming my way.

The German troops had reformed on the slope of Hill 253 and were advancing toward the crest. Here they were being met by a deadly fire from American machine-guns. These must have been set up on our side of the hill while the Germans were busy with my tank. The minute a German head rose above the top of the hill it became a target for our gunners on the farther slope. I found out afterward that they were the 7th Machine-Gun outfit.

The Germans were being kept busy enough. I suppose they thought that fifth shell had put me out of the game, for they weren't even watching the tank now. Their dead were piled thick everywhere on the slope in front of me.

I drew back inside the tank and closed the door. The stock of my machine-gun was canted up against the roof. I figured that that was what had hit me in the face. I moved the gun, and outside something slid down off of it. I didn't know until I worked it out afterward that it was the caterpillar chain of the tank. The shell had torn it loose, and it had hit the top of the tank, then bounced over so that it rested on the gun barrel where it projected from the turret.

I found that part of the stock had been cracked and loosened. I fixed that by binding it with an empty machine-gun belt. Otherwise the gun seemed to be all right.

I swung the turret very slowly and relocated the seventy-seven. There were a good many Germans around on the hillside now, but it was that gun I was interested in.

I wasn't at all sure how my gun would shoot at such a long range, but I was certainly going to take a chance. I opened several boxes of ammunition and inserted a new belt in the gun. The rest I hung across the sling, except two that I dropped over my left shoulder where I could get them in a hurry.

I was all set again—if the gun still worked.

I could see several men, probably gunners, clustered about the seventy-seven. I pushed my muzzle out—I was using battle sights because of the long range—I laid the gun exactly where I wanted it, and fired.

I gave that seventy-seven a whole belt before I stopped. I fired under it and over it. To the right of it and to the left. Several bursts I sent straight at it. I wanted to get the gun itself as well as the men who were firing it.

There was no more trouble from the seventy-seven. But the Germans all around there had waked up to the fact that the tank hadn't been put out of commission after all. They reopened on me with rifles and machine-guns. I went back to my old tactics of swinging from the woods at my right to the slope of Hill 253 at my left, and back again.

Now the gun began to give real trouble. I had a jam every three or four shots. A few minutes of that, and it became a single action. I had to pull the operating crank for almost every shot.

I knew I'd come to the end of my row. Bullets were spattering against the tank from all sides. They couldn't send a patrol out for me as long as that kept up. But neither could I get out of the tank and make a break for the woods.

Yet that was the only way I had any chance at all. The driver's compartment was in the end toward the woods. I decided to crawl through into that, wait until there was a slackening in the fire, then run for it.

But just inside the door of the driver's compartment I found a can filled with thin oil. I scrambled back into the turret. I broke all speed records dismounting the gun, getting in the new barrel, and setting the gun up again. I poured oil in the water jacket until it overflowed.

I'd salvaged a little water from the old jacket, but not much.

I took a look at the woods through the port. The nearest group of Germans had started a patrol my way. I whirled the turret toward them, and they ducked for cover.

I poured a little oil in the breech mechanism, inserted a belt of shells, and thrust the muzzle out through the port. Then I pulled the trigger. The old girl came right through with a purr.

I felt better. But just at that moment a spud-masher burst against the turret.

The patrol had come up so close that I couldn't depress the gun enough to work on them successfully. But I kept on firing short bursts at them, and they were afraid to leave their cover in the shell holes. All of a sudden I noticed that, when one of them ducked into a hole, he'd left a big bag of grenades outside. I knocked off my helmet, placed the stock on top of my shoulder, laid on that sack of grenades, and gave it a burst.

It went off with the roar of a six-inch shell! The concussion shook the tank. Flying pieces of the grenades got several of the patrol. The rest watched their chance and got back to safety in the woods.

I took up my old job of peppering first the hillside and then the woods. I fired as accurately as I could, and slowly. But the gun began to overheat again, and this time it fried oil. It wasn't long before the turret stank so that I could hardly breathe. Worse than that, the smoke around the gun was so thick it was almost impossible to see through it to aim. It was beginning to grow dark outside, too, and targets were much less distinct.

About this time I found I had nearly used up my ammunition. I eased the door open a little way and dragged in several of the boxes I'd piled outside.

I kept on firing, but the gun began to have a stoppage every now and then. When I had to take a few seconds off to cool the gun I'd drag some more boxes of shells into the tank. One such time I spent trying out my Luger and my forty-five. I wanted to be sure that I had a shooting chance, if a patrol got to me, or if I stuck it out and made a dash for the woods after dark.

I didn't like those intervals between fighting. They gave me too much time to think. And my thoughts were getting pretty black.

The gun began to stutter so badly after a while that I knew I'd have to give it a real rest. I didn't even try to keep a lookout for patrols. If they were coming, they were coming. There was nothing I could do about it.

I just sat there, with my head in my hands, waiting. I told myself I was waiting for the gun to cool off. But it was really the end I was waiting for. I couldn't hold out much longer with a gun that would fire only once in a while.

Suddenly a new sound came crashing through the noise the bullets made against my tank. I jumped up and swung the turret toward it to look out. Shells from our artillery were bursting all over the slope of Hill 253.

My gun had cooled down a little and I joined in, firing as fast as I dared. The next time the gun began to stutter, I swung the turret around where I could get a view of Woods 250 away in the rear.

I could see troops filing out toward the Bois de Cunel. I supposed it was the 4th moving forward. But it turned out to be some of the

30th Infantry relieving our men. I learned afterward that one of their observers had kept watch of my tank all that afternoon and telephoned everything that happened back to their headquarters. Of course they didn't know who it was in the tank.

I started firing, but it was no good. The oil in the jacket was so hot I was afraid it would catch on fire. I poured in a little fresh oil, and waited.

But I never fired that gun again. When I thought it was cool enough I took a look through the port to get my aim. The Germans on Hill 253 were running like rabbits for the woods!

Our barrage had shifted now from the side of the hill to the edge of the farther woods. But the Germans ran right through it. Behind them, the lines of the 7th were sweeping down over the top of Hill 253.

I threw open the tank door and climbed out. I was pretty sick at my stomach.

A group of the 7th was coming toward me, an officer and twenty-five or thirty men. The officer asked me what company I belonged to.

"Company K, of the 4th Infantry, sir," I said.

"What the devil are you doing over here?"

I told him I'd been holding the fort in that tank.

He took a look at the tank, then one inside it, then one at me. He must have noticed the blood matted in my whiskers.

"You certainly look like hell. Who hit you in the chin?" he said.

I was too far gone to answer. I asked him where my outfit was.

"I don't know," he said. "But you'd better find out and rejoin them!"

I saluted and started off toward Woods 250. He led his men on in the opposite direction.

I'd made it back about to where my old shell hole was. A terrific crash came behind me. I swung around toward it. A six-inch shell from a German heavy artillery gun far in the rear had exploded a few feet from the tank. As I stumbled through the woods I could hear the shells crashing all around the tank.

The Germans had at last got the range of the tank back to the heavy guns behind their lines.

As I came closer to Woods 250 details kept passing me carrying dead and wounded men back from the slopes of Hill 253. Just outside the door of the battalion headquarters dugout the new Intelligence officer who had talked to me the evening before was lying on the ground. He'd been mangled by a shell. He was still breathing, but that was all. A detail was preparing to take him to the rear.

I stumbled down the steps into the dugout. There were a couple of officers in there looking at a map. Sergeant Nayhone was sitting at a table. His head was in his arms down on the table.

I reported to one of the officers. Nayhone looked up.

He said, "You got back after all, Jack!"

He pulled himself up out of his chair and came across the room to me. He put his arms around my shoulders and started to cry.

He kept saying, "My God, you got back after all!"

"Hell!" I said. "I'm not good-looking enough to be an angel, am I?"

Nayhone and I started back. We passed the place where the kitchens had been set up and chow was nearly ready. We made it to the aid station. Just outside, Nayhone stopped.

I felt him slipping, and tried to hold him. But he collapsed and crumpled up on the ground just as one of the pill-rollers came out of the aid station to help us.

16

The Quality of Mercy

I didn't see Jesse until the next morning. He wanted to know all about the business in the tank, but I was too tired to go into many details. I did tell him, though, about the rifle that had been shooting all afternoon from over around headquarters. By that time I had a pretty good idea who'd been shooting that rifle. There weren't many men in the outfit who could make one hit after another at a thousand yards' range.

He grinned when I accused him of it. "Huh! Didn't I tell you that whenever you got into trouble I'd be somewhere around? When Nayhone told me where he'd put you I knew who was in that tank all right. But I didn't do so damned good for you at that. I missed two of those Heinies."

I was kept back of the lines for several days, and Floyd stayed back there with me. He had a way of falling out whenever he got so tired he couldn't stand up. He'd get back behind the line companies and sleep until he was rested, then go up to the front again. He never asked anybody about it, and no one ever seemed to know it.

It wouldn't have made any difference to him if anyone had. You couldn't do anything with him. What Floyd wanted to do he did.

If an officer bawled him out for anything, he would snap back, "Yes sir! . . . Yes, sir!" He'd pile on the military courtesy. The officer would go off very much impressed.

As soon as he was out of hearing Floyd would say: "To hell with that bird! He's so damned ignorant he don't know whether Jesus Christ died of pneumonia or was shot by the Indians."

The worst trouble I was having was my head. It was a mass of yellow blisters, like a burn. If one of the blisters broke and the water from it got on the skin anywhere else, there'd be a new blister. I dried them up as much as I could by doctoring them with a weak solution of iodine. But they gave me a pretty rough time.

On the night of the twelfth we formed up and made one of those blind marches which are almost as bad as a battle. It was raining. Our route took us through woods that had been uprooted by shell fire, and across old trenches, and over open ground that was all deep pits of mud or mounds of slippery earth. Our battalion halted near the eastern edge of the Bois de Naulemont. The 2nd pushed on into the Bois de Foret.

We had no more than got there than the Germans attacked the 2nd Battalion. Our battalions re-enforced it, and we drove the Germans back. But there were plenty of casualties on both sides. We found out from the prisoners we took that the Germans facing us there were members of the 1920 class. They were first-class fighting men, young and fresh and full of confidence.

After that attack the 1st Battalion was re-enforced by a company from our battalion. Jesse and I were in it. There wasn't much left of our old 3rd Battalion by that time.

The next day was a day of red-hot fighting. We found ourselves tangled up with the Germans in the worst kind of local scrap. By afternoon everything was mixed up. The officers who were left were going around commanding men without respect to organization. One of them came along and ordered Jesse and me to go with him. We told him we were Intelligence men.

"That doesn't make a damned bit of difference," he said. "Obey orders!"

He put us in a shell hole. He said, "Stay there until you're relieved. And shoot hell out of anybody that doesn't talk English well and quickly!"

The Germans had some of the best snipers I've ever seen, there in those woods. One of them got Major Smythe, our battalion commander. Jesse and I had some pretty close brushes with them.

By night we had cleared the Germans out of the Bois de Foret. But they still held Hill 299.

In the course of the fighting I ran out of rifle ammunition, so I took a shotgun and a lot of shells off the body of a dead runner. I had got separated from Jesse. Mike came along and I asked him if he'd seen Jesse.

"Sure! Little while ago. He's O.K."

I knew he was lying. He hadn't seen Jesse. He was trying to cheer me up.

It was raining but the Germans patrolled our front all that night. They shot gas into us with rifle grenades. That was a new way to use gas, but it was effective.

I think that next day was the worst day I ever spent at the front. The skin on my head was cracked. I was half sick. I was so exhausted that I could hardly move. When we were re-enforced with a part of the 7th Infantry, and also with a company of the 6th Engineers, I moved back into the woods for a while.

They were trying to reorganize back there. Officers were so scarce that Colonel Dorey himself was taking an active part. They were merging the 3rd Battalion with the 1st and 2nd, and distributing all the ammunition they had.

I found Jesse sleeping in the rear of one of the newly organized outfits. I fell down beside him. It was more like fainting than going to sleep.

I don't know how much later it was when somebody shook me and said something about attacking again. Jesse was gone. Everybody seemed to be moving forward. But they weren't moving very fast. They were dog-tired and they showed it.

I'd had a little rest, and the movement seemed to be waking me up. I worked myself forward and caught up with the first wave of troops just as they were leaving the woods. Our artillery was roaring away behind us. Ahead of us the Germans were answering.

It's all pretty hazy to me. When we left the ravine and began to climb another slope the Germans opened on us with rifles and machine guns.

I remember that the Germans were in a woods on the opposite side of a road that ran parallel to our front. There were not many of us left by the time we'd made the woods, but we waded on. The few Germans left in there tried to make a stand; but we shot them down. All our men were so tired that they were in a sort of sullen rage.

I saw that a real fight was developing down to my right and I made for it. But when I got there the fight was over. A bunch of our men, from half a dozen different organizations, had cleaned up a crowd of German machine-gunners planted in a ditch. Jesse and Floyd were in the gang.

On the other side of the road from the ditch was a stone quarry. At the same moment that Luger and rifle fire began to spatter us from the quarry, a number of machine-guns opened up on us from a woods to the right.

Jesse said, "Let's rush them out of that quarry."

We rushed the quarry. I was really warmed up and alive again for the first time that day.

The quarry was dug out of the bank just across the road and at the base of a steep hill. The hill sheltered it from artillery fire, and it commanded the road in both directions. It was about three hundred feet square inside, but the mouth wasn't more than thirty feet wide.

In a fight like that my small size was always an advantage. The big fellows got rushed first. There were about fifty of us when we boiled down into the mouth of the quarry. A few minutes later there weren't more than forty, including the wounded. There didn't seem to be any Germans left except dead ones. Their wounded died almost right away.

There must have been about as many of the Germans to start with as there were of us. And they had put up a good fight. But their Lugers and the few Mausers they had were no match for our shotguns, Springfields, and Colts. One squatty little Italian had got into the fight with a light Browning. We shot a German in the head always if we could.

When the smoke from the firing cleared away, we saw what a mess the quarry was in. The floor was covered with the bodies of the dead and wounded. The walls and our clothes were spattered with blood and brains.

We set about dragging the Germans outside and throwing them in the ditch across the road with the machine-gunners. They were all either dead or so near it that there was nothing we could do for them. On our way back from these trips we'd carry in any of our wounded that we found outside. We brought in the machine-guns from the ditch and set them up.

We took care of the wounded men as well as we could. We wrapped them up and put them in the decentest part of the quarry. Then we fixed up our defenses. We had plenty of ammunition, and we put it where it would be easy to get at. Across the entrance to the quarry we made a barricade of rocks to keep out shell fragments and bullets. We posted sentries there and at the opening in the top of the quarry and up at the crest of the hill.

I saw what looked to me like a boot sticking out of a crevice between two big rocks back in a dark corner. I held my forty-five in one hand, grabbed the boot with the other, and yanked.

A man came out, clutching at the rock with both hands.

He kept yelling, "Nein! . . . Nein! . . . Nicht! . . . Nicht!"

I rolled him over on his back and jabbed him in the belly with my pistol. He had a Luger in his belt and I took that. I had to kick him in the side to make him understand that I wanted him to get up. He was holding his arm over his face, and he was so weak from fright he could hardly get onto his feet. He couldn't stand without leaning against the rock.

I yelled at him, and he took his arm down. He was just a kid, tow-headed and with baby-blue eyes. He was built more like a girl than like a man. He began to cry like a baby.

Some of that hard-boiled bunch had heard the commotion in our corner. They began to crowd around. One of them growled, "Kill the yellow son-of-a-bitch!" He didn't mean it for any joke.

I whirled around and faced the gang, my forty-five in one hand and the Luger in the other. I brought them both to a level. Most of the faces in the crowd were just curious. But some of them looked mighty mean.

I said, "Cut that stuff."

Before anybody had a chance to say anything a big sergeant edged his way up to the front. He had a cocked pistol in his hand. "Put up your guns," he ordered me. "Someone'll have to go through him."

The words "go through" didn't mean anything rougher than a searching. But something told me that the little German wouldn't live very long if that sergeant got his hands on him. I shifted the forty-five. It was lined directly on the sergeant.

"You can't do any kidding around here," I said. "I'm an Intelligence man and I'll do my own searching. I'm through talking. Back up—all of you!"

Instead of that they crowded closer. Several new faces appeared at the back of the gang. But just then someone started shoving them out of the way. Two men were shouldering their way through. They were Jesse and Nigger Floyd.

"What kind of show you running, Jack?"

Jesse lined up on one side of me, Floyd on the other. Then Jesse said to the crowd: "What the hell are you stalling around here for? What do you think this is—a side-show?"

Nobody answered.

"All right," he said. "Get busy. Police out this place. Finish organizing it for defense."

Some of the men moved away and started to work. Others stayed where they were. The sergeant was one who stayed.

Jesse looked at him. "Move out, damn you!" he said. But the sergeant didn't stir. "Like hell I will!" he said. "I'm in command here."

Jesse had two forty-fives in his waistband and a shotgun in his right hand. "I'm a sergeant myself," he said. "We'll talk about rank later!" The barrel of the shotgun seemed to move just a little as he spoke.

Floyd had had his back turned to us while he looked my prisoner over. In each hand he had a piece of German-issue bread that he'd got out of a captured pack. He would tear a bite first out of one piece then out of the other. Just about this time he finished the piece in his right hand. He faced about slowly. He looked the sergeant over.

He didn't say anything. He didn't have to. The look in his black eyes would have scared the devil. The sergeant moved out.

Jesse went with the rest of the crowd to see that they got the place fixed up for the night, and I wasn't much better off than I'd been before. Floyd had been for me, against the gang. But his sympathies were all with them about the proper way to treat a prisoner.

As soon as the sergeant had faded Floyd turned that same look on the little German, who was plastered against the wall and shaking as if he had a chill. Floyd had two guns in his belt. His straight hair hung down to his eyes. All the time I was arguing with him, he kept those eyes on the prisoner's face. I never saw anything whiter than that face. The kid wasn't crying any longer. He was too scared.

But I'd made up my mind that I'd shoot Floyd before I'd let him have his way with my prisoner. He saw that I meant business after a while and he gave in, but he insisted on staying right beside us until I'd turned the boy over to someone else. He was going to be sure that half-dead little German didn't pull any dirty work!

"You're all right, Punk," he said. "But you're too damn chicken-livered!"

It got dark and the firing died down outside. A detail of prisoners were marched along the road. There were twenty of them, guarded by two privates and a sergeant. I took my prisoner out to turn him over to them. He had pretty well recovered from his fright, but when he found out he was leaving me he went to pieces again.

One of the prisoners in the detail tried to reassure him. But another prisoner, a non-commissioned officer, began to abuse him.

"Shut your damned mouth!" said one of the guards. "Who told you to butt in?"

He gave a kick with his hobnails on the German non-com's pants.

My prisoner was very grateful when I gave him back the trinkets I'd taken from him. He made quite a speech to me. Another prisoner who could talk English said he was thanking me and that he hoped God would take care of me.

Floyd said: "Let's get to hell out of here!"

We went back to the quarry.

They'd got it all ready for the night, and it was safer than being outside in the open. A few of the men had found German packs with food in them, but they hadn't distributed it around. Someone found a keg of schnapps in a box near the hoist engine, and we all took a drink. Most of us hadn't had a real meal for days. That schnapps had plenty results.

Those of us who hadn't found any food were pretty hungry, but we had enough water. There was a spring in the quarry, but at first we drank only what was in the boiler of the hoist engine. Then we decided that the Germans had been driven out in too much of a hurry to have had time to poison the spring. We tried it, and it was all right.

A few shells fell in our neighborhood that night, and some of our sentries were fired on. But I got a little sleep in a shell hole outside of the quarry, and woke up to find rain beating down on me.

We had a council of war that morning in the quarry, and we decided it wasn't necessary to send back a detail to report our condition. Nobody even spoke of dropping back to safer ground in the woods. They were a hard-bitten lot, the toughest of half a dozen regiments. They'd bought that ground with blood and they didn't propose to give it up until they had to.

While we were talking, one of our sentries reported that the Germans were massing in the edge of their woods as if they meant to attack. And they did attack, about two hundred of them supported by several heavy machine-guns.

But we'd had plenty of time to get our guns manned, and all the advantage was with us. They gave it up after a while and dropped back. We had a few casualties, but we knew that they had suffered much worse.

About ten o'clock in the morning a chow detail of fifteen men joined us. There were also several signal corps men and six officers. They'd been lucky enough to make the quarry without drawing fire.

But their coming wasn't as lucky for us as it looked. The chow they had brought was canned salmon and canned apricots. I drew salmon. It made me sick, and I retired to a crevice in the rocks behind the spring. And I wasn't the only one.

The new officers began making themselves unpopular as soon as they arrived. They were replacements. Not a front-line officer in the lot. The men were all too desperate to be bothered with forms, and they weren't very respectful.

One of the officers said, "What's the matter with this goddam hard-boiled outfit? They go round here getting sick like babies!"

Jesse said, "Well, I'll tell you. This outfit took the quarry without help from anybody. They're all good soldiers. But they take it for granted that a new officer coming up here don't know a hell of a lot about conditions. And they aren't in the mood for parade-ground stuff. I'm doing everything I can to show you the respect that's due an officer. But you'll have to take my word for it that these men are good soldiers. They're veterans. And they know their business."

The officer opened his mouth to reply. Somebody yelled, "Sit down before you get knocked down!"

He started to draw his pistol, then put it back in its holster. "I'll put you under arrest!" he said.

Somebody snickered. Several voices yelled, "Horse collar!"

That officer gave it up for a bad job. "I'll put you under arrest!" became a byword with us.

The most decent one of the lot hunted Jesse up later and talked to him. Jesse told him the men had been through too much to be expected to click their heels every time stripes were flashed in front of them. He said if they'd just leave the men to him there wouldn't be any trouble. They must have decided that was so, and things quieted down.

We learned from the chow detail that Colonel Dorey had been badly wounded the afternoon before.

Jesse said, "So that's the reason those fancy officers got up this far. If the colonel had been on the job he'd have had them tamed before we ever saw them!"

About noon a lieutenant from one of the 7th Infantry companies worked his way up to us. He was a front-line officer, and he got plenty of respect. He had three of his own men with him.

The lieutenant told Jesse we'd done pretty well and ordered us to stay where we were. He left us one of the new officers and took the rest away with him. They came under fire just as they left the quarry. One of the new men we hadn't liked was knocked off. He'd been at the front just long enough to get his boots muddy.

Early that afternoon the Germans began bombarding the quarry. The signal corps men had set up a telephone, and word came over it for Jesse. He was to locate the guns that were firing on us. He took me with him, and we crawled out, up the slope of the hill above us.

The sun was shining now, and we located one of the guns without much trouble. We had followed a brush fence up our hillside from the quarry. In front of us, when we came to the top, was a wide, level field. Beyond that was Hill 299. The gun was firing from the edge of the woods on the northern slope of 299.

On our way back we ran into fire from what seemed to be two eighty-eights. We ducked for cover, and made the quarry. But Jesse had been hit in the back by a rock the size of a man's fist. It paralyzed him for a while, and I had almost to carry him the last part of the way.

He was about all in when we got to the quarry, and I telephoned the whereabouts of the gun we'd located. Late that afternoon several German planes flew over us and threw down light bombs. But we fired at them with our automatics, and they gave it up without having made a hit.

It was four o'clock when our artillery began a heavy shelling of the woods back of us and to our left. Fifteen minutes later a considerable number of our troops rushed across the road and advanced into the valley on the other side of it. Then the Germans did something I'd never seen them do before. They burst out of their woods and began to fight right there in the open.

If we'd had any idea of what was going to happen we could have turned our machine-guns on the Germans as they advanced. By the time we'd got over our surprise, Germans and Americans were all mixed up. We couldn't have fired then without hitting our own men.

It was a stubborn, bloody fight. But in the end the Germans were chased back into their own woods.

About dark one of the signal corps men who had been left with us began yelling for Sergeant James. He was wanted at the telephone. I answered.

The voice at the other end of the wire said, "I'm talking for the adjutant."

I said, "I'm talking for Sergeant James. He's been knocked out."

He asked me who was speaking and I told him.

There was some talk I couldn't hear. Then a new voice spoke into the phone. I can't explain it exactly, but I knew I was talking to an officer now. He asked me about Jesse, and I told him what had happened.

He said, "All right. You'll do. I want you to investigate the woods to the west. Don't go on any private machine-gunning details! Just find out everything you can and report it to me. You'd better take somebody with you."

I said, "All right, sir."

"Remember, you're to get that information back!" he repeated. "Call for the adjutant."

Jesse was out of it. I looked for Floyd and couldn't find him. I didn't know anything about the rest of the fellows in the quarry, and on that kind of a patrol you're a whole lot better off by yourself than with someone you don't know. So I set out alone.

I made the belt of woods from which the Germans had advanced that afternoon and followed it for about three hundred yards. Presently I heard what sounded like a small group coming along a trail toward me, in the direction of our lines. I flattened out in the bushes. They were skylined as they passed me. I saw three German helmets. I followed them for about two hundred yards. They disappeared.

I flattened out again and waited for some more to show up. The next group was going the other way. I waited a minute or two, and just then a man came down the trail alone, headed the same way the first three had been going. I followed him, and he led me to a big dugout. I saw a faint gleam of light as he disappeared in the passageway.

I watched that place for about fifteen minutes. There was a lot of traffic in and out of it. I figured I had found something worthwhile.

I got back to the quarry and reported to the adjutant. I told him I thought the dugout was a German headquarters.

The adjutant said, "Very good," and rang off.

I wasn't satisfied with that. It seemed to me my discovery was important. So I rounded up a group from the men in the quarry.

"I'm looking for a couple of men to go on patrol," I told them.

A corporal from the 7th Infantry looked me over. Then he said, "What kind of a patrol?"

"I've located the Heinie battalion headquarters."

He said, "What's your plan?"

"Go up there with a bunch of grenades and blow hell out of those Germans. Somebody's got to go with me to cover my actions. I want two good men."

He said, "Will I do?"

"Count me in," a man from the Fourth Division said.

I stopped the others. "That's enough. The next thing's to get the grenades."

"There are a lot of Heinie spud-mashers lying around outside," the corporal said. He was a Swede, and he looked like a good fighter.

He and the other fellow rounded up a couple of armfuls of grenades and borrowed about two hundred yards of French wire from the signal corps boys. We made up a bomb that weighed at least thirty pounds and put a wire handle on it to carry it by. We wired several of the firing strings on the grenades, so that there'd be no chance of misfire.

Then we laid our plans. I was to go first. The corporal would follow, slightly to the rear and five yards to the right. The other man was to carry the bundle of grenades and keep five yards behind the corporal. They were to walk when I walked, crawl when I crawled, and stop when I stopped.

The corporal and I had our shotguns, but the fellow with the grenades had load enough without any long arms. We followed the brush fence to the top of the hill and then headed for the woods.

Several small parties of Germans passed close to us. But they weren't making any effort to keep quiet, and we had plenty of time to get out of their way. Within forty yards of the dugout we halted. I took the grenades and turned over my shotgun to the man who had been carrying them.

I warned them to be sure to cover my approach. "And in case of a mix-up be damned careful where you send your buckshot!"

I didn't know anything about those boys. I was almost as afraid of them as I was of the Germans.

I didn't try to hurry the last few yards to that dugout. I found that the wires around our bunch of grenades had worked loose. They rattled a little, no matter how carefully I moved. So I took off my blouse and tied it around the bundle.

Five yards from the dugout I stopped and waited. It was a hole dug in the ground, as deep as a large room. Across the top, big timbers were laid even with the ground. Dirt and brush were spread over them, above that several sheets of steel. These had been taken from old cannons; they were to protect the dugout from shell fragments. Wooden steps led down a passageway to the door.

While I waited, several Germans arrived in a group. They stopped at the entrance to the passage and stood there, talking. One of them was smoking a pipe. I could smell the smoke. And whenever he drew on his pipe the glow from the burning tobacco would light up his face and be reflected from the underside of his helmet. I couldn't make out his features. There was just that quick glow when he took a puff, then darkness again.

After what seemed a long time to me the Germans turned and started down the steps toward the dugout. I waited a minute, then pulled the strings of my grenades, ran a few steps after them, and heaved the bundle as far from me as I could. I heard the grenades rattle and thump as they hit.

Just in time, I whirled on my heel and ducked out of the passageway.

17

Far Gone

The other two fellows were waiting for me. As I reached them the grenades went off with a roar behind us. Back at the dugout somebody started howling. Things were falling out of the air all around us as we ran. After about a hundred yards of this we dropped to a walk and began to pick our way with more care.

When we were halfway back to the quarry the Germans shot off a number of flares not far from it, and our seventy-fives opened up on the woods around there with high explosives. But we got through safe and found everybody waiting to know our luck.

I went to the phone to report. It was out of order, but the signal corps man had gone out to see if he could locate the trouble. Floyd waited at the phone with me, and when I'd finally got the report through he took me out to where he'd made a bed for Jesse.

He had him hidden in a crevice in the rocks where it looked like he'd be safe from anything unless maybe it was a bolt of lightning. Floyd had collected a lot of clothing from the battlefield down in the valley and had made up a pretty fair bed for him.

I told them about our raid on the German headquarters. Jesse laughed. "Feed the little soldier, Floyd," he said.

Floyd had also made a collection of food from German packs down in the valley. Part of it was some sort of canned sausage, and the smell of it almost knocked me out. But the taste wasn't so bad.

Floyd made me stay there and sleep with Jesse. I woke the next morning with rain sifting in my face. I picked out an American blouse from our bed and put it on. My mother's picture had been in the blouse I wrapped around the grenades. There were some papers too, which might have identified us. I knew no one would ever read those papers, but I hated to lose that picture. It was in a little leather case like a pocketbook, with isinglass over the picture. I felt kind of lonely without it.

But it was gone and there was nothing to do about it.

I left Jesse still asleep and went into the quarry. There was a lot of excitement there. Our troops had moved up and they were turning our quarry into a regular regimental headquarters. The wounded had all been taken back. Chow had come up, and there was still some of it left. It was warm! Beef stew, sliced onions, and bread. I piled all I could on the lid of a container, filled the container with coffee, and went back to our crevice.

Jesse was awake, and Floyd had crawled in beside him. Floyd's arm was in pretty bad shape. Jesse was working on it, but he stopped for food. We ate most of it, and I put the rest away.

Floyd was about half out of his head, and quarrelsome. We had to let him have his way about everything until he finally dropped off to sleep.

Jesse was worried. He said, "We'll have to get something on that arm, or it's going to rot off!"

I crawled out and hunted around until I found some pill-rollers. But they said I'd have to see the lieutenant doctor. I couldn't find the lieutenant doctor, so I went back to the pill-rollers. They didn't have any iodine, but they promised to save me some when it came up.

I reported my failure to Jesse, crawled into the crevice, and went to sleep. When I woke up Jesse was gone. Floyd was still asleep, but he was mumbling and moaning. It looked to me as if he was delirious. I didn't dare leave him.

In about half an hour Jesse came back. I never found out how he got it, but he had a half-pint of whisky, some iodine, and a small supply of clean gauze. He waked Floyd up and gave him a drink. They'd chased everybody out of the quarry, he said, except the headquarters personnel.

We dressed Floyd's arm, and it looked so bad to me I told Jesse I thought we ought to get him to the doctor. Up to that time Floyd hadn't been taking any interest in what we were doing. He came to life at that.

"Damn it, Punk! There you go getting chicken-livered again! What the hell do you think I am? Anybody can live with an arm off. It don't make a damned bit of difference to me."

I said, "All right, Floyd, it's your arm. But I don't like the looks of it."

We went around to the other side of the quarry where a lot of digging had been done and there were plenty of holes. Most of the men who had been ousted from the quarry were camped in here, and we found a hole that had more space in it than our crevice.

Jesse gave Floyd another drink. He went to sleep, and we started out to rustle up some guns and ammunition. We had our pistols, and we got hold of two rifles and a shotgun. We felt a little easier then. Our troops seemed to have things pretty well in hand around there, but there was plenty of fighting still going on to our right.

About the middle of the afternoon I went around to the quarry to see if there was anything to eat. There wasn't. But one of the runners waiting there was Mike.

I asked him if he'd heard anything about Tom. It seemed to me weeks since I'd seen Tom. Mike didn't want to tell me at first, but I pinned him down. Tom had been riddled by machine-gun bullets.

Mike said he had seen him on a stretcher at regimental headquarters. He had asked for me.

I asked Mike how badly he thought Tom was hurt.

He shrugged his shoulders. "Bad. I guess he's through."

I didn't ask any more questions about Tom. When I asked about Norosoff, Mike said he didn't know. He guessed Norosoff was gone too.

When I told Jesse and Floyd what I'd heard, Floyd raved, "That's what'll happen to all you Irish, if you don't watch your step. We've got to kill this outfit whenever we find them. You're all too damned chicken-livered!"

He sat there for a while without making a sound. He had a high fever, and his arm must have felt pretty bad. He'd look at it every now and then, the way an animal looks at a wounded leg. Then he'd burst out again. He and Tom had been great friends. It hit him hard. The more he thought about it the wilder he got.

"I'll cut the guts out of every goddam German I can find! This is a goddam war anyhow!"

Then he'd say: "You're too goddam chicken-hearted, Jack. It's gonna get you in trouble. Ain't that so, Jesse?"

"How do I know? Shut your mouth for a while and give us a rest."

Floyd went right on. "It makes me mad all over seein' you so damned chicken-hearted! I'd have finished that little bastard up in the quarry the other day. I'd have cut his heart out."

By this time he was making so much noise that the lieutenant left in charge of us came around and bawled him out. Floyd stood at attention and took the bawling-out. It was a mean one. It wound up with something about court-martials.

Some soldier in another hole didn't like it much. "Fer Christ's sake!" he yelled. "Shut up, Court Martials!"

The lieutenant tried to find out who'd yelled at him, and they all began to razz him. He gave it up and went back to the quarry.

Then Floyd started in on me again. One of the men in another shell hole called out, "Oh, shut up, Schnapps!"

Floyd had a weakness for schnapps, but he didn't like that nickname. He pulled out his trench knife. He went straight over and walked into the soldier who'd spoken to him. I had to go after him and get him back into our hole. I tried to take his trench knife.

"Let that boy alone," I said. "He likes to live just as much as you do."

"I don't give a damn about living!" Floyd said. "I don't give a damn whether I live or die. What the hell difference does it make?"

But he quieted down after that, and seemed to feel a little better.

About dark I went around to the quarry to see if there were any prospects of food. At the entrance I met a boy who had just come through from headquarters.

He said, "We're smashing through on all the fronts! It can't last much longer."

There seemed to be a pretty general feeling that things were looking up.

Inside the quarry a big lieutenant was organizing a raiding party and asked me how I felt. I told him I felt pretty good.

"Fine!" he said. "If you know of any other good men, go and get them."

Jesse was gone when I got back to our hole. But I told Floyd what was up, and he insisted on going along. I took the shotgun, and we reported to the lieutenant.

Somebody got a shotgun for Floyd and gave us twenty rounds of ammunition apiece. There were about twenty in the patrol, but the others had already been given their orders, so the lieutenant talked to Floyd and me.

"You will patrol Hill 299, and find out all you can about the disposition of the German troops. Barkley will be the getaway man for the patrol in case of trouble." He said to Floyd, "You are to stick with Barkley. If there's a tie-up, see him through."

The patrol didn't start until eight o'clock. The lieutenant joined us then. He told us to leave behind all papers, and anything else that might give information to the Germans. That didn't bother me. By that time I hadn't even my dog tags left. I'd lost those the day of the tank fight, and all my papers had been deposited in German headquarters the night before.

The lieutenant led us through the woods in a northwesterly direction toward Hill 299. A little belt of woods lay on the southeastern slope of the hill. We cleared that and started up the slope. The men in that patrol knew their business. We made no noise. As we went forward the sound of movement among the Germans became quite clear. But the banging away of artillery had drowned out smaller sounds, and we were almost upon them before we started hearing them.

We halted, and hit the ground. Germans seemed to be withdrawing from the western end of the woods; others moved up onto Hill 299 from somewhere at our right front.

We had been lying there, listening in, for about ten minutes when a German rifle company walked out of the woods behind us. We were all so intent seeing what was taking place ahead of us that we'd forgotten to watch the woods we had left. When we discovered those Germans, they were coming straight toward us.

They had no way of knowing we were there. But that was our only advantage. They outnumbered us about three or four to one, and they were between us and our only line of escape. So far as we knew we were completely surrounded by Germans. There was nothing for it but to try to shoot our way out.

The Germans were coming toward us in a loose column of fours. One of the leading files was carrying a light Maxim. We let them come until they were within about fifty feet of us. By that time we had them skylined. We got in about two charges of buckshot apiece before they had time to scatter.

They were badly rattled. But what they did would have been the right thing if it had been daylight. They ran out to the flanks, forming a sort of skirmish line. They would have been better off in the darkness if they had flopped down on the ground and crawled. As it was they were outlined for us against the sky.

My shotgun was working very stiffly. When paper shells get wet they swell up, and make a gun slow. Sometimes they jam it altogether. The Germans were firing by this time. The man on my right quit shooting, and when I spoke to him there was no answer.

Just beyond him somebody began firing rapidly with a pistol. It came from where the lieutenant had been, and I worked over that way.

As I passed the dead fellow I took part of his ammunition. Mine was going fast. I lost some of his in the darkness, but it helped. When I got to the lieutenant I told him I thought we'd better try to get out of there.

He said, "No, we're getting the best of this!" It looked as if he was right. Most of the Germans had thrown themselves on the ground by now, but they kept jumping up and trying to run. Every time one of them did that he skylined himself, and we grabbed those chances.

Suddenly the light Maxim went into action almost directly in front of us and not more than forty feet away. But the gunner was either excited or inexperienced. He was firing into the ground halfway between himself and us. There were lots of mud and rocks flying our way from that gun, but no bullets. I lined up and let drive at the gun flash. It didn't flash again.

Then the Germans up on Hill 299 shot a flare. The lieutenant yelled, "Let's go!" We jumped to our feet and charged to the rear, in the direction from which we'd come. When we'd gone fifty yards the Germans shot half a dozen flares in low arcs right over us. They lighted things up so that a bunch of Maxims opened on us. There were both heavy and light guns. They were firing from Hill 299. We hit the ground again, and waited for the flares to dim. We were being fired on from the right now, too. And the Germans we had run back into the woods were shooting from there.

The Germans on the hill kept on sending over their flares. But whenever their light dimmed for a moment we'd make a rush back toward the quarry. Each time we made one of those rushes there were fewer of us to make the next one. We didn't try to do any firing. It would only have slowed us down and given away our location.

The fourth rush carried us pretty well out of the light from their flares. We kept on going—those who were left. There weren't more than seven of us by that time.

As I turned the corner of the little woods three figures rose from the ground in front of me. A Mauser blazed. It wasn't twenty feet away, but it missed me. I think it got one of the men behind me, though.

I had only four charges of buckshot left, but they were all in my gun. I crouched and sent two of the charges where the Mauser had fired. There were evidently two hits. Only one of the three figures I'd seen at first came lunging toward me. From his movement I knew that he was charging with his bayonet ready.

My sticky shotgun was too slow. I parried with everything I had and the bayonet missed me. But my left hand was knocked loose from the shotgun.

Our helmets came together with a clang. With my free left hand I grabbed the German by his collar, and ducked under his left arm. My helmet was brushed off. I stepped in it, and the chinstrap looped across my instep.

I remembered one of Tom's tricks then. I brushed the German's helmet off with the butt of the shotgun in my right hand. Then I brought the butt down as hard as I could on the back of his head.

At that instant somebody charged into us like a football tackle. We all three went down together. The newcomer was Nigger Floyd. As we lit he drove his trench knife with a grunt deep in between the German's shoulder blades.

There were six of us when we got back to the quarry. I reported, and then we went outside to look for Jesse. He wasn't in our hole, and nobody knew where he'd gone. Gas shells were falling around there with their *uck-ul-lucka-uck-ul-lucka-pluck!* We found the wind was blowing it away from the other side of the hill, so we moved around there for the night.

We huddled up with about ten of our old quarry gang, posted double sentries to watch for gas, and went to sleep.

When I woke up in the morning the first thing I saw was little Norosoff grinning at me. He'd spent the night in the shell hole next to ours. I couldn't remember having seen him since that morning after I got the letter from my girl.

"How are you?" he said.

I was still sort of dazed to see him there. Mike had been so sure he was gone. "I'm all right," I said.

I was glad to see him. He'd come in as a runner after we left on our patrol. When we went around to the quarry we found Jesse there. His back still bothered him. Otherwise he seemed to be in pretty good shape.

Jesse had a lot of things to tell us. They had already evacuated a bunch of gas casualties that morning. There was no chow up. And from the way the Germans were shelling the roads behind us it didn't look as if there'd be any right away. The regiment was in bad shape.

We'd been cut to pieces half a dozen times, and the remains reorganized so often that nobody knew what he belonged to.

The 7th Infantry were in about the same shape we were. But they reenforced us with a battalion that day. What was left of our provisional 1st Battalion was pulled back around the quarry and reorganized as a reserve. Our provisional 2nd Battalion, together with the battalion from the 7th, held the line.

That night plenty of food came up.

Jesse had got hold of some medical supplies and set to work on Floyd again. He also had some greasy stuff that he smeared over my bald head.

Floyd said, "That's a waste of time. The only way to get hair back on top is to cut his head off and set it on upside down!"

The sun came out for a couple of hours and we all felt a little better. In the afternoon Jesse and I were sent out to secure information. Floyd was worse again, and just before we left Jesse gave him a small flask of whisky.

He flashed his gold tooth at us. "An officer gave it to me," he said. I doubted whether that officer knew how generous he'd been.

The Germans were in the habit of occupying Hill 299 at night and pulling back from it in the daytime. We covered the same ground the patrol of the night before had covered, and we ran across several of their bodies. The big lieutenant had been shot in the head with a rifle held very close. Some of the wounded had been bayoneted. All of their pockets had been slit. Sometimes the slits went right on through the flesh.

Jesse and I managed to crawl to the top of the hill without being seen. When we got there we were pretty safe. The ground had been so torn up by shell fire that there were plenty of hiding places. The light was fair, and Jesse had brought a pair of powerful French binoculars.

We could see signs of a good deal of activity among the Germans on the other side of the Meuse, but not much on our side. We took turns at using the glasses and wrote out everything we saw. We were particularly careful about noting the map coordinates. I wanted to give enough information so our artillery could blow those Germans down there to hell.

In the late afternoon a German plane must have spotted us. It circled over us two or three times, then ducked back over toward the Meuse. A few minutes later we were shelled off that hill. But before we left we located the battery of seventy-sevens that was doing the shelling, and included them in the report. We were proud of that report. It was good, especially from an artilleryman's standpoint.

When we got back to the quarry we made our report together. There was an artillery captain at regimental headquarters—our seventy-fives had been moving up that day.

When they finally dismissed us, and we got outside, Jesse chuckled. He said, "I'll bet some Dutch outfit is going to be ducking a hell of a lot of hardware before morning!"

I said, "Well, I hope to hell they start ducking too late!"

We found Floyd where we'd left him. He was pretty sick, but he wouldn't even talk about reporting to the doctor.

"If I go back," he said, "you're both goin' back with me. That's what we said. If I go back you're both goin' back with me. And if I go back I'll have to be carried back!"

We finally took him down the road south of the quarry to some old shelters the Germans had used. We made him a bed in there and built him a fire. We kept water boiling in canteen cups and put hot compresses on his arm until midnight. He fell asleep then, and we went back to the quarry to see if there was any chow.

There wasn't. Jesse went back to Floyd and I waited in the quarry. Food came up by and by, and I carried a supply to them. It was all I could do to make the trip; something had happened to my foot when it got tangled in my helmet strap. It felt as if the instep was broken. While I was using it it wasn't so bad, but the minute I kept still it began to stiffen up.

The next day the 7th Infantry and a provisional company from our outfit captured Hill 299.

When chow came up that night Floyd was too sick to keep his down. But he still wouldn't talk about going back. Jesse and I split the night watching him. The thing that worried me most was that he was too far gone to be quarrelsome any more.

But the next day when we told him we had decided to turn him over to the pill-rollers, he snapped back into form. He refused to go, and he cursed us until we all felt better. Jesse went off to call on some officer friends. He came back with part of a bottle of whisky. That Indian could find liquor in Andy Volstead's house![56]

About that time our provisional 1st Battalion suddenly drove eastward and cleaned out the northeastern section of the Bois de Foret. The Germans didn't put up much of a resistance. They were pretty far gone too. Jesse and I were in on this, but it didn't offer much in the way of excitement.

Parts of the 13th and 38th Infantry re-enforced our battalion.[57] The attack drove eastward and northward. Brieulles was taken to the east, and the attack pushed as far northward as Cléry-le-Grand.

In the middle of that day I played out. Jesse and I had been sitting down for a few minutes, and when we were ready to go on I couldn't get up. My legs just wouldn't work.

Jesse was almost as far gone as I was, and it was dark before we managed to get back to the quarry. We found Floyd where we had left him and crawled in with him. If chow came up we didn't know it. Not one of us was able to go and find out. I don't remember anything that happened the next day except that now it seemed to be Floyd taking care of Jesse and me. Some other soldier helped him. I kept thinking it was Tom and I couldn't understand it. I knew Tom was in the hospital or dead.

That evening Jesse shook me. He shook me until I finally answered. He said, "Jack! We've got to get going, Jack. We're relieved!"

I got up. The three of us started back along the road toward Montfaucon.

The only thing I remember about that night is sitting on a dead man while Jesse and Floyd rifled some packs. They didn't find any food, but they got several blankets. They had run across a German Howitzer, surrounded with straw ammunition cases. We made a bed out of them under the gun, and covered ourselves up with blankets. I was in the middle. And it was raining.

18

Armistice

When we woke up in the morning we were soaking wet. We crawled out and headed toward Montfaucon again.

Combat wagons kept passing us, loaded with our dead. Once a long train of them went by us. They were trucks twelve or fourteen feet long, four feet deep, and three or four feet wide, each drawn by six mules. They were loaded to the top. It seemed to me that not another leg or another arm could have been crowded into them.

It was still raining. The road was a quagmire. The mules were struggling and straining through the mud. As one of the wagons passed us a body fell out, and we helped put it back. He was a young fellow. His back was so stiff you couldn't bend it.

There were lots of other groups working their way toward the rear. In one of them was an officer who said he'd been with a burying detail. They'd buried the Germans where they fell. Their orders were to put one man to a grave and leave a German helmet on top of it. But he'd had a colored burying detail under him and he'd had a lot of trouble.

"It was all right in the daytime," he said. "But we had a hell of a time keeping those niggers up there after dark. They were scared half to death at night. If we didn't watch them every minute they'd pile all the Germans they could see into one shell hole. Then they'd fill it in, stick one helmet on top of it, and call it a day!"[58]

Most of the time we were too tired to talk to anyone, and we didn't dare to stop for rest. We were afraid if we once sat down we'd never get up again.

Along in the afternoon we found a soldier lying in the mud at the side of the road. He was through, he said. He'd made up his mind to lie down there and die.

We had a tough time getting him up and making him try to go on with us. Every few minutes he'd stop, and start to lie down again. When we wouldn't let him, he'd cry and say all he wanted was to die.

Finally Floyd jabbed him with his trench knife and said, "Damn you, I'll kill you if you don't shut up and keep goin'!"

He staggered along after that. We didn't hear any more about his wanting to die.

We got to a little place south of Montfaucon at last. Our kitchens were there, all fired up. Everywhere you looked men were sprawled out on the ground. We located an aid station, but Floyd began to rave as soon as we mentioned it.

He pulled the dressing off his arm. "There's nothing the matter with me. I'll cut this goddam thing off," he said. He held it out to Jesse. "Tie it up!"

Jesse said: "Damn it, do you think I want to stand here and put on a demonstration? I've tied up your damned arm two or three times already and you can't leave it alone. The pill-rollers have got to see it now."

"Get the hell out of here!" Floyd said. "Get to hell down the road, both of you!"

When we didn't move he started down the road himself. We got him back, cursing the pill-rollers.

"Yes, goddam it," he said, "you want to go off and leave me, you two fellows!"

By that time the captain doctor had noticed us. He came over with a couple of pill-rollers. We had started toward the kitchens, and he asked us where we were going.

Jesse told him we were going to the kitchen, to get something to eat.

The captain said, "I'm going to give you a drink first."

He gave us some kind of mixture, which Jesse and I got down all right. But Floyd couldn't make the grade.

The doctor looked at him. "Grab that man!" he said to the pill-rollers.

He put up a fight, but he was so weak they soon got him down on a stretcher. They had to tie him, though, to keep him there. The doctor began to talk to him.

"I'm sorry, son," he said. "But you're in bad condition. Let me see what's the matter with that arm."

Floyd stopped cursing and let the doctor examine it.

When he got through he looked at Jesse and me. "He'll have to go back," he told us. "What about you two fellows?"

"I ain't goin' back as long as they stay up here!" Floyd said.

The doctor said, "That's all right, son, but you're in bad shape. You want to get over this, don't you?"

Floyd said, "I told you I don't care a damn what happens to me. But nobody ever said Nigger Floyd had laid down! I'm damned if I'm goin' to quit!"

The captain smiled at Floyd. "You'll be all right," he said. "Just leave it to us. You'll find out we're a bunch of fighting doctors too!"

Floyd gave up then. He begged me to take his trench knife. "You keep it for me, Jack."

They took him away to the aid station on the stretcher.

I was about all gone. Jesse put his arm around me and held me up. "Straighten up, kid, or they'll get you too," he said.

We went to the nearest kitchen and they gave us some chow on tin plates. But I couldn't eat mine. I put the plate down and stretched out on the ground. The sky seemed to turn black and drop toward me. I heard Jesse say something that sounded to me like "Plugh wough."

"I'm no squaw!" I mumbled. I don't remember anything more.

Somebody shook me awake. Jesse was stretched beside me, and someone had thrown a blanket over us.

It was a sergeant, with a fine brogue, who had waked us up.

"I'm afraid you boys'll have to move," he said. "Or would ye rather I drove me water-cart over the top of ye?"

We crawled over a little closer to one of the kitchens, dragging the blanket after us.

"How you feeling, Jack?" Jesse asked me.

"Guess I'll make it," I said.

Jesse grinned. "She's a rough old road!" he said.

One of the K.P.'s heard us talking, and brought us out something to eat. I'd seen him before! This was the K Company kitchen. We must have stumbled into it by instinct.

When he found out who we were, the mess sergeant brought us a canteen cup of coffee. That coffee surely had authority! It must have been half whisky. The mess sergeant was a tough old soldier. He knew what we needed.

Jesse asked him how many were left.

"Not enough to eat all the chow we've got," he said.

He fixed up a bed for us, and we went to sleep again.

Around midnight he brought us another cup of his special brew, and more food.

We slept late the next morning, but the mess sergeant had our breakfast saved for us. He told us to get set to move, but he said that we weren't likely to move far. The men couldn't stand it. Everybody we saw seemed to be in about the same shape we were.

The sergeant gave me a quart of warm water in the top of a chow-wagon can. I washed my hands, my face, and my head. My head had a protecting crust on it by this time, and I ruined that. I washed off scabs with the hair sticking to them. But just the same I felt better after that wash.

Jesse and I went up to the aid station to see if they'd taken Floyd back yet. They were just getting ready to move him. He seemed to have made up his mind there was no use to fight any longer, but he was still the same old Floyd. When Jesse said something nice to him, and a little bit soft, he said, "Get to hell out of here. I ain't no damned squaw!"

The doctor talked to us and told us they'd do everything they could for Floyd. He thought he had a fighting chance to get well. We felt better after that and started back to where they were collecting the men for another march.

That captain doctor's kindness to us got me thinking about all the officers that had been sent up with our division. They were fine men.

And the medical officers took all the pains they had time for, to find out what was the matter with you. Except once in a while a man who was pretending sickness in order to get a tag. The doctors would dig into him all right.

They had all the consideration in the world for the men who were shell-shocked. I remember one time when I was at battalion headquarters, a lieutenant who was pretty nearly all in himself brought in a shell-shocked fellow. He was raving and trying to fight everybody who came near him.

The lieutenant's nerves were shot. He started cursing the crazy fellow, and talking about court-martialing him.

The doctor stopped him. "Wait a minute. Wait a minute! How did he get this way?"

"I don't know," the lieutenant said. "All I know is that I found him out there like that and I had a hell of a time bringing him in here!"

"All right," the doctor said. His voice was as kind as the lieutenant's was harsh. "You don't have to worry about him any more. We'll look after him. When a man comes in here in this shape he belongs to me. I think if you're wise, lieutenant, you'll get a little rest before you go back out there."

A few minutes after Jesse and I had left the aid station, we ran across Mike. He was in about the same shape we'd been in the night before.

We were so glad to see each other that we all shook hands. And that's something not often done in the army. They might pound you on the back, but they hardly ever shook hands with you.

Mike had come in late in the night, and he was looking for some food. After we had told him how to find the K Company kitchen we went on.

Jesse said, "I knew that damned Dago would come out all right. You can't kill a Dago!"

The regiment moved back about a kilometer shortly after this. Jesse and I got hold of Mike and put him between us. He seemed actually to be asleep as he walked. As soon as we halted we put him to bed near the kitchen. Then I borrowed a razor and some soap, and shaved. I drank a cup of coffee to brace me up, and reported to the pill-rollers. I figured I could get by now without being sent back, and I wanted something to put on my head. They gave me some greasy stuff, like Vaseline, and I spent the rest of the day nursing Mike. Jesse had disappeared. No one had seen him since morning.

During the afternoon six or seven hundred replacements came into the camp. They were in good condition. They certainly made us look like tramps.

That evening Jesse came back. He had caught a ride on a truck to some little town. And of course he had some liquor. Several quarts of cognac, in canteens. We drank a little, gave part of it away, and saved the rest for emergencies. Jesse and Mike and I went to bed together. For the first time in days I took off my shoes. It was twenty-one days, as nearly as I could remember.

The next morning I wished I'd made it twenty-two, my feet were so swollen. My instep was as sore as a bad tooth. I thought I'd never get my shoes on again. We were in for a pretty good hike that day, and I came mighty close to not making the grade. I'd caught cold the night before, too. I guess if it hadn't been for Jesse's cognac I'd have had to fall out by the road somewhere.

The day after that I was pretty sick. I got separated from Jesse, and we were piled into trucks and jolted all day over terrible roads. I had thought marching was as bad as anything could be. But it seemed to me now that this was worse. I was so miserable that I hoped I would die.

We billeted that night in a town by the name of Culey. Mike and I were assigned to a cow barn. I couldn't eat any supper. I wrapped myself up in a blanket, rolled into the straw, and passed out. The next morning I was delirious. Mike went to the French family that owned the barn and told them about me.

I have misty recollections of being carried somewhere in a woman's arms. I'm not sure whether I remember being put to bed in a house, or whether I heard about it afterward from Mike. But a couple of days later I woke up in a big feather bed.

A sturdy, good-looking young woman was trying to pour some kind of hot toddy down my throat. She was the one who'd carried me into the house.

When the girl saw that I knew her, she called in the rest of the family. There was her mother—a widow—and a feeble old man who was madame's brother.

The young woman was about twenty years old and had two little children.

They all seemed glad to find me awake. They brought food, and fed it to me. I had on a heavy cotton nightshirt six sizes too large for me. I asked where my clothes were, but they didn't understand a word of English.

I pulled myself up in bed and made motions as if I were putting on a coat and buttoning it. I kept saying, "Clothes," while I was doing this.

Madame got the idea first. She laughed. "Ah, clothes," she said. "Non! Non!"

She pushed me back onto the pillow. I was asleep almost before my head touched it.

That evening the two women bathed me as if I were a baby. I made an awful fuss at first, but it didn't do a bit of good. I'd pull the sheet up over me and they'd pull it down again and go on with their work. I gave up after a while. I was so weak the girl alone could have handled me. And, besides, it began to feel damned good!

They gave me an alcohol rub. They washed my head and put some kind of ointment on it with a white powder sprinkled over that. When this was all finished they put me into a suit of pajamas instead of the nightshirt I'd been wearing.

I learned later that the pajamas had belonged to one of madame's sons, who had been killed in the war. There were also two other sons who'd been killed, and one still living. He was a captain in the army.

After the bath they picked me up, wrapped a blanket around me, and put me in a big armchair in front of a fire. They placed my feet in a crock half full of hot water and something else that smelled like whisky. Then they fed me. That was the best meal I ever ate.

There was a large piece of breast meat on the plate. "*Capon!*" the widow said. She made motions as if she were lifting something very heavy. Then she blew her chest out and thumped it. They all laughed, and I laughed with them.

After supper Mike came in. He knew a little French, and the old man had a French-English dictionary. Between us we managed quite a conversation. The two women kept dipping water out of the crock my feet were in, and adding more hot water. Every now and then they gave me a hot toddy. By the time they put me to bed at nine o'clock I felt as if I owned the world!

I asked Mike about Jesse. He said Jesse was all right but was too drunk to come to see me.

Mike looked natural enough to put it across. But I knew that when the occasion demanded it, he could be the best little liar in the A.E.F. And I knew how much liquor Jesse could stand. Mike stuck to his story, however. I couldn't get another word out of him.

The truth was that Jesse had given out too. He was in a French bed, being taken care of by a French family, just as I was.

I stayed in that home several days. They took such wonderful care of me that I couldn't help getting well fast. They cooked eggs for me and all sorts of good things. They made me marvelous salads. They doctored my head and feet. I don't know which was in the worse condition. Madame said it was trench feet I had.

When she'd see the scar in my side, she'd roll her eyes and say, "La baïonnette! C'est terrible!" I figured that Mike must have been talking to them.

Finally I insisted on getting up and dressing; they brought me the clothes I had been wearing when they took me in. But I certainly wouldn't have recognized them. They had been washed and darned and patched and pressed until they looked better than the misfit uniform I drew when I got back to the company.

There was nothing left of my shoes, so the old man gave me a pair of slippers. It had been weeks since I'd had any leggins. I limped down to the company orderly room, where I explained to the top sergeant what had happened to me.

They'd been carrying me A.W.O.L., but he promised to fix me up. He must have kept his promise, for I never heard anything more from it. He told me to get it on record with the pill-rollers. I reported to them and they fixed up an ointment for my feet; the captain doctor gave me an order to my company commander authorizing me to miss drills.

I went back to the company to draw new clothes and equipment, and that afternoon the company commander sent for me. When I got to the orderly room I found Jesse waiting there too. They had called us both up to tell us we'd been detailed to go to an officers' school.

We went outside to have a little private conference over that, and we decided to pass it up. We figured that one more good fight was about all there was likely to be before the war was over. We couldn't see ourselves back of the lines at an officers' training school while that was going on.

We told the captain we wanted to stay with the outfit, and asked him to check us off. He said, "All right. Maybe you're wise," and dismissed us.

There were all sorts of rumors now. We heard that Pershing was planning a drive toward Metz with an American army of two million men. We had a good deal of faith in this one, because it was clear that *something* big was on the way.

We had replacements that brought us up nearly to full strength. And they were being whipped into shape fast. The old men were assigned to their places in the new organization, but we didn't have to do any work. Just recuperate and be on hand for roll-call.

We were moved over into another little town, and I said good-by to the people who'd been so kind to me. They didn't understand at first. So I tried making motions to show that I was going to the front, and blowing *tat-tat-tat-tat* as if I had a bugle.

Then they caught on. "Oui!" they said. "Oui!" The two women kissed me, the old man threw his arms around me, and the children cried. It was a long time before I could get away.

In our new quarters we kept on hearing the rumors about Metz. Jesse and I got hold of some maps of the Metz region and studied them until we knew everything about the topography that could be learned from paper. One thing was clear: If the Germans fought half as well as we'd seen them fight on other fields, our troops would have stiff going.

Metz wouldn't be easy to take. It had disappearing guns that would roll out from under the mountain to fire, then roll back again under cover. Our long-range guns had been battering at those placements, but had done them mighty little damage. To get to Metz the attacking troops would have to cross an open valley eighteen or twenty miles wide. This valley could be raked by the fire of those disappearing guns.

The rumor went that the Americans were to back up the French there—and that our division was to open the fight.

On the ninth we were turned out in full packs, ready to move. But the orders were canceled.

On the eleventh we turned out again. We were all fixed up, ready to load on the trucks. We were sure this time we were headed for Metz.

But the final orders to move didn't come through. About nine o'clock in the evening we heard a wild commotion in the little town. The French people, old and young, were running through the streets. Old men and women we'd seen sitting around their houses too feeble to move, were out in the streets yelling. "Vive la France! Vive la France! Vive l'America!"

We couldn't imagine what was the matter. "Hell seems to have broken loose. What's it all about?" Jesse said to me.

"Search me!" I said. "It looks like all the Frogs in town are going nuts."

Down the street came a soldier. He was telling everybody the armistice was signed.

I said, "What's an armistice?" It sounded like some kind of a machine to me.

The other boys around there didn't know what it meant either. That was one thing we hadn't heard any rumors about. We figured out after a while that it had something to do with fighting, but we thought it was a kind of temporary pause, like a truce.

We went back to our old quarters that night. But we didn't do much sleeping. We'd got so cannons didn't bother us, but we weren't used to the kind of noise that went on in that French town, all night long.

There were mobs in the streets. French people didn't get drunk often, but they were all drunk this time. The children were drunk and the old men and women were drunk, and the young people were drunk. They danced and sang. They sent up rockets and flares and laughed and shouted and cried.

And all the time they were yelling, "Vive la Marne! Vive la France! Vive l'America!"

The next morning everybody was up when the bugles blew. And everybody was determined to find out what this armistice was.

When the official word came through that it meant peace, we couldn't believe it. The recruits in our division went as wild as the French, but the older men just sat still. They thought there must be a catch in it somewhere. Peace! It was too good to be true.

Finally Jesse said, "Well, kid, I guess it really does mean the war's over!"

I said, "I just can't believe it's true!"

But it was.

19

Into Germany

Orders came through on the fifteenth. The next day we piled into trucks and started somewhere. We rode most of that day, but it was a long time before we did any more riding. They put us out at Nonsard and we hiked to Beney, where we spent the night.

We all said, "If the war's over, where the hell are we going?" We got up to the line. Here was the shell-torn country we knew—the old trenches—the miles of barbed-wire entanglements. We started looking for the Germans then. Thought they might have changed their minds, and we'd better watch our step. We wouldn't have been surprised any day to find that they'd established a new line somewhere. But as we went on and nothing happened we got over that feeling.

In all the little towns we passed through the French people made a lot of fuss about us. They would crowd into the streets and wave American flags that they'd made themselves. Most of the flags were pretty good, but there were funny ones too. Some had red, white, and blue stripes, with one or two stars. Some had the stripes running the wrong way.

We had found out by this time that we were headed for Germany. The German army was retiring just ahead of us, and every now and then we had to slow our march in order not to get mixed up with them somewhere.

I liked Alsace-Lorraine. The fields looked rich and fertile, like Missouri country. Where we'd been in France the sun always went down behind the hills. Here it would set in a big red ball. It would drop slowly down over the horizon of the open country, just like the sun at home.

I got a real thrill when they told us we were marching over one of the famous roads Napoleon used; we were following in the footsteps of his army. It was a good wide road. On each side of it were big cottonwood trees.

When we'd get to a high point I liked to look back and see the long line of our troops marching up the hill.

I was glad to be going into Germany, for I wanted to see what the German people were really like. We'd heard so much that it didn't seem possible they could be like the rest of the world. But when we marched through the little German towns, and they crowded out in the streets to watch us go by, they didn't seem much different from the people I'd always known. Not as different as the French.

Aside from the clothes some of them wore, and their language, the only thing that seemed queer about them was the scared look on their faces. We couldn't figure that out at first. But when we called out friendly things to them they'd look at each other in surprise, and their faces would light up. After that they wouldn't act afraid any more. It dawned on us then what was the matter. They'd been told worse things about us than we'd been told about them! They were just finding out that they'd been fooled.

The ex-soldiers still felt pretty bitter. When there was one of them in the crowd he'd look at us if we were some kind of wild beasts. But when you thought what he'd probably been through to try to win this war, you couldn't exactly blame him.

Nayhone was back with us again, and Floyd and Mike were with us too. Norosoff had been gassed and had stayed behind. He rejoined the outfit soon after we got to Germany. But it was a long time before we had news of Tom.

Almost a month from the day when we took up the march into Germany, we came to our first real halt. One of our battalions stopped at one town. A second went on to another. We settled down in

Meisenheim, and went back to the routine of garrison life again. It made a difference knowing the war was behind us instead of ahead. We drilled enough to keep in good shape and discipline was still strict; but there was time now to think about something else besides the army.

We liked the Germans we met in the little town. They were friendly, as soon as they found out we weren't really monsters.

Soon after we settled down in Meisenheim, Corporal Rissey got permission to look up his German relatives—and found them living in a village only three miles from the camp. There were several German soldiers in the family, but just the same they staged a big celebration for their American cousin. He came back to camp so full of liquor and food that it took him two or three days to get over it.

He kept saying, "After the chow we get in the army, it was swell! They sure do know how to cook!"

One of my principal activities that winter was trying to get my hair back. I spent most of my pay—and all the money I could get hold of shooting crap—on my scalp. By the time we got into Germany there was beginning to be a little hair on the back of my head, but the top was still perfectly bald. I found a German barber who said he could make the hair grow again. He used some stuff that stunk so that nobody would bunk with me. They scattered when they saw me coming.

Even Floyd. "You smell like an old dead horse!" he'd say. My regular name was "Limburger Cheese."

But I stayed by it, and pretty soon my hair began to grow. It grew like everything. By spring I could stop using the stuff, and by the time I left Germany I had a real head of hair.

On the sixteenth of March the company commander called Jesse and me into the orderly room. He told us to brush up our uniforms and get everything about us spick and span. That's all he told us. It sounded like an insult to us. I'd been made a corporal in spite of myself by that time, and we both prided ourselves on always being smart soldiers. We went out of the orderly room pretty sore.

The next day the outfits formed up and marched to Andernach. At the Aviation Field there we found the 1st and 2nd American divisions ahead of us. The field was choked with soldiers.

We formed according to our numerals, First Division on the right, Second Division center, our [Third] Division on the left. There were a lot of bands and they were all playing. Out in front was a bunch of generals and generals' aides, both Allied and American.

After a while several officers came and posted themselves along our line, and a lot of orders were read. I figured those were officers' business, and didn't pay any attention to them.

All of a sudden I heard my name called. "Corporal John Lewis Barkley, Company K, 4th Infantry." I looked around to see what it was all about, and the company commander yelled, "Answer your name!"

I did. My voice sounded so loud to me it made me jump. The captain told me to get out there in front. I started out toward the officer who was reading the list of names.

There was another name that had been read before mine. It was Lieutenant George P. Hays of the 10th Field Artillery.[59] I figured maybe the lieutenant knew what was going on and what we were supposed to do about it, so I timed my pace to arrive at the same time he did. He marched up to the officer, halted, and saluted. I followed suit. I felt better now that the lieutenant was taking the lead. I figured that we weren't going to be shot, anyway.

A tall, skinny officer in the center yelled, "Persons to be decorated, front and center. March!"

There was a circle drawn on the ground with lime, opposite the front and center of the Second Division. They marched us up there. They placed the lieutenant on my right, and General Sladen on my left.

Somebody said, "This is one day when a corporal ranks a general!"

I was standing at the very best attention I could, but I was getting more nervous every minute. I glanced around at the lieutenant. It seemed to me that he looked pale, and sort of green around the gills. I began to feel the way he looked.

About then somebody told us to stand at ease. I think it was a major out in front. He laughed and said: "I'll bet Hays and Barkley are worse scared than they've been for a long time!"

While this was going on they were placing a lot of men ranging all the way from colonels and majors and captains down to privates on the line at our left. This took some time, as they seemed to be doing it according to a roster.

When that was done, someone called us to attention. A tall officer mounted a little platform that had been set up to our front. I'd never seen him before, but knew him at once. It was "Black Jack"—General Pershing.

I heard him say something about decorating as brave soldiers as the world has ever known—but that was all I could get. It wasn't that I couldn't hear. I had a ringside seat as far as hearing was concerned. But I couldn't get used to standing up there with a bunch of generals and colonels, while three divisions stood at attention behind me. I hoped they'd make it snappy.

At last General Pershing finished his speech and climbed down from his platform. He came straight toward Lieutenant Hays. I kept my eyes glued to the front, but I knew what he was doing. He stopped before the lieutenant, plopped his heels, and did something with his hands. I heard him speak to the lieutenant. Then he was standing in front of me.

He saluted, and I almost snapped my right arm off in answering. But I did it automatically. My head had about quit functioning. The general stepped up close to me, did something with the front of my blouse—and a pin went straight through the blouse into the flesh on my chest! He shook hands with me and congratulated me, and said something about a "fellow Missourian."[60] Then he knocked his heels together, gave a low, snappy salute, sidestepped to the right, and began decorating the next fellow.

There was a bunch of brigadier generals with him, and I heard one of them say to the general's aide: "Hell! He's just a kid!"

Since Lieutenant Hays weighed some hundred and eighty pounds, and General Sladen certainly couldn't be called a kid, I figured it must be me that he was talking about. After the decorating had all been finished, brigadier generals kept coming up and shaking hands with us—and they were a fine-looking lot of men.

As soon as Pershing had passed on, his aide said: "Let's fix this thing right for you!" He took the pin out of my chest and fastened it in my blouse where it belonged. General Sladen told me then that I could stand at ease, and I was altogether more comfortable physically than I'd been before. But I was still upset in my mind. I kept thinking how awful it would be if there'd been some mistake, and they'd picked out the wrong fellow to decorate.

I still didn't know what it was General Pershing had pinned on me, so as soon as I dared I squinted down along my nose. I couldn't see anything but a little blue ribbon with white stars. But that was enough. I knew that the medal beneath it was the Congressional Medal of Honor.[61]

There'd been two of those in our family before. The first one had been given to a major-general who was related to my mother's family.

When the decorating part of the ceremony was over they marched us around and placed us on the reviewing line behind General Pershing.

That review was the grandest sight I've ever seen. The First Division went by with its scarlet "One." The Second with its Indian Head. Jesse had been given the D.S.C. and was somewhere in the reviewing line, and I wondered what he thought of that head. Last came our own Third Division, with its blue and white bars.[62]

Infantry, line after line, poured past us, machine-guns, engineer and special troops—clicking like a machine. Caterpillar tractors kicking up the dirt. Seventy-fives traveling in a cloud of dust.

I looked at General Pershing. It seemed to me he was growing taller and straighter all the time. He'd rare up on his toes, as he watched, then come down on his heels again. He was a soldier from the ground up!

And I didn't blame him for being proud of our outfits that day. When I looked back at the lines of men, marching and marching past us, at the flags and the artillery and the horses, I felt cold chills running over me. I felt all stirred up and warlike inside. I was almost sorry the war was over.

After that I got some other medals.[63] In fact the medal business got monotonous after a while. Every time they gave out new ones, the outfits would have to line up and stage a review—that is, if a medal was going to one of their men. It happened several times that I was the only man in our battalion being decorated, but they all had to be marched seven miles and reviewed just the same. Twice they got rained on, and I came in for a lot of unpopularity.

Whenever it clouded up after that, somebody would say: "All right, Barkley. Assemble a few generals, and let's pull off another review!"

Floyd, like Jesse, had a D.S.C., and some other medals.[64] But he never got tired of rubbing it into me about my "tin shop." "What the hell!" he'd say. "Every time the kid goes outdoors somebody gives him a Croix de Guerre. He's gettin' so he can't sit down without stickin' a pin in himself!"

There was one of those decoration parties when I didn't do the outfit much honor. We hadn't known it was coming, and the night before Mike and Jesse and I had got into a row with some German soldiers in a restaurant. I had to turn out for that decoration with a large and very prominent black eye!

Spring was coming on now, and I got more and more homesick every time a letter came from Missouri. The only thing which helped that feeling was getting out into the woods.

Jesse and I used to do a little hunting and fishing on the sly. We'd slip back into the hills with our Lugers, and I got so I could shoot one of them from a squatting position, two-handed, almost as accurately as I could a rifle.

Mostly we went after hares. But one day we ran across a beautiful buck deer, not more than seventy-five yards from us. We froze in our tracks.

"Gosh!" I whispered to Jesse. "Wouldn't he make a meal for Company K?"

Jesse said, "It's a damned shame it's against orders to shoot him!"

"You bet!"

By that time we'd both eased down into shooting position. "Count one, two, three," said Jesse.

We counted slowly, together. The two pistols cracked almost at the same instant. The buck dropped. We dragged him back to a tree, butchered him, and hung him up by our belts out of reach of dogs.

After that we went back to a cottage we'd seen just outside the woods. The German farmer was awfully scared of getting in trouble, and it took plenty of marks to persuade him to haul the deer down to the company for us after dark.

His mother was a very neat, withered little old lady. When she found out what was going on she was horrified. We gathered after a while that she was saying the kaiser would put us in prison.

Jesse flashed his gold tooth at her. "Nein!" he said. "The kaiser's lost his job. Me—I'm the son of the new American kaiser."

The old lady couldn't make out what he was saying, so he showed her an American penny, pointing from the Indian head on it to himself. She couldn't see very well, but she did make out a resemblance. There was no doubt about Jesse's looking like the Indian on the penny. She didn't raise any more objections after that.

We took the farmer back to where the deer was, and he kept his promise. The company had a venison feast the next day. I tanned the pelt and brought it home.

When he turned our game over to the company we saved out a ham for the major. The major believed in enforcing orders, so we didn't leave our cards with the ham when we deposited it at his quarters. But from the way he looked at me the next time I saw him I think he suspected where his venison came from.

Floyd came into the barracks one day to tell me that Tom was back with the outfit. Floyd had been doing a little celebrating in honor of the occasion, and he'd decorated himself up with all the medals he had. But he'd run out of money—and he wasn't nearly through celebrating.

He said, "I'm broke. That damned outfit took me for a crow in that crap game this morning. They picked me clean! An' I want enough money to get drunk on. I gotta get drunk to celebrate, Punk."

I told him I was sorry, I was broke too. "Why don't you try some of the fellows who skinned you?"

He said, "I'm in debt now so I ain't gonna live long enough to pay it!"

I said, "All right, I'll see what I can do."

But I couldn't do anything. I tried every soldier I knew who'd be likely to have any money. They all said they were broke. They all said Floyd had borrowed everything they had. He seemed to have borrowed all the money in the outfit. It certainly must have been a cutthroat game he'd been in that morning.

Finally I went to the major. I'd always give him a snappy salute when I went in, but after I'd been there a while he'd usually ask me things about myself, and draw me out until I stopped being nervous about talking to him like a friend instead of a major.

He'd been shot over the heart—straight through the front and out the back. But they had done a great operation on him and he'd recovered entirely. That was luck for the outfit. He was a wonderful officer.

I told him my story. He said, "I'm not lending any money. How much do you want?"

I went back to Floyd with fifty marks, then I set out to find Tom. But when I found him it didn't strike me that there was much reason to celebrate. He was in the hospital, and he was only to stay a few days for a visit.

I said, "Gosh, Tom, but I'm glad to see you! How are you?"

"I'm damned glad to see you," he said, "but outside o' that—hell, don't you know what they've told me?"

"No. We tried to find out where you were and what happened to you, but we never could."

"Well, they say my chances are pretty damned thin!" He unbuttoned his blouse. His whole chest was punctured with machine-gun bullets. His lungs were punctured. I couldn't see how he'd lived through it.

He said, "You can't kill a good Irishman!"

But there wasn't much left of Tom. He managed to get around a little before he went back to France, but it wasn't a happy party. I took him to the companies where he'd had friends. A lot of them weren't there any more. They never would be. He asked about one officer after another.

"He went west," I'd tell him.

"Well, he was a hell of a good officer," Tom would say, and go on to the next one.

Jesse had been away for some sightseeing, but he came back the day Tom had to leave. I was glad, but I think it only made it harder for Tom. He cried when he said good-by to us. Old hard-boiled Tom! I never heard from him after that. I'd give a good deal to know what became of him.

During all that winter in Meisenheim we were getting more and more friendly with the people in the town. The German ex-soldiers held out longest, but something happened finally which made even them warm up to us. One of them—he was about twenty-three, and he'd been a fine soldier—had his iron cross framed in his house. Two or three of our boys went in there one night when they were drunk, broke the glass, and stole the cross out of the frame.

Some of the rest of us heard about it, and we were sore. We did a little private-detective business and found out who'd taken the cross, and got it back. When we turned it over to that German we made American soldiers pretty solid with him.

It didn't work, though, with those whose girls had jilted them for some of us. And you couldn't exactly blame them. There was one, by the name of Gruenther, whose girl seemed to prefer me to him—or at least she was pretending to. Maybe she really did—almost anyone could have beaten that fellow's time. Whatever the truth was, Gruenther was determined to make trouble for me.

One night Corporal Rissey's girl came to his billets, scared to death. Gruenther had been getting drunk and telling everybody how many of their comrades I'd killed. He and some of his friends were planning to stick a knife into me and throw my body into the canal. She was terribly afraid they'd find out she'd given them away, but she had to warn me.

Rissey sent another soldier home with her, and came over to tell me what was going on. I got out of bed, slipped my forty-five in my waistband, and dropped an extra clip in my pocket. The two of us set out to find Jesse.

He was in bed too, but he dressed and got his gun and went with us to call on the major. It was after midnight, but the major listened to our story. Then he sent Rissey after the girl who'd told it to him. That poor little fraülein was scared white. But she didn't back down. She told the major all she knew.

He sent us back to our barracks, with an order for me to stay in my quarters until he sent for me again. That was next morning. An orderly came and took me to the major's office, and a few minutes later the burgomaster arrived.

When the burgomaster heard the story he was horrified. He kept assuring the major that it couldn't possibly be true. That nothing of that sort would be allowed to happen.

The major said, "Well, it better not! If one of my men is injured in any way, I'll pull my troops out of the town and blow it off the face of the earth!"

He looked so fierce that I think the burgomaster believed it.

The major ordered the burgomaster to get hold of Gruenther and three other Germans whose names he mentioned, and bring them to him. I don't know how he found out about the others. One of them was related to the little fraülein who had brought us the story.

The burgomaster hurried away. But he never kept his promise to deliver Gruenther to the major.

The reason was that Jesse, Floyd, and Mike saw Gruenther first. After they got through with him he wasn't to be found by anybody in that part of Germany. It was Mike who gave me the details that morning, after drill.

The three of them had skipped breakfast, and set out to find

Gruenther in the town. When they saw him coming, Floyd and Jesse ducked into an alley, while Mike waited on the corner. He gave Gruenther his prize-fighter's sock on the chin, and dragged him down the alley to the others.

Then Mike stood behind Gruenther and held him by the collar while Jesse talked. Jesse loaded his pistol in front of the German.

"I've killed plenty of Heinies with this pistol," he said, "and I've no objection to killing a few more. If anybody hurts Barkley—I don't care a damn who it is—I'm going to shoot *you* with this pistol. I'm going to shoot you eight times. I'll follow you for ten years if necessary. And there's one thing you can be damned sure of! I'll keep my word!"

About this time Floyd brushed Jesse out of the way with his arm. "Now let a *real* Indian talk!" he said.

He took out his dirty, rusty old trench knife. He'd never allowed the knife to be cleaned or oiled, and it was enough to give you blood poisoning just to look at it. He waved it back and forth in front of Gruenther.

"Do you see this knife?" he demanded. "It ain't been cleaned since I killed a damned German with it in the Argonne. The war's over now. I won't need this knife much any more. If I ever see you, or hear you, or *smell* you." He stopped to sniff Gruenther over. "An Indian can scent like a hound," he told him. "If I ever see you, or hear you, or smell you in this part of Germany, I'll stick this knife into you and I'll break the handle off!"

He jabbed Gruenther in the belly with the point. Gruenther jumped back, and Mike tripped him up. Floyd crouched over the German, thrusting the point at him, while he howled and begged and swore that he'd been lied about.

"Shut your mouth!" Floyd said. "No one's gonna listen to your damned lies."

He grabbed Gruenther by the collar and jerked him to his feet.

"Be damned sure you don't forget what I told you!" he said.

Then he jabbed about an inch of the knife into Gruenther's pants and turned him loose. That was the last any of us ever saw of him.

20

British Trouble

About this time Jesse and I decided that we ought to get a look at some of Germany while we had the chance. We'd already been to Bonn and several towns not far from Meisenheim, but what we wanted to see was Cologne. We had enough money, and our medals made it easy for us to get passes. But Cologne was different. It was in the British area, and we weren't supposed to visit it except in organized parties.

These parties were conducted by Y.M.C.A. men, which was all right if you wanted to go that way. But Jesse and I couldn't see ourselves in a party like that, so we decided to take a chance without passes. We caught a boat to Cologne. We were spick and span and had all our medal ribbons on our blouses. We ran into several M.P. details in Cologne, but they didn't bother us, and we were beginning to feel like having a little fun.

We hung around for a while outside a beer garden with a couple of British Tommies on guard at the door. We could hear music and singing, and we kept seeing good-looking fraüleins at the windows. When we saw that the Tommies at the door were only armed with swagger sticks, and had no belts on, we decided to make a try for it.

Jesse said, "We've been outstaring our own M.P.'s all day. We ought to be able to get by those babies."

When we started through the door the Tommies crossed their canes in front of us.

"You can't go in there," one of them said. He didn't have any front teeth and that made it sound funny.

"Oh, we can't, can't we?" Jesse said. "Now just watch and see!"

He took a swagger stick in each hand, pulled them away from their owners, and threw them on the ground. Then he swung the doors open, and we marched into the beer garden.

It was evidently a very exclusive hangout, reserved for British officers. We couldn't see anyone else at the tables. But we didn't stop for that. We found an unoccupied table and sat down. The waitresses were unusually pretty German girls, and when Jesse pulled out a row of bills two inches thick several of them floated over to our table.

Jesse flashed his gold tooth, and ordered half a dozen bottles of white Moselle wine. They brought a tray with a dozen bottles for him to inspect, and a pasteboard box to pack them in.

"Never mind the boxes," Jesse said. "We'll furnish our own containers."

He knocked the head off a bottle, tipped his head back, and set the bottle down empty. Then he gave the fraüleins a handful of change and told them to buy pretties with it. Jesse and I could both talk pretty fair soldier German by this time, and we had a lot of fun with those girls. Our line was new, and they got quite a kick out of it. One of them asked if Jesse was an Indian.

"Sure!" Jesse said. "My name's Squatting Calf. My father's name was Sitting Bull." He pointed across the table to me. "That's Pain-in-the-Face. He's Indian too."

The girls laughed and crowded around. About then, several British officers got up from one of the tables and came over to ours. They pushed the girls aside and sat down.

I had the British D.S.O. ribbon on, and one of the officers was very inquisitive about it. I got the feeling that he thought there must be something funny about my having it.[65]

I answered as politely as I could because he was an officer. But I was uneasy about Jesse. He was doing very little talking, but his face was getting as innocent-looking as a papoose's. I'd known him long enough to recognize that look. It always spelled trouble for somebody.

The other officers couldn't help being amused, but they didn't like the attitude of the one who was doing the talking. They showed that plainly.

One of them suggested that they go on, and leave us alone. "They're behaving themselves," he said, "and they look like good soldiers!"

But the captain who'd been doing the talking took that up. "They *ought* to be good soldiers," he said, "they're descended from the English!"

Jesse broke his silence. He smiled sweetly at the captain and said: "You've got us wrong there. Barkley here is a cross between an Irishman and a Hunyack.[66] And I'm damned proud to say there's not a drop of English blood in me!"

The captain pretended he hadn't heard. He went on discussing Americans. He said they'd done well for untrained men. In fact had come nearly up to his expectations.

Here a lieutenant joined in.

He said to Jesse, "My word! You must be one of the bloody aborigines!"

Jesse paid no attention to that, but answered the captain.

"My word!" he said. He knocked the head off another bottle and took a drink. "My word! Just what did you expect of us? We knocked hell out of the Boche on every front we met them on. What kind of luck did you have?"

Just then a squad of British soldiers, led by an officer, marched into the beer garden. The two men who'd been on guard at the door pointed us out to the officer. The squad marched down on us as if they expected to engage in a desperate battle, and the officer in charge placed us under arrest.

The officers who had come to our table tried to intercede for us, but the officer in charge of the guard insisted that we were his prisoners and must come with him.

Jesse smiled at the German girls. "The wine's all paid for," he said. "Drink it yourselves."

He stood up and addressed the officer of the guard. "All right, sir," he said. "You're just in time. I was getting frightfully bored!" And he pretended to yawn.

They marched us off to their guardhouse. But the lieutenant in charge of the detail had noticed my British medal ribbon, and it must have bothered him. When we got to the guardhouse he pointed it out to the British major, who seemed to be provost officer. The major looked bothered too. He talked to us for quite awhile, and finally said that he was afraid he'd have to put Jesse in the cells. That was what they called the prisoners' room. He couldn't seem to make up his mind what to do with me.

I settled it by saying: "It's all right with me. I'd just as soon go into your cells."

The major looked relieved, but still worried. "I have no choice but to detain you until we hear from your commanding officer," he said.

We spent the night in the prisoners' wardroom. But we didn't do any sleeping. And we didn't let anyone do any either. The other prisoners would tell us something that was against the rules, and then we'd do it. We must have broken every rule in the place at least once.

The British prisoners and some of the privates in the guard were having as much fun as we were. But the non-commissioned officers were wild. We were careful not to go too far, and every time they cursed us for doing something we shouldn't have done we apologized and pleaded ignorance.

We found that those Tommies had a real sense of fun. I asked one of them what he was in there for.

"For stealing a battleship," he said.

I overheard the British sergeant's report to the officer of the day next morning or whatever they call the officer of the guard. I couldn't follow all of it, but there was no mistaking the fact that the sergeant didn't like us. He didn't like us at all. He must have been relieved when they turned us over to two British M.P.'s who were to deliver us to the American authorities at Andernach.

I think those two M.P.'s had been tipped off by the sergeant, and had promised to even up for the trouble we'd given him. Instead of going straight to the boat landing they paraded us around town like a pair of tame bears. And they didn't care what they said to us. Jesse was so mad I had a lot of trouble to keep him from "leaving the reservation," but we finally got to the boat without his letting loose.

We found the boat guarded by a bunch of our Marines under the command of a lieutenant. But the lieutenant was plainly under the command of his sergeant. Soon after the boat started we saw that the American M.P.'s didn't like the way the British M.P.'s were bossing us around. Particularly the sergeant.

One of the Britishers began to get abusive, and the American sergeant gave him a dirty look. "It's your business," he said, "and they're your prisoners. But if I were you I'd be damned careful how I handled those two guys!"

He took the lieutenant with him up to the front end of the boat. The other Americans drifted away too. We were alone with our guards.

Jesse glanced at me out of the corner of his eye. "Let's get their guns," he whispered.

We lined up at the rail and began discussing the scenery. The M.P.'s crowded up behind us and listened in, but they couldn't do anything to us for admiring the scenery. When they were quite close to us, Jesse called my attention to an English flag in front of some building on the bank of the river.

"That's a fair-looking piece of bunting," he remarked in a loud voice, "but I've seen prettier."

I glanced back over my shoulder. Both of the M.P.'s had turned to look at the flag.

"Now!" I said, and we whirled and took them. I had the gun off the one behind me before he knew what it was all about. Jesse's man was a little more troublesome, but he didn't hold out long. With their guns in our hands, we stepped back to the rail and looked them over.

They let out a howl, and the American sergeant came running to our end of the boat. There were several Marines with him, and when they saw what had happened they just grinned.

The British M.P.'s began to try to tell their troubles to the American sergeant. He said, "I told you not to fool around with these guys! If you want your guns, go get 'em. It's your funeral, not mine!"

He rounded up his men and went back to the front end of the boat. Our guards were worried. But not Jesse. "You'll get your guns when we get good and ready to give them to you. In the meantime you'd better be damned polite or we'll feed you to the fish!"

The lieutenant came back. He didn't know what to do. The sergeant was with him and advised him to let things alone. He said: "All we're expected to do, is to run this boat in an orderly manner. The rest of it's not our business."

The lieutenant finally went forward again, and the sergeant asked Jesse what we were going to do when we got to Andernach.

Jesse laughed. "Well, we thought we'd turn our two prisoners over to the authorities."

The sergeant said, "There are several orphanages in Andernach. I figure that might be a better way to get rid of them."

When we got off the boat at Andernach, we unloaded the guns and gave them back to their owners. But they seemed to have forgotten we were prisoners. They set off in the direction of headquarters at a run, leaving us to do as we pleased.

We wanted them to have plenty of time to tell their story first, so we loafed around awhile before we started for headquarters too. But they were still talking when we got there. They were talking to the sergeant major—one of the roughest old soldiers in the outfit. They were both talking at once.

The sergeant major was saying as we came in, "Save your wind for an officer. I can't understand your goddam lingo anyway!"

"Stick around," he said to us. Then to the M.P.'s: "*You*—can your bull till the officer of the day gets here."

He grabbed up a handful of papers, sat down at a desk, and paid no more attention to us.

The major showed up before the officer of the day did. "What's going on around here?" he said.

The sergeant major stood up. "Damned if I know, major, I can't understand these birds' lingo." He began to get mad again. "But they come bustin' in here like they owned the place. And there ain't any goddam English goin' to run this headquarters!"

The major didn't say anything. He walked into his office and ordered the four of us to follow him. We lined up before him and stood at attention while he sat down at his desk, took a cigar out of a drawer, and lighted up. Nobody said anything. The Britishers weren't sure what was the right thing to do. And Jesse and I knew that major! A friend when you were in trouble—but a fiend for discipline. He never talked much, and he didn't like anyone who did.

When he had his cigar going, he said: "What's all this row about?" The tone of his voice was quiet. But he had a trick of clicking his words so that they seemed to snap at you.

Before Jesse or I could open our mouths, those two M.P.'s began to talk, both at the same time, and neither of them telling anything like a connected story.

The major held up his hand. "That's enough!" he said. He ordered everyone out of the room but me, and told Jesse to send the sergeant major in.

"Herd those three out of hearing somewhere," he ordered the sergeant major. He waited until the door had closed, then he motioned to a chair. "Sit down," he said to me.

He blew a smoke ring, watched it drift toward the ceiling, knocked the ash off his cigar. When he spoke again it was in a conversational tone. "Now, I want facts, Barkley. Make it snappy!"

I told him the story in as few words as I could. I didn't say much about the M.P.'s hard-boiled treatment of us, or anything about the pistol business.

Then he called Jesse in. Jesse told the same story, except that he quoted a lot of the insulting things that had been said to us, both by the captain in the beer garden, and by the M.P.'s later. But he forgot to put in the trouble we'd made for the sergeant in the guardhouse the night before, and he didn't tell about taking the M.P.'s pistols, either.

He wound up his story with: "I didn't mind their insults for myself, sir. But I couldn't stand by and see them wipe their feet on a medal-of-honor man!"

The major looked him over with a sort of unblinking stare. That was a hard look to meet, but Jesse was an expert. He stared right back, and his face never changed expression.

One of the M.P.'s was a sergeant, and the major called him in. As soon as he understood that the major was asking for a report from him, he jumped into a long-winded story.

The major stopped him. "I don't want a speech. I want facts. Just answer my questions."

The questions didn't include anything about our little mutiny on the boat because the major didn't know anything about it, and that was all the sergeant was interested in.

So between the sergeant's excitement and the major's impatience, the story got so confused no one could have made sense out of it. We were safe so far. But the major asked one last question: "Have you any other important facts to report?"

We held our breath. But the M.P. was through. All he wanted was to get out of there. "No sir!" he said.

The sergeant major brought in a receipt for the M.P.'s; the major signed it, and they were dismissed.

Then the major held Jesse and me in his office. He was a master of about fifteen ways to bawl people out. He chose the worst one he knew. He talked to us as kindly as could be. He said he was proud of our records, and hated to see us do anything that wasn't worthy of them. He kept saying how sorry he was that he'd have to discipline us.

I was in a cold sweat, and Jesse came nearer being pale than I'd ever seen him before.

I don't know what would have happened if the officer of the day hadn't rapped on the door and interrupted the major's speech. The O.D. was very indignant about our behavior. He made the mistake of suggesting what should be done with us. The major stiffened up and said that he was handling the case.

But that didn't stop the O.D. He had a lot to say about our disrespect to the British officers, and he was still talking about the discipline we deserved when the major interrupted him.

He said, "Captain, I'm perfectly able to run this battalion. I intend to run it without your help. I find my time very well occupied with taking care of the American army and looking after its interests. I have little leisure to devote to taking care of the British. I am handling this case. If you have nothing of importance to report, that will be all."

The captain looked dazed. He saluted and went out.

The major had smoked up his cigar. He got out another, lit it, puffed on it, blew a few smoke rings. Then he said: "Sergeant James ... Corporal Barkley ... I hope you will not find it necessary to get into any more trouble. I know you *can* be good soldiers. I expect you to be. Return to your company. That's all!"

I know when I'm through. The major never had any trouble with either of us after that.

21

Fraternization

Not long after this I was detailed for special duty at the Schloss outside the town. The man who owned it was a baron, and the people in the village said he was a distant relative of the kaiser. He'd had three sons killed in the war, and another was still in a hospital in a pretty hopeless condition. There was a daughter, too. Once in a while she'd come into town with a maid and everybody would turn around to stare at her. She was a damned pretty girl.

The officers had some suspicions about the baron's frequent trips away from home and decided there had better be someone at the Schloss to check up on him. I was glad to have a chance to see the inside of the place. It was even grander than the château at Blesmes. Outside it was sort of rough looking, but inside it had been fixed up with modern things and decorated like a palace in the movies. I was almost afraid to touch anything, and it seemed funny to be living in a place like that.

I felt more at home in the park that surrounded the house. It was early spring, and the grass was green already. The leaves were coming out on the trees, and there were lots of flowers in bloom, some outdoors and some in big steam-heated greenhouses; but I only saw them through the glass. The head gardener never invited me inside. Under the circumstances, I could have gone in without an invitation, but he was an ex-soldier and I wasn't looking for trouble.

I was there for some time before I saw anything of the daughter except distant glimpses. Of course the baron and baroness hated having me there, and the whole family stayed out of my way. I was beginning to get pretty tired of my job.

One day I was sitting in the big drawing-room, wishing I could either get something on the baron or be sent back to barracks, when the girl came into the room. She stopped at first when she saw me there and looked as if she'd turn around and go out again. I got up and went over to her.

"I wish you'd stay and talk to me," I said in the best German I could manage. "I'm lonely as the devil."

"That is too bad, but my father says I must not talk to you."

"Well, he isn't here today, and I won't tell him." She laughed, and then we sat down on a sofa and she began to ask questions about America. She could talk English much better than I could talk German. She couldn't seem to understand the difference between our farmers and the German peasants, and I could think of a lot of things I'd have rather been talking to her about. But I could see she was getting over the idea that Americans were as bad as she'd been told they were.

Margaretta did about everything she wanted to. The baron was furious when he found her talking to me and threatened a lot of punishments if she ever did it again. But she didn't pay much attention to him, and after that things began to get interesting around the Schloss.

She took me all over the park and told me about the funny-looking statues that were all over the place—gods and goddesses and animals from India. One day we went into the greenhouses. The head gardener made some objection to opening the door, but Margaretta soon settled him. He muttered something, and he looked sullen—but he opened the door. There were not only flowers in there, but all sorts of hothouse fruits and vegetables. The peaches growing on the little trees were ripe and the prettiest things I'd ever seen. But when she gave me the biggest one to eat it was disappointing. It looked much better than it tasted.

I didn't feel that I was wasting time being with Margaretta so much, because through her I got more of a line on the baron than I'd been able to before. I found out where he went on his trips, and how it happened that he could afford to run a big establishment like that when nearly everybody in Germany was living from hand to mouth. Early in the war he'd had enough of his wealth converted into gold to take care of his family no matter what happened and had stored it in safety-deposit boxes in several banks.

You could see that he was a shrewd old fellow. He was tall and thin and straight, and he had white chin whiskers. There were plenty of cars in the garage, but they never used them. The baron used to go into town on his bicycle, so he was often dressed in some sort of golf clothes. But he looked just as much dressed up in those as he did in anything else.

Margaretta's mother was a plump, red-haired woman who couldn't speak a word of English. I don't know whether she was more worried over her husband's rudeness to me, or her daughter's friendliness. The baron usually just looked right through me as if I wasn't there.

From wishing that I'd be relieved from the duty of watching the Schloss, I began to be afraid the baron would complain to headquarters about me, and someone else would be sent there in my place. I explained that to Margaretta, and we decided to act indifferent when anybody was around. We found a place in the park where we could be pretty sure of being alone. It was a stone bench right against the wall, and it was screened on all sides by trees and shrubbery. No one ever seemed to come there except occasionally the men, working on the grounds, and we could see them in time to get away behind some bushes that grew almost up to the wall. We called it our "cave."

We would sit there and talk and talk. About America and Germany and ourselves. There seemed to be a lot to tell about ourselves. We never mentioned the war. Margaretta was different from the girl I'd been engaged to at home and the girls I'd known in France. She had a way of looking at me, when I did something she didn't like, that made me feel small enough to climb down an anthill. And then her voice—if she would speak to me at all—would drop below freezing. But that didn't happen very often as we got more friendly. She didn't like me to swear and she didn't like the way I thought about some things, and

I tried to change to please her. And she wouldn't let me touch her or kiss her. All we could do was sit and talk.

One night everybody had gone to bed, and I was sitting on a bench in the garden, looking at the moonlight on the little lake that had a fountain in the middle. There were eight swans swimming around in it—two of them brown and the other six pure white. Margaretta had hardly come near me for a week, and I was feeling sore about it, and mad at myself for letting it worry me.

I had about decided to throw a pebble against her window and try to get her to come down, when something white brushed my hand and fell on the walk in front of me. It was a flower and I knew it had grown on the clump of bushes at my back. I wheeled around. Margaretta was running away from me along the path that led in the direction of our cave.

It was a long way from the house and it was dark under the trees by the wall. I thought at first she wasn't there. I stood at the entrance, wondering where else to look for her; then I heard her laugh and felt her hand on my cheeks. I swung around and caught her in my arms and kissed her. I don't think she had quite expected that, but I wasn't in any state of mind to care if she did look at me in that displeased way of hers. Anyway, it was too dark to see it, if she did. She had something loose and silky on, and there was perfume on her hair. I kissed her again and then I picked her up in my arms and carried her through the bushes into the cave.

After that we were more careful than ever not to be seen alone—and we were alone much oftener. I don't think the baron suspected anything, but about that time the baroness began to be very nice to me when her husband wasn't around. She asked me questions about my family. Their standing, their religion, how much money they had, what they looked like.

Between my poor German and her ignorance of American ideas and customs, I don't think she got a very clear picture. I don't know what Margaretta had told her to make her so interested in me, but I was getting uncomfortable about the whole thing. It was easier to be with the baron, who acted as if I didn't exist, than with Margaretta's mother, who went out of her way to be pleasant.

Once I asked Margaretta if she wasn't afraid of what her father would do if he found out we were seeing each other so often. Her head went up, and she said in her chilliest voice: "No. Are you?"

I said: "No, I don't think so. But I don't want you to get in trouble on my account. It's not worth it to you, is it?"

She got very angry and said I didn't really care for her, and then she cried. I never spoke about it again.

The worst of it was, I was getting to care a great deal for her. I thought about all sorts of wild schemes and knew all the time none of them would work. I was worried. I hadn't figured on falling in love with her.

Then one day without warning I was ordered to move back into the barracks at once. And the same day our outfit was transferred from Meisenheim to another little town five or six kilometers away over the hills. Margaretta was out somewhere with her mother when I got the orders, so I couldn't explain to her what had happened.

As soon as we got to the new town, though, I hunted up someone to write her a letter for me. She couldn't read or write English any more than I could read or write German. I had to be very careful what I said, because there was always a chance it might get into her father's hands. So I just told her about our sudden transfer and asked her to write to me. I suppose, considering her position and mine, it would have been better to let the thing drop, but at the time I felt as if I couldn't leave her like that.

I didn't hear from her for more than a week. Then she turned up at my billet one morning. Her father was away and she'd got permission to spend the day with some Catholic sisters in the town. She said she'd meet me at dusk, and I could walk home with her to the castle. We talked about it as if it were only a few hundred yards.

That was a wonderful walk over the hills. It was nearly twelve when we got to the Schloss, and I had to walk all the way back again. But it was worth it. There were plenty of places along the road where we could slip off and be as much by ourselves as in the castle park.

It was then we made our plans about seeing each other. She'd figured out a safe way to get my letters, and I told her I knew I could get over the Schloss wall at a certain spot I'd noticed quite near our cave. Whenever I could get away I'd write, and she would wait for me in the park.

We met there all through July. There was a big tree on the outside of the wall and a smaller one just inside. Tree climbing was an old story to me, and I never had any trouble but once, when a branch on the smaller tree broke under me and I hit the ground hard.

We had several quarrels. At least Margaretta would hold her head high and try to freeze me into being ashamed of myself for some little thing, and then I'd get mad instead of feeling the way I used to. We always made up, though, until the time I got my thirty-day furlough.

I wanted to see a little of Europe while I was there, and I certainly didn't want to go home without seeing Paris. Margaretta wanted me to stay around there so we could see each other. And Paris was the last place she wanted me to go. She didn't seem to think there was anything in Paris but girls. She'd never shown any signs of being jealous before. I suppose because she was so used to being admired and looked up to wherever she went. She wasn't afraid of any other German girl, but it seemed French girls were different.

I didn't see what right she had to tell me where I could go or couldn't go, and said so. She looked at me very steadily for a minute, and then she said she never wanted to see me again. I left a few days later without telling her good-by.

When I stopped being angry, I felt damned ashamed of myself. The only thing I wanted to do was get to Paris as fast as I could and get good and drunk.

22

Paris and Home

I hadn't taken much part in camp activities for some time. I'd even drifted a little away from Jesse and Floyd. But they hadn't held it against me. I didn't tell them much, but it was hard to fool those two Indians. I'm sure they knew just what was the matter with me.

Those last two or three days before my furlough started, I came back with a vengeance. I got into every crap game I could find. I didn't care whether I won or lost. I lost. Lost all the money I'd saved up and the month's pay I'd just got. Then I had to win, or give up my trip to Paris.

I borrowed a stake from Jesse and went over to regimental headquarters. Then my luck changed. The dice wouldn't fail me. I won all the money in sight. Finally everybody else gave up, and I came back to my own town. I was puffed out like a balloon with francs, but I had the feeling that my winning streak wasn't finished.

I found Jesse and asked him about any games that were going on. He said there'd been several but they were all over. Three or four men had cleaned out everybody else in town. I flashed my roll then, and everybody who heard about it wanted to borrow from me. I loaned to all my friends, and the word got to the K men who'd cleaned the company that I had a bigger wad than they had.

They sent me word that a game was starting in the room back of K Company's barbershop. I went over there to meet them, and told them I felt my luck; and they said I was afraid I'd lose my roll.

That was enough. I went into the game, and I went in to win. For a while everything came my way. Then I lost.

Finally my luck came back. I doubled every bet. I couldn't lose. At three o'clock I had practically all the money in sight.

It was a square crowd. One of the boys had been counting—or trying to count. He offered to stay with me the rest of the night to help me protect my winnings against outsiders, and I was glad to have him. There was a bushel basket full of francs. I thought we'd never get them stacked up so we could handle them.

The next day I was banker to all my friends, but it hardly made a dent in my money. I loaned some to Jesse and to Floyd. Jesse got into a black jack game and won some more. Floyd got drunk and went over to call on another company and came back with all *their* money. We sort of had a corner on funds around there.

But Jesse didn't lose his head. He tried to persuade me to leave most of my money behind when I went on my furlough, and when I refused he had it changed into larger bills, and tied it all up carefully in rolls.

He said, "Goddam it, don't you lose this money! And don't spend it all on the Frogs. It'll do you a lot of good after you get home."

I told him it was probably the only chance I'd ever have to see Paris, and I was going to see it right. But he made me promise to deposit the money in a bank the first thing I did, and then take out each day what I wanted to spend. He had my name and organization written on my bag, and on adhesive tape labels that he plastered all over me.

"If you get knocked in the head, we can at least identify the body. You'd better take a gun."

I reminded him that we weren't allowed to take guns on furlough.

He said, "That don't make any difference. You aren't supposed to be carrying a mint around with you either. You're going to stuff the old forty-five right into its old den!"

And before he'd let me get on the train at Andernach he made sure that my gun was safely hidden in the back of my shirt. He also made me repeat my promise about the bank.

In Paris I took a taxi from the station to the bank, deposited all my money except several thousand francs which I took with me, and set out for the Y.M.C.A. Not that I had any interest in the Y.M.C.A., but I had to have some place to leave my bag until I knew what I was going to do. And we were supposed to keep in touch with our outfits through the Y bulletin boards.

The man who had opened the account for me in the bank spoke English and had given me pretty clear directions how to get to the Y.M.C.A., so I set out on foot.

It looked to me as if I could have a good time in Paris. There were lots of sidewalk cafes and taxis and big buildings, and the people looked cheerful and friendly. I wished Jesse and Floyd were along, though.

I came to a sharp corner where two streets ran into each other and a little fruit shop was set in the angle. I stopped. I didn't want any fruit, but the shop was run by a pretty girl. She had on sort of lumpy-looking clothes, but they didn't fit badly enough to hide her figure. And she didn't need a tongue. Her eyes would do the business for her.

I asked her for some fruit and when she answered in English I bought everything in sight. I told her I was on leave.

"Oui? That is nice. And what will you do here?"

"Oh, have a good time. See some of the sights. Do you know this town real well?"

She looked surprised but nodded her head. I was getting what I thought was a big idea.

"Will you show me around? I'm afraid I'll miss something if I do it alone, and I want to do this right. Lots of wine, lots of food . . . everything the damn town's got."

She seemed rather doubtful.

"That will take a great deal of money. And I have my shop to keep."

"Can't you get somebody to take care of that for you? Hire somebody if you have to. I'll pay the expenses."

Her eyes got very big.

"Are you an American millionaire?" she asked.

I tried to tell her I won the money in a crap game, but her English didn't go that far. We finally left it that I was an American millionaire. She seemed pleased, and it was all right with me.

She told me her name was Marie, and she had a sister who would take care of the shop. I waited about half an hour until she came back with such a homely girl I didn't see how they could be sisters, and then Marie and I went to the Y, which was only a few blocks away. I left my bag there, but I took my medals with me. It struck me they might be handy to have around if I got in a tight place sometime.

My sister had sent me a list of things I ought to see in Paris, but I'd lost the paper and the only thing I could remember was the Eiffel Tower. That sounded as if it might be interesting anyway, so I told Marie I wanted to see that.

It was a good thing we went there that first day, because afterward we didn't bother about sightseeing, and I'd have felt sort of foolish to have come away from Paris without even one landmark to talk about.

When we'd finished with the tower, I said, "Let's have a drink."

She took me into a dirty, dingy little hole, down some steep stairs. It was run by a one-legged man, and the drinks were cheap enough.

I said: "This isn't the kind of joint I want, at all. Don't you know any classy places?"

I couldn't understand why she looked so worried. She knew I had money, because I'd shown her my roll when we started out, and yet the next place we went to wasn't an awful lot better. But we had some drinks there and I began to be more and more bothered by her clothes. Marie was pretty and I liked her a lot, but her clothes didn't come up to my ideas of how women in Paris ought to dress. So I said: "How about a whole new outfit—you know, new dress, new shoes, new hat, new from the inside out? I like you fine, but I don't like your clothes."

She shrugged. "They are all I can pay for," she said. "I do not like them, but what would you? The war has made us very poor."

"Hell, I'm going to take you. You don't have to worry about what it costs."

That was different. She got up so quickly I nearly choked on the last of my wine. She was going to walk to the place she said was the best store in Paris. I was sorry for her, it was taking her so long to get used to spending money.

I said, "Listen. I've walked all over this damned country. It's not my idea of a good time. We're riding!"

So we took the swellest taxi I could find and when we got to the store, I saw she'd picked the right place. Marble and gold trimmings, and clerks dressed up in sort of evening clothes. I found one who spoke English and told him I wanted Marie outfitted from head to foot, and everything she had on now thrown into the furnace.

He gave me a chair and told me to wait. I waited an hour and a half, but it was worth it. I didn't know her until she came up and spoke to me.

"I am the way you want now?" she said.

My gosh, she looked great! I could hardly wait to get out in the street and show her off. As soon as I'd paid the bill, we went to a big cafe with tables on the sidewalk, and had a drink. We had several drinks.

Then we went to a hotel and got a room. Marie was a smart girl. She'd given the store the name of the place where we were going to stay, and by the time we got there, all the other things she'd bought were there too. I took back what I'd thought about her getting used to spending money. I never saw so many clothes in my life. All sorts, and they all looked as if they wouldn't last more than a minute.

In the evening we went to a cabaret, and when we got tired of that, we went on to another. All I remember about the last part of that night is standing up at a bar and treating everybody in sight.

The next day I woke up to find Marie standing beside the bed with something for me to drink. I don't know what it was, but it fixed me up all right. There was just time for me to get to the bank to draw out more money, and then we started all over again. Once in a while, we'd ride out through the Bois de something or other, to get our heads clear. Not that Marie drank very much. She drank slowly, the way I'd noticed most French people do.

In the evenings we went to cabarets, and once or twice to the theater. Everybody turned around to look at Marie, and I felt damned proud of myself. I didn't see a girl in Paris any better looking than she was, after she got dressed up.

Nearly every place we went I stood treat to a gang of people I'd never seen before. I don't know . . . I wasn't having as much fun as I expected.

Marie was a good sport. There were some things we didn't agree on, but she seemed to like me, and any place I wanted to go was all right with her. She had gone to school in England for a while, and I guess her people must have had some money before the war. Their home was in the path of the first German advance and they got to Paris by the skin of their teeth. Her mother and father died during the war, and the two girls had had a hard time. She never told me much about how they managed—just shrugged her shoulders and said, "*Que voulez-vous?*"—but I could make a pretty good guess.

One evening I was so fed up with cabarets and places like that that I decided we'd go to the most exclusive restaurant we could find. We ordered a grand dinner and some expensive wine. When the waiter brought the wine, he said it was thirty-five years old. That was within a few years of Marie's age and mine put together.

I noticed a group at another table, in a sort of arcade opening off the main room. There were two men in civilian clothes who looked like Americans and an American major. They kept looking at us and it seemed to me they were talking about us. After a while the major got up and headed toward our table. He had some trouble keeping his balance, but he made it. He was a handsome, well-set-up man.

I stood at attention. "Sit down," he ordered. Then he sat down himself at the other side of the table. "Let's see your pass."

I handed it over. He looked at it and threw it down on the table. "That pass isn't worth a damn," he said. "We've got orders to run all you Johns out of town."

I said, "Are you with the military police?"

He scowled at me. "Damn it, don't talk back to me. I'll put you under arrest."

I stood up. "Come on, Marie," I said. "Let's get out of here."

He reached across the table and grabbed her by the wrist. "I'll take care of her," he said.

I reached toward my back pocket. "Oh, no, you won't. Turn her wrist loose."

He jumped to his feet. "You damned little bastard!" he yelled.

I ducked as he picked up the bottle on the table. It smashed against the wall behind me, and I came down with the butt of my pistol on his head.

The two men who were with him had hurried over and they picked him up. That major was tough. He was only out for a minute and then he began fighting and cursing again. "Where's that son of a bitch . . . I'll get him for this."

"Is this man an M.P.?" I asked one of the men in civilian dress.

"No," he said. "But what the hell did you hit him for? How long have you been over?"

It looked as if this was the time to flash my medals. If there was any way out of it, I wasn't going to spend the rest of my leave in the guardhouse. So I hauled out the Medal of Honor and one or two others and laid them on the table without saying anything.

The major's friend gave one look and said, "See here, major, you'd better cool down." And then he said something to him in a low voice that I couldn't understand.

The major was getting pretty shaky anyway, and he let some men who had crowded around take him into a room at the back of the restaurant. Then the other two men asked me for my name and looked at my pass. They told me there might be some news about my outfit. I'd better keep in touch with the bulletin board at the Y. Then they said not to worry about the row that had just been pulled off.

I asked them what their rank was, and they said they were lieutenant colonels. But I wasn't to spread that news around. They weren't supposed to be out like that in civilian clothes.

They went out to see the major, and I sat down again. The head waiter, or whatever he was, was just about having a fit. He was trying to get everybody to sit still and pretend nothing had happened and he didn't give me any kind looks.

Marie was quite cool and began eating dinner again.

"Do you think you will have trouble with those officers?" she asked.

"They said I wouldn't, but I don't know," I said. I felt as if I needed a drink. The major'd wasted our perfectly good wine, so I ordered some more. The decorations had done the trick so far, but I wondered how long they were good for.

Pretty soon the two officers came back with the major between them. He looked a mess but a lot more sober. One of the officers took me aside.

"We've got the major to apologize," he said. "He's a damn good officer, but when he's drunk he doesn't know what he's doing. We want you to accept his apology."

The major apologized all right and then he said, "Well, kid, what outfit?" When I told him, he said: "You better transfer to mine. It's a damned good one. No hard feelings about this?"

I shook hands with him. "No, not on my side," I said.

He laughed. "All right. We're good fellows again. I'm going to get out of this damned town . . . drink too much here."

They took him away, and then Marie began to ask about how I'd got my medals. I guess that was the first time I ever told anybody about my fight in the tank, but it was easy to tell Marie. She knew how to listen and the right kind of questions to ask.

After we finished eating, we went back to the hotel. I said I was too tired to go anywhere else, but the real trouble was that when I came to pay the bill, I found I didn't have money enough for any more than that.

The next morning I stopped at the Y on my way to the bank. There wasn't anything about our outfit on the bulletin board, but the man in charge said there had been rumors that we were to move before long. I'd better keep close watch of the board.

"By the way," he said, "where have you been? Have you been keeping in touch with home? Don't forget that your people like to hear from you."

I felt a little guilty, but I wasn't going to show it. "I've been busy," I said. "I've been stopping with friends."

"Oh, that's fine! But what about seeing the important things in Paris? We have guides to take you around."[67]

Well, at least I'd seen the Eiffel Tower!

I left as soon as I could and went on to the bank. My funds were running awfully low. It scared me when I stopped to think how much money I'd spent in a little over a week. I'd done what I wanted to do in Paris, anyway. I knew Marie had got a lot of money from me, one way and another, but I didn't mind that. I was sorry for her and I figured she needed it more than I did.

I thought she'd feel pretty badly when it came to saying good-by, and I was sure I would. I was thinking about that as I took out the key to our room. I was back earlier than she expected . . . and the girl she'd said was her sister was with her.

I wanted to beat her up, but I packed my things as quickly as I could and got out.

———⊷◆⊶———

I stayed at the Y for the next few days and waited to see the notice go up that would let me get back to the outfit, without anybody asking questions about why I cut my leave short.

The day after I got back to Germany our sailing orders came through. We were leaving at once. Jesse and Floyd and I stuck pretty close together, and when we got our first sight of New York and knew the trip was over, it was queer how mixed up I felt. I was glad to be almost home, but home didn't seem real any more.

Our gang broke up at Hoboken.

Except Tom, of course. I never knew what happened to him after he left us in Germany. Mike and Norosoff were close to home when they got to Hoboken, and I suppose they made out all right. I never heard from them either. Nayhone didn't stay in this country long after the war. He went home to Syria and has done very well there as some sort of broker.

Floyd gave me an address in Oklahoma. "That old lady'll always know where I am. An' if you don't write to me, Punk—"

"Hell, you know I'll write," I said. But when I did, the letter came back. It had been readdressed in a woman's hand to some place in Nicaragua, and returned with "Not known" written on it. The Nicaragua part made it look as if peace had been too much for Floyd and he'd joined the Marines. But why was the letter marked "Not known"? After that both Jesse and I tried to get trace of him, but we never could. I'd give a lot to see Floyd again.

As for Jesse . . . I heard from him every now and then after I got home, but nothing particularly exciting. Then one day I got a telegram saying that if I needed any money, all I had to do was tell him how much. And I was to come down to Oklahoma at his expense right away.

Of course I went. They'd struck oil on his government reservation land, and Jesse was living like a prince and having the time of his life. We had a great time together, and I went home feeling mighty happy about him.

Not very long afterward I got word that his body had been found thrown in a creek near the town. It was murder for money, of course. There were two bullet holes in the back of his head. No one could have got Jesse from the front.

***

Two Indians, an Irishman, an Italian, a Jew, a Syrian, and a middle-western farm boy . . . that was an honest-to-goodness American gang.

***

THE END

John Lewis Barkley—After the Great War

Joan Barkley Wells

After the Great War, my dad, John Lewis Barkley, returned to Missouri on August 27, 1919, a day before his twenty-fourth birthday. This was truly a happy birthday for him, his family, and friends. Returning to farm life gave him an inner peace and a sense of stability. Plowing the fields and tending to various daily chores helped to focus his mind and to dim memories of the horrific Great War. He did not allow his medals or the lure of potential fame to alter his common-sense perspective on life. His Barkley-Doggett ancestors were of Ulster Scotch, Dutch-English, and Native American ancestry. An adventurous lot, they settled the early frontier of colonial Virginia, Pennsylvania, Kentucky, and finally Missouri. His parents, Frank and Leona Barkley, were unpretentious people who built a log house on Scalybark (or Scaly Bark) Creek. Years later they moved into a frame farmhouse on the brow of a hill overlooking the rolling countryside of Johnson County, Missouri, near the town of Holden. The Barkleys actively contributed to their church and community, and in 1917 and 1918 they raised and sold mules for the war effort. Frank and Leona believed in higher education for their eight children. Before entering the U.S. Army, John attended the Warrensburg Teachers College and played football.

After his return from overseas duty, my dad received many invitations to speak to civic and military groups who wanted to hear of his war exploits. He wasn't very comfortable with these situations. He did, however, enjoy working as an instructor at John Tarleton College in Stephenville, Texas, where he taught war tactics and marksmanship. While at Tarleton, he started to write down his memories of the Great War, and he met Captain Mike Mulcahy, the campus drill instructor, who became my dad's literary collaborator. Together, they worked on an account of my dad's military service titled "Scarlet Fields." King Features, a newspaper syndicate, became interested in the memoir in 1930 and arranged for publication through the Cosmopolitan Book Corporation. Several months before the book was published as *No Hard Feelings!*, King Features summoned my dad to New York City to work with a team of editors. While there, he took part in promotional tours—and attended chic New York cocktail parties in the homes of the very rich and famous such as the Harrimans and the Vanderbilts. For my dad this was all a bit much.

After meeting my dad at one of these high-society gatherings, Howard Chandler Christy, a noted American illustrator and painter, stated that he wanted to paint a full-length portrait. This statement shocked my dad; he was a poor Missouri farm boy, and he didn't have money to pay the artist. But there was no charge. Christy saw my dad as the quintessential American soldier of the Great War and wished to honor this veteran's service and courage. He completed the painting in five days. It was exhibited in the window of the Scribner building in New York City and later at the Nelson-Atkins Museum of Art in Kansas City, Missouri. Today it hangs in the National World War I Museum at Liberty Memorial. Once the editing of *No Hard Feelings!* was completed, my dad gladly returned to Missouri and shed his double-breasted suit for overalls.

At a family picnic, my dad met Marguerite Mullen, a resident of Johnson County, Kansas. They married in 1936, and he moved there, where he helped my mother and my maternal grandmother operate their dairy farm until dad's death in 1966. The couple had one child—me. I was born on July 30, 1938.

Throughout his life after World War I, dad belonged to various veterans' organizations such as the American Legion, the Veterans of Foreign Wars, the Army and Navy League, the Regular Veterans Association, and the Medal of Honor Society. He believed strongly in preserving the memory of America's fallen soldiers, and as a trustee of the Liberty Memorial Association he helped support one of the largest and most important World War I memorials in the nation; he remained on the board of trustees until 1966. He corresponded with many of the commanders of the societies to which he belonged, as well as with prominent World War I leaders such as former secretary of war Newton D. Baker and Major General (ret.) James G. Harbord, who commanded the AEF's Service of Supply. Dad's civic memberships included the Rotary Club and Sertoma International.

Years after the publication of *No Hard Feelings!* dad occasionally interviewed with journalists, and in the late 1930s they wanted to know his thoughts about potential U.S. involvement in a conflict with Nazi Germany. He favored American neutrality. However, once the United States entered World War II, he supported the war effort enthusiastically. John Lewis Barkley, age forty-three, volunteered to serve if needed.

Dad believed that one of the reasons he survived the war was because he had learned to live off the Missouri woods as an expert rifleman and tracker. He wasn't afraid to face the outdoors alone, and he could depend on an inner strength. He enjoyed the beauty of nature. His experiences in the woods and swamps near Holden prepared him for his adventure overseas and inspired his public service in later life.

In the late 1950s, after efforts to establish a public park system in suburban Johnson County failed, Sertoma appointed dad as the club's committee of one to oversee the purchase and development of new parkland. Under dad's supervision, Johnson County acquired 44 acres for Antioch Park, then another 1,250 acres for the Shawnee Mission Park and Dam. He believed that children and adults should not be confined to a small suburban lot. Contact with nature would enhance their lives. He often worked twelve to fourteen hours a day or more on problems connected with park development. A few years later, Johnson County hired him, at $350 per month, to serve as its first park system superintendent. He delighted in people's enjoyment of the parks, especially their use of the lake at Shawnee Mission Park. In 1962, *The Kansas City Star* called him the unofficial "Mr. Parks" of Johnson County. And in 1996, thirty years after my father passed away, the Johnson County Park & Recreation District honored him with the opening of the John Barkley Visitors Center in Shawnee Mission Park. A plaque with his likeness hangs in the lobby. And later, [John] Barkley Drive, which hugs the southern edge of Shawnee Mission Park, was dedicated to honor both of my parents.

My own three children, who never knew Grandfather Barkley, have a great respect for and appreciation of nature, and they are mindful of the sacrifices that the doughboys made for our marvelous country nearly a century ago. All three have visited the National World War I Museum at Liberty Memorial many times, and they have been proud to see their grandfather's medals and portrait on display.

Notes

Introduction

1. Richard Reed to Michael Briggs, University Press of Kansas, December 14, 2010.
2. For a more lyrical but less informative account of service in an AEF intelligence platoon, see Albert Earl Robinson, *An Epic Day: Personal Glimpses of the Great World War I* (New York: Carlton, 1968). Robinson served as a scout in the 140th Infantry, part of the Thirty-Fifth Division.
3. Thomas A. Britten, *American Indians in World War I: At Home and at War* (Albuquerque: University of New Mexico Press), p. 102. According to Britten, "A scout platoon [this seems to correspond with what Barkley calls an 'Intelligence platoon'] consisted of one sergeant, two corporals, and seven privates from each infantry company. Four scout platoons made up a complete battalion scout company."
4. Mark Ethan Grotelueschen, *The AEF Way of War: The American Army and Combat in World War I* (Cambridge, UK: Cambridge University Press, 2007), p. 28.
5. Leonard P. Ayres, *The War with Germany: A Statistical Summary* (Washington, DC: Government Printing Office, 1919), p. 117.
6. Ibid.
7. Laurence Stallings, *The Doughboys: The Story of the AEF, 1917–1918* (New York: Harper & Row, 1963), p. 377.
8. John Lewis Barkley, *No Hard Feelings!* (New York: Cosmopolitan Book Corporation, 1930), p. 65.
9. Ibid., p. 69.
10. Emilio Lussu, *Sardinian Brigade* (New York: Knopf, 1939), p. 170.
11. Robert Graves, *Good-Bye to All That* (London: Jonathan Cape, 1929), p. 175.
12. See Adrian Caesar, *Taking It Like a Man: Suffering, Sexuality, and the War Poets* (Manchester: Manchester University Press, 1993).
13. Ernest Hemingway, *A Farewell to Arms* (New York: Simon & Schuster, 1995 [1929]), 63.

14. John Lewis Barkley to Mike Mulcahy, February 4, 1930, File 99.33.7, John Lewis Barkley Papers, National World War I Museum Archives, Kansas City, Missouri; hereafter Barkley Papers.

15. Barkley, *No Hard Feelings!*, p. 226.

16. Ibid., p. 227.

17. Ibid.

18. Ibid., p. 230.

19. Ibid., p. 229.

20. Britten, *American Indians in World War I*, 101.

21. Ibid., p. 102.

22. *History of the Third Division United States Army in the World War for the Period December 1, 1917 to January 1, 1919* (Cologne: M. Dumont Schauberg, 1919), pp. 388–389.

23. William M. Floyd to John Lewis Barkley, August 13, 1946, File 2010, Barkley Papers.

24. Barkley, *No Hard Feelings!*, p. 28.

25. Ibid., p. 46.

26. Ibid., p. 47.

27. Ibid., p. 327.

28. John Lewis Barkley to Mike Mulcahy, January 2, 1930, File 99.33.7, Barkley Papers.

29. John Lewis Barkley to Mike Mulcahy, January 21, 1930, File 99.33.7, Barkley Papers.

30. John Lewis Barkley, Notes for "Scarlet Fields," p. 5, File 96.33.8, Barkley Papers.

31. Barkley, *No Hard Feelings!*, p. 37.

32. John Lewis Barkley to Mike Mulcahy, September 23, 1929, File 99.33.7, Barkley Papers.

33. John Lewis Barkley to Mike Mulcahy, October 27, 1929, File 99.33.7, Barkley Papers.

34. John Lewis Barkley to Mike Mulcahy, November 12, 1929, File 99.33.7, Barkley Papers.

35. John Lewis Barkley to Mike Mulcahy, March 4, 1930, File 99.33.7, Barkley Papers.

36. John Lewis Barkley to Mike Mulcahy, March 16, 1930, File 99.33.7, Barkley Papers.

37. John Lewis Barkley to Mike Mulcahy, September 9, 1930, File 99.33. 7, Barkley Papers.

38. John Lewis Barkley to Mike Mulcahy, March 4, 1930, File 99.33.7, Barkley Papers.

39. John Lewis Barkley to Mike Mulcahy, January 19, 1931, File 99.33.7, Barkley Papers.

40. King Features Syndicate, Royalty Statement for *No Hard Feelings!*, January 15, 1931, File 99.33.7, Barkley Papers.

41. A. E. Pfrommer to John Lewis Barkley, October 27, 1932, File 99.33.7, Barkley Papers.

42. Stanley M. Rinehart Jr. to John Lewis Barkley, March 16, 1938, File 99.33.7, Barkley Papers.

43. Lambert Davis, Review of *No Hard Feelings!* by John Lewis Barkley, *Books* (September 28, 1930), p. 29.

44. James B. Wharton, "Armageddon," *The Nation* 131 (November 12, 1930), p. 530.

45. E. G. Taylor, Review of *No Hard Feelings!* by John Lewis Barkley, *The New Republic* 65 (December 10, 1930), p. 120.

46. Review of *No Hard Feelings!* by John Lewis Barkley, *The Bookman* 72 (October 1930), p. 200.

47. Leon Whipple, "Talking Through Their Brass Hats," *Saturday Review of Literature* 7 (October 11, 1930), p. 282.

48. Barkley, *No Hard Feelings!*, p. 327.

49. For more on the American Legion and its construction of war memory, see Steven Trout, *On the Battlefield of Memory: The First World War and American Remembrance, 1919–1941* (Tuscaloosa: University of Alabama Press, 2010), pp. 42–106.

50. For a sustained comparison of *All Quiet on the Western Front* with *Hell's Angels*, see Robert Baird, "*Hell's Angels* above *The Western Front*," in *Hollywood's World War I*, eds. Peter C. Rollins and John E. O'Conner (Bowling Green, OH: Bowling Green State University Popular Press, 1997), pp. 79–99.

51. See Mark Meigs, *Optimism at Armageddon: Voices of American Participants in the First World War* (New York: New York University Press, 1997); and Jennifer Keene, *Doughboys, the Great War, and the Remaking of America* (Baltimore: Johns Hopkins University Press, 2001).

52. Barkley, *No Hard Feelings!*, p. 36.

53. Ibid., p. 39.

54. Ibid., p. 79.

55. Ibid., p. 82.

56. Ibid., p. 52.

57. Ibid., p. 143.

58. James G. Harbord to John Lewis Barkley, January 9, 1933, File 99.33.7, Barkley Papers.

59. For more on the 1929 war novel competition, see Trout, *On the Battlefield of Memory*, pp. 101–106.

60. John Lewis Barkley to Mike Mulcahy, January 18, 1934, File 99.33.7, Barkley Papers.

Notes to the Chapters

1. Situated on the government reservation at Fort Riley, Kansas, Camp Funston was the largest of the training cantonments built by the War Department in 1917. Its vast complex of two-story wooden buildings could hold up to 50,000 troops, and it was the only cantonment to feature a privately funded Zone of Camp Activities, where soldiers could enjoy healthy forms of recreation sponsored by the Young Men's Christian Association (YMCA), Knights of Columbus, and other charitable organizations.

2. The Eighty-Ninth ("Middle-Western") Division contained mostly draftees from Kansas, Missouri, Colorado, Nebraska, and the Dakotas. The 356th Infantry Regiment consisted almost entirely of Missourians.

3. While in their larval stage, trombiculid mites (also known as "redbugs" or "chiggers") burrow into the skin of animals and feed on the inner skin, producing severe itching and swelling. They are a nuisance throughout the states of Kansas and Missouri during the spring and summer months.

4. The Spanish Flu of 1918 affected millions and actually broke out in the region of Kansas where Barkley was stationed. In March 1918, more than 500 soldiers at Fort Riley and the adjacent Camp Funston facility contracted the virus, which quickly spread to the East Coast and then on to Europe. The mortality rate peaked during the fall of 1918, as the Great War drew to a close. Estimates of the global death toll from the virus range from 50 million to 100 million; more than half of the approximately 100,000 American soldiers who died in the Great War were victims of the pandemic.

5. "Moros": Muslim revolutionaries in the Philippines who fought a guerrilla campaign against U.S. forces between 1899 and 1913. "Juramentado": a Moro who, after ritualistic preparation, used an edged weapon to kill Christian soldiers.

6. "Gurkhas and Senegalese and Moroccans": colonial troops known for their stealth and ferocity. Gurkhas, who served in the British army, came from Nepal and achieved notoriety in both world wars. Senegalese and Moroccan soldiers hailed from French colonial North Africa.

7. During the late summer and fall of 1918, nearly 8,000 American

troops arrived in Vladivostok as part of a multinational expeditionary force; keeping Allied war supplies out of Bolshevik hands was ostensibly their mission. Tom makes this reference to "Siberia" during the spring of 1918, when American intervention in Russia was being hotly debated in Washington, DC.

8. The 4th Infantry was one of four infantry regiments in the Third Division; the other three infantry regiments were the 7th, 30th, and 38th. The 4th and 7th Infantry formed the 5th Infantry Brigade; the other two regiments made up the 6th Infantry Brigade. In theory, the Third Division was part of the Regular Army; in reality, it contained thousands of draftees like Barkley.

9. In 1911, the 15th Infantry Regiment arrived in Tientsin, China, where it joined an international force assembled to protect civilians during the Chinese revolution. The United States would maintain a military presence in China throughout the next three decades.

10. The 38th Infantry and the 7th Machine-Gun Battalion were additional units in the Third Division. The former would earn renown as the regiment that bore the brunt of the German army's July attack across the Marne River at Château-Thierry.

11. The 4th Infantry arrived in Brest, France, on April 15, 1918.

12. The *History of the Third Division United States Army in the World War* (Andernach-on-the-Rhine, Germany: M. Dumont Schauberg, 1919) confirms that far from being routed, the 7th Machine Gun Battalion fought valiantly in the streets of Château-Thierry on May 31 and June 1, so much so that the unit received a commendation from Marshal Philippe Pétain. Though ultimately driven from the town, the battalion bought crucial time for the rest of the Third Division to move into position along the south bank of the Marne. Barkley's memoir faithfully depicts the fog of war. The *History* confirms that rumors of a debacle involving the 7th Machine Gun Battalion reached the 4th Infantry on June 1.

13. The military action that Barkley witnessed near Château-Thierry during the summer of 1918 falls into three distinct phases. Phase one: In early June, the Third Division helped stop the last of the German spring offensives, which were made possible by Russia's withdrawal from the war and a massive transfer of German manpower from the Eastern Front to the Western Front. This is the battle that Barkley describes in this chapter. Phase Two: On July 15, the German army launched its final offensive, an all-out effort to win the war in one stroke. Amid what came to be known as the Second Battle of the Marne, the Third Division once again helped block the German advance. Phase Three: As it became clear that the

German army was exhausted and overextended, Allied forces, including the Third Division, counterattacked (this battle is known as the Aisne-Marne offensive), ultimately rolling back German gains between the Marne and Vesle rivers.

14. According to the *History of the Third Division United States Army in the World War,* on "June 3rd/4th a company of the [9th Machine Gun] Battalion relieved the 7th Machine Gun Battalion and held their positions against determined and repeated attempts by the enemy to cross the Marne River" (ibid., p. 185). These are the soldiers Barkley describes.

15. "cooties": lice. These pests were a bane to all armies on the Western Front.

16. In later life, Barkley became a gun collector, particularly of firearms associated with the Old West. His collection contained several hundred specimens.

17. Appointed head of the U.S. Food Administration in 1917, the future president Herbert Hoover introduced a number of domestic austerity measures designed to increase the availability of food for the U.S. military. Among Americans on the home front, doing without certain foodstuffs, such as meat or grain, on specified days of the week became known as "Hooverizing."

18. "Automatics": Colt-Browning Model 1911 .45-caliber automatic pistols. A large-caliber handgun, the Colt-Browning .45 remained a standard U.S. Army sidearm for much of the twentieth century. "Trench knives": the Model 1917 Trench Knife issued in World War I featured a fearsome studded metal hand-guard and a triangular blade. Designed to puncture, rather than cut, it was an impractical and unpopular weapon. "Trench club": Usually made from whatever materials a soldier had on hand, World War I trench clubs were indeed "wicked-looking weapon[s]." Many of these clubs (or "conches") feature nails or spikes, giving them the appearance of medieval maces.

19. For this action, Jesse James earned the Distinguished Service Cross. His citation reads, "After many attempts to get patrols across the Marne had failed, Sergeant Jesse James alone swam the river, taking with him a wire, by which a boat containing 2 of his comrades was drawn across without attracting the attention of the enemy." As is often the case, there are minor differences between Barkley's account and the official record. James's citation places his river-crossing on the night of July 13; Barkley remembered the incident occurring on the night of July 10. Moreover, in Barkley's account, the boat contains three soldiers, not two.

20. In other words, Barkley could hear a German machine-gunner

cock his weapon by pulling back on the lever located on the right-hand side of the gun's receiver.

21. Manufactured by a French bicycle company, the Chauchat automatic rifle (or light machine gun) was a notoriously unreliable firearm. The gun's half-moon–shaped clip featured a cutaway design that enabled the weapon's operator to see how many rounds were left after each burst; as a result, dirt frequently entered the clip, causing the firing mechanism to jam.

22. Although widely used by American soldiers in World War I, the term "Austrian whizbang" is a misnomer. No such gun existed. Barkley refers most likely to the German 77mm field gun, which, like the famous French Seventy-Five, sometimes fired at a flat trajectory.

23. "one-pounder": a breach-loading 37mm cannon typically used, much like the bazooka in World War II, against fortified positions. Most of the AEF's one-pounders were French-made.

24. Extremely accurate and well designed, the 9mm Luger, or Parabellum Model 1908 Automatic Pistol, was the standard German sidearm in World War I. Doughboys coveted the firearm as an iconic souvenir.

25. The shoulder straps (also known as "shoulder boards") on a German soldier's tunic designated his regiment and branch of service; for Allied soldiers, German shoulder straps were important sources of intelligence information—and became popular souvenirs.

26. For close fighting amid trench conditions, the U.S. Army adopted the Winchester Model 1897 12-gauge shotgun in 1917. American soldiers on the Western Front found the weapon invaluable.

27. These soldiers were probably Senegalese, not Algerian. In the classic memoir *Fix Bayonets!* (New York: Scribner's, 1926), John W. Thomason describes the fearsome knives wielded by Senegalese troops, as well as their fondness for human ears as war trophies (ibid., p. 106). Though likely exaggerated (American and European soldiers eagerly cast Africans in the role of the exotic "savage"), these details are consistent with other accounts.

28. "Heavy" and "light" machine guns used by the German army in World War I differed primarily in terms of their carriage design; both were bulky, water-cooled weapons. The German Model 1908 heavy machine gun rested on a complicated sledge mount, designed to be lifted or pulled by two men. The Model 08/15 light machine gun, introduced in 1915, featured a simple bipod, which made the weapon somewhat more portable.

29. "star gauge": tubular instrument used to measure the precise diameter of a rifle bore at any given point inside the length of the barrel.

Inspectors at American arsenals took multiple star-gauge measurements on every Model 1903 Springfield rifle, thereby adding to the weapon's mystique as a precision firearm. Barkley seems to have used the term as a slang expression for his Model 1903 rifle.

30. "flash hider": a conical device mounted at the end of a machine-gun barrel and designed to conceal the muzzle discharge (or "flash") created as each round is fired.

31. The 110th Infantry Regiment was part of the Twenty-Eighth "Keystone" Division, a unit made up primarily of Pennsylvania National Guardsmen. For a superb account of the Aisne-Marne campaign from the perspective of a soldier in the Twenty-Eighth Division, see Hervey Allen's memoir *Toward the Flame* (1926).

32. "Annamese": an archaic term referring to Vietnamese. Barkley's contemptuous reaction to these truck drivers from French Indo-China typifies American racial attitudes at the time.

33. The YMCA was one of several civilian organizations that provided recreation and canteen services for American soldiers. Because the YMCA charged for apples, hot chocolate, and so forth (the Salvation Army typically did not), its representatives receive a good deal of scorn in American World War I memoirs. *No Hard Feelings!* is no exception.

34. "French Blue Devils": the nickname for *Chasseurs Alpins,* alpine light infantry. "Italian troops": Italy entered World War I on the Allied side in 1915. Incompetently led and riddled with political and regional factions, the Italian army suffered approximately 600,000 casualties while fighting Austro-Hungarian and German forces in the Alps and on the Carso Plateau.

35. "Roll of gold stars": gold stars symbolized dead American soldiers. "Go west": British slang for "dying."

36. Directed at a German salient southeast of Verdun, the Saint-Mihiel offensive (September 12–19, 1918) marked the first time that American forces on the Western Front went into action as a single national army under Pershing's direct command. The offensive succeeded in eliminating the salient (in part because the Germans had already decided to withdraw), and American casualties were light in comparison with other operations.

37. "Game of pitch": a card game.

38. "Hotchkisses": French heavy machine guns issued to American forces.

39. Barkley's final battle, the Meuse-Argonne offensive (September 26 to November 11, 1918), was the bloodiest in American history, with more

than 26,000 American fatalities. The U.S. Army attacked along a twenty-mile front, which stretched from the Argonne Forest in the west to the Meuse River in the east, and faced three lines of German fortifications. The Third Division entered the battle during its second phase, after German artillery and machine-gun fire had shattered untested divisions like the 35th and 79th (the former suffering more than 6,000 casualties in five days) and added weeks to Pershing's timeline for the advance.

40. "Montfaucon": A village, reduced to rubble, atop the imposing hill of the same name, which was located at the center of the Meuse-Argonne front. The German crown prince used the summit of Montfaucon as an observation post during the Battle of Verdun in 1916. During the opening phase of the Meuse-Argonne battle, the inability of doughboys in the Seventy-Ninth Division to capture this critical position slowed down the entire operation. Montfaucon is today the location of the imposing American Montfaucon Memorial, a monument to the AEF divisions that fought in the Meuse-Argonne offensive.

41. "slum": a stew, often reviled by doughboys, made of meat, tomatoes, onions, and potatoes.

42. "dog-robbers": orderlies.

43. "block": removable firing mechanism for a German Model 1908 or 08/15 machine gun.

44. "Mauser": the informal term for the Gewehr 98, the standard rifle carried by German infantrymen in World War I. The weapon's bolt action was essentially the same as that of the American Model 1903 Springfield rifle.

45. "Light Browning": The Browning Automatic Rifle (BAR) was issued, in place of the Chauchat, to some American units during the Meuse-Argonne offensive. Comparatively reliable and accurate, the BAR remained in service during World War II.

46. Under the right conditions, mustard gas changes from a gaseous state to a solid, forming a fine, toxic powder. When mustard gas comes into contact with human skin, it produces painful blisters.

47. "pill-rollers": medics.

48. "pin a tag": Wounded doughboys sent to the rear received diagnostic tags that indicated their condition and required treatment.

49. "the 79th and 5th": American divisions that fought earlier, over the same ground, in the Meuse-Argonne offensive. By the time of the Armistice, most American combat divisions had participated in the battle at one time or another.

50. "one-fifty-fives": 155mm howitzers, standard heavy artillery in the French army and the AEF. The French manufactured nearly all of the AEF's howitzers.

51. "a light tank": a French Renault FT17 Light Tank. Used by both the French army and the AEF, this two-man vehicle was the first tank to feature a turret. It was armed with either a 37mm cannon or a Hotchkiss machine gun. Contrary to myth, tanks at this time were hardly war-winning weapons. Mechanically unreliable and vulnerable to artillery (as well as the antitank rifle that Barkley later mentions), few remained functional for very long on the battlefield. Appropriately enough, the Renault FT17 on display at the National World War I Museum in Kansas City (just a few feet away from Barkley's medals and his portrait by Christy) bears the scars of German artillery fire that disabled it in 1918.

52. "Jager": a corruption of the German term *Jäger*, which refers to a light infantryman or skirmisher.

53. A water-cooled machine gun, such as the German MG 08-15 or the British Vickers, features a tubular casing—a "water jacket"—that surrounds the barrel. To keep the barrel from overheating, an inevitable problem with rapid-fire weapons, the gun's operator would feed water into the jacket via a hose attached to a reservoir roughly the size of an ammunition box.

54. Resembling an elephant gun, the Mauser 13.2mm antitank rifle fired a huge slug that, as Barkley notes, could penetrate armor.

55. "spud-mashers": German stick grenades, also known as "potato-mashers." The grenade consisted of a metal can, filled with explosives, attached to a wooden handle. To activate the grenade, one removed a cap from the end of the handle and pulled on a cord, which ignited the fuse. To increase their explosive force, stick grenades could (as Barkley notes) be bundled together.

56. Andrew John Volstead, a Republican member of the House of Representatives, helped create the National Prohibition Act of 1919, otherwise known as the Volstead Act.

57. "13th" is almost certainly an error in the original edition. Men from the 30th and 38th Infantry would have reinforced Barkley's battalion at this point.

58. Within the racially segregated U.S. Army of 1917–1918, African-American troops received little respect from their white counterparts. Although some African-American units, such as the famous 369th Infantry (the "Harlem Hellfighters"), served with distinction in combat, the vast majority of black soldiers spent the war as laborers; many

performed the unpleasant tasks required of the army's Graves Registration Service. White soldiers often shared anecdotes, like the one offered here, that underscored the supposed inferiority of African Americans in uniform. Once again, Barkley's memoir reflects a racial sensibility that was typical of the time.

59. George P. Hays, a first lieutenant in the 10th Artillery Regiment, earned the Congressional Medal of Honor through his actions near Greves Farm, France, on July 14–15, 1918. His citation reads, "At the very outset of the unprecedented artillery bombardment by the enemy, his line of communication was destroyed beyond repair. Despite the hazard attached to the mission of runner, he immediately set out to establish contact with the neighboring post of command and further establish liaison with two French batteries, visiting their position so frequently that he was mainly responsible for the accurate fire therefrom. While thus engaged, seven horses were shot under him and he was severely wounded. His activity under most severe fire was an important factor in checking the advance of the enemy."

60. John J. Pershing was born in Laclede, Missouri, in the north-central region of the state.

61. The citation for Barkley's Congressional Medal of Honor, awarded for his actions near Cunel, France, on October 7, 1918, reads as follows: "Pfc. Barkley, who was stationed in an observation post half a kilometer from the German line, on his own initiative repaired a captured enemy machinegun and mounted it in a disabled French tank near his post. Shortly afterward, when the enemy launched a counterattack against our forces, Pfc. Barkley got into the tank, waited under hostile barrage until the enemy line was abreast of him and then opened fire, completely breaking up the counterattack and killing and wounding a large number of the enemy. Five minutes later an enemy 77-millimeter gun opened fire on the tank point blank. One shell struck the drive wheel of the tank, but this soldier nevertheless remained in the tank and after the barrage ceased broke up a second enemy counterattack, thereby enabling our forces to gain and hold Hill 25."

62. "scarlet 'One,'" "Indian Head," "blue and white bars": Barkley refers to divisional shoulder patches, which the U.S. Army adopted for the first time in late 1918. The patch for the First Division featured a red numeral set against a shield; the patch for the Second Division depicted the profile of an American Indian, superimposed on a star; the patch for the Third Division (Barkley's unit) consisted of a blue square with three white diagonal stripes, one for each of the division's major battles (the

Marne, the Saint-Mihiel, and the Meuse-Argonne). The U.S. Army still uses all three of these insignia today.

63. Barkley's additional decorations included two medals from France (the Médaille Militaire and the Croix de Guerre with Three Bronze Palms), the Montenegrin Medal of Bravery, and the Italian War Cross.

64. William Floyd's DSC citation reads as follows: "The Distinguished Service Cross is presented to William M. Floyd, Private, U.S. Army, for extraordinary heroism in action near Les Evaux, France, July 13, 1918. After seeing several patrols fail in the attempt to cross the River Marne, during the night, Private Floyd, with three companions, successfully crossed in broad daylight and in full view of the enemy, remaining in hostile territory throughout the day."

65. "D.S.O.": the Distinguished Service Order, a British medal for gallantry. According to Joan Barkley Wells, Barkley, who disliked most Englishmen, later gave away his British decoration. Thus, it is not known whether the DSO was, in fact, the medal that he received. Because the British army reserved the DSO for officers, Barkley may have been mistaken about the title.

66. American slang, of Native-American origin, for a mischievous child.

67. Along with other charity organizations attached to the AEF, the YMCA sought to keep American soldiers away from European fleshpots. Though plenty of soldiers (like Barkley) avoided the chaste recreations offered by the U.S. Army's civilian partners, the rate of venereal disease in the AEF was far lower than that of other Allied armies.